Tayloring Reformed Epistemology

The Veritas Series

VERITAS

Tayloring Reformed Epistemology

Charles Taylor, Alvin Plantinga and the
de jure *Challenge to Christian Belief*

Deane-Peter Baker

scm press

© Deane-Peter Baker 2007

The Author has asserted his right under the Copyright,
Designs and Patents Act, 1988, to be identified as the
Author of this Work

British Library Cataloguing in Publication data

A catalogue record for this book is available
from the British Library

Hardback 978 0 334 04153 5
Paperback 978 0 334 04140 5

First published in 2007 by SCM Press
13–17 Long Lane,
London EC1A 9PN

www.scm-canterburypress.co.uk

SCM Press is a division of
SCM-Canterbury Press Ltd

Typeset by Regent Typesetting, London
Printed and bound in Great Britain by
MPG Books Ltd, Bodmin, Cornwall

Contents

Centre of Theology and Philosophy

www.theologyphilosophycentre.co.uk

Every doctrine which does not reach the one thing necessary, every separated philosophy, will remain deceived by false appearances. It will be a doctrine, it will not be Philosophy.
Maurice Blondel, 1861–1949

This book series is the product of the work carried out at the Centre of Theology and Philosophy, at the University of Nottingham.

The COTP is a research-led institution organized at the interstices of theology and philosophy. It is founded on the conviction that these two disciplines cannot be adequately understood or further developed, save with reference to each other. This is true in historical terms, since we cannot comprehend our Western cultural legacy unless we acknowledge the interaction of the Hebraic and Hellenic traditions. It is also true conceptually, since reasoning is not fully separable from faith and hope, or conceptual reflection from revelatory disclosure. The reverse also holds, in either case.

The Centre is concerned with:

- The historical interaction between theology and philosophy.
- The current relation between the two disciplines.
- Attempts to overcome the analytic/Continental divide in philosophy.
- The question of the status of 'metaphysics'. Is the term used equivocally? Is it now at an end? Or have twentieth-century attempts to have a post-metaphysical philosophy themselves come to and end?
- The construction of a rich Catholic humanism.

I am very glad to be associated with the endeavours of this extremely important Centre that helps to further work of enor-

mous importance. Among its concerns is the question whether modernity is more an interim than a completion – an interim between a pre-modernity in which the porosity between theology and philosophy was granted, perhaps taken for granted, and a postmodernity where their porosity must be unclogged and enacted anew. Through the work of leading theologians of international stature and philosophers whose writings bear on this porosity, the Centre offers an exciting forum to advance in diverse ways this challenging and entirely needful, and cutting-edge work. Professor William Desmond (Leuven)

VERITAS

Series Introduction

'. . . the truth will set you free.' (John 8.31)

Pontius Pilate said to Christ, 'What is truth?' And he remained silent. In much contemporary discourse, Pilate's question has been taken to mark the absolute boundary of human thought. Beyond this boundary, it is often suggested, is an intellectual hinterland into which we must not venture. This terrain is an agnosticism of thought: because truth cannot be possessed, it must not be spoken. Thus, it is argued that the defenders of 'truth' in our day are often traffickers in ideology, merchants of counterfeits, or anti-liberal. They are, because it is somewhat taken for granted that Nietzsche's word is final: truth is the domain of tyranny.

Is this indeed the case, or might another vision of truth offer itself? The ancient Greeks named the love of wisdom as *philia*, or friendship. The one who would become wise, they argued, would be a 'friend of truth'. For both philosophy and theology might be conceived as schools in the friendship of truth, as a kind of relation. For like friendship, truth is as much discovered as it is made. If truth is then so elusive, if its domain is *terra incognita*, perhaps this is because it arrives to us – unannounced – as gift, as a person, and not some thing.

The aim of the Veritas book series is to publish incisive and original current scholarly work that inhabits 'the between' and 'the beyond' of theology and philosophy. These volumes will all share a common aspiration to transcend the institutional divorce in which these two disciplines often find themselves, and to engage questions of pressing concern to both philosophers and theologians in such as way as to reinvigorate both disciplines with a kind of interdisciplinary desire, often so absent in contemporary academe. In a word, these volumes represent collective efforts in the befriending of truth, doing so beyond the simulacra of pretend tolerance, the violent, yet insipid reasoning of liberalism that asks with Pilate, What is truth? – expecting a consensus of non-commitment; one that encourages the commodification of the mind, now sedated by the civil service of career, ministered by the frightened patrons of position.

The series will therefore consist of two 'wings': 1, original monographs; and 2, essay collections on a range of topics in theology and philosophy. The latter will principally be the products of the annual conferences of the Centre of Theology and Philosophy (www.theologyphilosophycentre.co.uk)

Conor Cunningham
Peter Candler
Series editors

Acknowledgements

This book is the end result of a fascination with Charles Taylor's work which started when I was introduced to his magnificent *Sources of the Self* in an honours course taught at the University of Natal by Ben Parker in 1996. In the intervening years I have benefited enormously from the interventions of the supervisors of my masters and doctoral theses (Simon Beck and Nicolas Smith respectively), as well as feedback from my immediate colleagues (particularly Douglas Farland, Ian Jennings, Deborah Roberts, Patrick Lenta and Simon Beck again) and the broader South African philosophical community. It was Douglas Farland who directed my attention to Taylor's work on transcendental arguments, which was in many ways the most important step in setting this project on its course. Beyond South Africa Ruth Abbey deserves special mention for the important role she has played in helping me to understand Taylor better, and both Michael Rea and Kelly James Clarke (perhaps unknowingly) made important contributions to my grasp of key features of this project. Alvin Plantinga himself has been impressively gracious and helpful in all his dealings with me, and he is in my mind unquestionably our generation's finest role-model as a Christian philosopher. I owe a deep debt of thanks to all of these people, and can only hope that each of them gains some satisfaction from seeing this book in print.

On the home front, the years leading up to this book have been nothing if not eventful. My wife Polly and I have welcomed three wonderful children into the world and said sad farewells to both our mothers, lost to cancer. Polly, you've never ceased to

Acknowledgements

believe in me, even when I doubted myself. Thank you. My parents, Peter and Merlyn, must also be thanked for supporting and encouraging me at every turn, even when they must sometimes have wondered at the direction I was taking. My deepest sadness is that my mother is not here to share my satisfaction at seeing this project reach its fulfilment. This book is dedicated to her memory.

Soli Deo Gloria

Introduction

For some years, due in large part to the pervasiveness of the verification principle, the philosophy of religion had all but ceased to be a recognized subject in the philosophy curriculum. In recent philosophical discourse, however, there has been a proliferation of work in the field of philosophy of religion, and in particular at the intersection between epistemology and philosophy of religion. Much of that interest has centred on the emergence of what has come to be known as 'Reformed epistemology'. The title of this movement reflects the Calvinist theology[1] shared by the exponents of this standpoint – Alvin Plantinga, Nicholas Wolterstorff, and William Alston being notable among them. The central claim of Reformed epistemologists is that belief in God is (at least in some cases) properly basic – that is to say, that 'belief in God can be rational and warranted apart from being based on any other propositions' (Koehl, 2001, p. 168). The purpose of the arguments offered by Reformed epistemologists is to oppose what Plantinga calls the '*de jure*' objection to theistic belief – the idea that it is somehow irrational, a dereliction of epistemic duty, or in some other sense epistemically unacceptable, to believe in God. This objection is distinct from what Plantinga labels the '*de facto*' objection – the objection that, whatever the rational status of belief in God, it is, in fact, a *false* belief. The primary (and

---

1 Calvinist theology plays an important role in the philosophical theory expounded by Reformed epistemologists, though Plantinga is quick to point out that his epistemological model draws on Aquinas as much as it does on Calvin (Plantinga, 2000a, pp. 168–75).

limited) goal of Reformed epistemology, then, is to defend Christian belief against the *de jure* objection, thereby showing that 'everything really depends on the *truth* of Christian belief' (Plantinga, 2000a, p. xiii).

As we shall see in the pages that follow, just what the *de jure* objection amounts to is not easy to establish. While I believe that Reformed epistemologists have, by and large, successfully argued their case, it is not clear that any of them have successfully rebutted the full range of objections that can be seen to fall under the *de jure* umbrella. A particular gap is the lack of a meaningful response to those critics of Reformed epistemology who raise the question of just how far Reformed epistemology takes its Christian adherents, especially in the light of the fact of religious pluralism. For while there is perhaps some level of satisfaction in being able to show that one's beliefs are, if true, warranted, as we shall see this does little to convince others that Christian belief is worth taking particularly seriously. For example, there seems little reason, as has often been observed,[2] to suppose that believers in other religions and adherents to non-theistic worldviews might not be equally warranted in holding their beliefs, if those beliefs turned out to be true, and as such Reformed epistemology offers no motive for the unbeliever to consider adopting Christian belief. As the Reformed epistemologist Michael Sudduth admits, for example, 'none of Plantinga's arguments entail that the conditions under which some people justifiably believe in God constitute an adequate reason for others to adopt this belief'.[3]

In this book I intend to demonstrate the feasibility of combining the Reformed epistemologist's position with an argument for theism that I draw from Charles Taylor's work, and to show the value that would be added to the Reformed epistemologist's position by such a combination. As will become clear, I believe Alvin Plantinga's contribution to Reformed

---

2 See, for example, Gutting's response to Plantinga's Reformed epistemology, Gutting, 1983, pp. 79–92.

3 In a posting to the 'reformed epistemology' e-group, 01/06/03.

epistemology to be the most comprehensive of the theories on offer, and, further, that the Taylor-inspired argument that I will outline withstands the most cogent objections that have been levelled against it.

It is worth noting from the outset that it is not at all obvious that arguments aimed at the same goal, defending or commending theistic belief, will automatically complement one another, even where both or all arguments are based in the same, Christian, tradition. The theological divide between Catholicism and Calvinism presents one possible obstacle in this case. Taylor's Catholic faith seems at first glance to ally him with the majority of Catholic philosophers of religion, who are on the whole critical of the Reformed epistemologist's position,[4] though it must be noted that Taylor himself has not referred explicitly to Reformed epistemology in any of his writings. As Linda Zagzebski has pointed out, the primary difference of relevance here 'is connected with the difference between Catholic and Calvinist views of the Fall. Although both traditions agree that natural human faculties have suffered damage as a result of original sin, Catholic theology has commonly maintained that the will suffered more than the intellect, and that our powers of reasoning can still hope to achieve much that points the way to Christian belief' (Zagzebski, 1993, pp. 3–4). Calvinists, on the other hand (as we shall see), consider sin to have caused serious cognitive malfunction, which can only be rectified by divine intervention, through the ministrations of the Holy Spirit.

Despite this potential difficulty, there is reason for some hope at the outset of this investigation. First, Taylor, though Catholic, by no means fits into the conventional mould of 'Catholic philosopher of religion'. He is unusual, for example, in pointing out the historical contingency of the classical arguments and strategies of natural theology that so preoccupy many Catholic philosophers of religion.[5] A second point is that

---

4 See for example the views expressed in Zagzebski, 1993.

5 This is implicit in, for example, Taylor's treatment of Aquinas on pages 141 and 143 of *Sources of the Self* (Taylor, 1989).

Taylor's argument, at least as I construe it in the pages that follow, is primarily phenomenological, which again differentiates it from most arguments that fall under the umbrella of natural theology.

In order to give the reader a roadmap of the argument of this book, I will in this introduction briefly set out Plantinga's epistemological model and the Taylor-inspired argument for theism and then outline the possibility and benefit of a fusion of the two. Before doing that, however, a brief history of the Reformed epistemology movement is necessary in order to set the background against which this work exists.

A Brief History of Reformed Epistemology

The label 'Reformed epistemology' is a relatively new one in epistemological discourse. While there is always some uncertainty as to the exact origin of such terms, Alvin Plantinga's use thereof in his paper 'The Reformed objection to natural theology', which he read for the American Catholic Philosophical Association in 1980, is the clearest and most unambiguous early usage of the term. While the label is new, however, the basic idea at the heart of Reformed epistemology is not. As Dewey Hoitenga succinctly points out, 'The central claim of Reformed epistemology is the immediacy of our knowledge of God' (Hoitenga, 1991, p. ix). The roots of this notion, as the 'Reformed' label suggests, go at least as far back as the theological work of John Calvin. As Hoitenga indicates:[6]

> The word Reformed identifies the theological tradition inspired by John Calvin and the epistemological claims derived from Calvin's famous words near the beginning of his *Institutes of the Christian Religion*:

---

6 In the only existing book specifically aimed at examining the philosophical lineage of Reformed epistemology, *Faith and Reason from Plato to Plantinga: An Introduction to Reformed Epistemology*.

There is within the human mind, and indeed by natural instinct, an awareness of divinity. . . . To prevent anyone from taking refuge in the pretense [sic] of ignorance, God has implanted in all men a certain understanding of his divine majesty. . . . Since, therefore, men one and all perceive that there is a God and that he is their Maker, they are condemned by their own testimony because they have failed to honor him and to consecrate their lives to his will. (I, iii, 1)

This conviction, namely, that there is some God, is naturally inborn in all, and is fixed deep within, as it were in the very marrow . . . It is not a doctrine that must be first learned in school, but one of which each of us is master from his mother's womb and which nature itself permits no one to forget, although many strive with every nerve to this end. (I, iii, 3)

Thus, although the term Reformed epistemology is new, its central claim lies at the heart of a modern theological tradition. (Hoitenga, 1991, pp. ix–x)

While Calvin is the most obvious source to whom Reformed epistemologists are indebted, Reformed epistemologists have also pointed to an even older lineage. Theologically, of course, like most such traditions, Calvinists see their doctrine as simply reflecting the teachings of the Christian Bible, and the epistemologists who take their direction from Calvinism similarly see their foundations as being ultimately 'biblical'.[7] Hoitenga, however, goes to great pains to delineate what he perceives to be Reformed epistemology's venerable and ancient *philosophical* heritage. In response to accusations that Reformed epistemology is basically the result of 'modern Cartesian assumptions', and that it is no more than 'some kind of "new bird" that its advocates have provided with "its own preening branch to

---

7 Witness, for example, Plantinga's regular quoting of Scripture in support of his 'A/C' epistemological model in *Warranted Christian Belief* (Plantinga, 2000a).

stand on"', Hoitenga dedicates himself to showing that Reformed epistemology is 'a serious philosophical theory with an ancient philosophical pedigree' (Hoitenga, 1991, p. xii).

Hoitenga sees the seed of Reformed epistemology lying in the writings of Plato. He begins with a consideration of the theory outlined in the *Republic*, with its notion that knowledge and belief are opposed, and argues that epistemologists on the whole have rejected that theory as too narrow. It is not a complete rejection, however, because this theory highlights the idea of the epistemic priority of 'direct acquaintance' with objects. As he puts it 'We did acknowledge with Plato . . . the priority of such direct knowledge by acquaintance, especially for the knowledge of the Good, which is Plato's analogue for God; and there we also found the ultimate philosophical source for the Reformed claim for the immediacy of the knowledge of God' (Hoitenga, 1991, p. 236).

Following a chapter of exposition of biblical texts, particularly those relating to Abraham, that 'support the Reformed claim regarding the immediacy of our knowledge of God' (Hoitenga, 1991, p. 237), Hoitenga moves on to show how Augustine applied his famous formula of 'faith seeking understanding' to a synthesis of this biblical idea with Platonic epistemology. He interprets Augustine as being most influenced by the epistemology of Plato's *Republic*, in that he maintains a sharp distinction between knowledge (which is basically understood in terms of direct acquaintance) and belief, and in that he subordinates belief to knowledge. 'Though belief is prior in the order of time, knowledge is prior in the order of desire. We have a deep desire to transform what we believe on authority into the knowledge of personal acquaintance' (Hoitenga, 1991, p. 237). This relationship of faith to understanding is construed in two quite different ways in Augustine's writing. 'In one, the understanding faith seeks is rational proof that God exists; in the other, the understanding faith seeks is deeper acquaintance with God himself whose existence the believer already knows by God's own presence in his or her mind' (Hoitenga, 1991, p. 237). Despite the acknowledged ambiguities in

Augustine's epistemology-related writing, and the consequent difficulty of interpretation, Hoitenga argues that it is the latter construal that is most authentically Augustinian. Sennett sums up this point when he writes that 'The key point here is one that incorporates both the biblical conception of faith as trust and commitment and the Platonic acquaintance doctrine. Believers begin with a trust of and commitment to God, grounded in belief based on testimony – i.e. they begin with faith. This faith creates a desire to know God – not just know about him. That is, the believer seeks a knowledge that comes from direct acquaintance with God' (Sennett, 1994, p. 343).

John Calvin, the Protestant Reformer from whose work the Reformed epistemologists gain their label, takes up and re-articulates Augustine's emphasis on direct knowledge of God. As Hoitenga puts it, 'For Calvin, as for the Bible and for Augustine, all human beings live in the direct presence of God, the sense of which is renewed in the believer by faith but avoided and even suppressed in those who lack such faith by unbelief' (Hoitenga, 1991, p. 237). This understanding of the cognitive effect of unbelief (caused by sin) is what sets Calvin apart from the majority of contemporary theologians and philosophers of religion, who on the whole do not think that sin so affects our cognitive faculties as to make God rationally inaccessible to us without his rectifying intervention. This belief in the cognitive effect of sin also clearly connects Calvin to the tradition that Hoitenga is set on identifying. Calvin, however, neglects Augustine's linking of faith to understanding, and gives no developed account of how direct knowledge of God is restored from the demise thereof caused by original sin.

It is Alvin Plantinga, in Hoitenga's view, who most centrally brings this tradition of epistemology into contemporary discourse, through his 'revival and reformulation of Calvin's ideas about our knowledge of God' (Hoitenga, 1991, p. 237). Hoitenga's work brings to light two main phases of Plantinga's work.[8] The first, earlier phase, epitomised by Plantinga's paper

---

8 Cf. Sennett, 1994, p. 344.

'Reason and belief in God' (Plantinga, 1983a), focused on establishing the direct knowledge of God. For Plantinga the direct knowledge of God is articulated as a 'properly basic belief', which is no more in need of evidence in order to be justified than are perceptual, memory and self-evident beliefs. It is on this basis that Plantinga articulates the objection (a long-standing one, according to Hoitenga) that Reformed epistemologists raise against natural theology's presupposition that rational argument must precede faith. The second 'phase' in Plantinga's work that Hoitenga recognizes is directed at the construction of a positive epistemological theory by which to explain how this basic belief in God can be understood. It must be added that since Hoitenga wrote his analysis of the roots and direction of Reformed epistemology, Plantinga has gone on, in his trilogy of books on epistemic warrant (and in particular in the final volume *Warranted Christian Belief*) to bring together and synthesize both these 'phases'. Furthermore, Plantinga goes on to do what Hoitenga notes as one of the things that is lacking in Calvin's epistemology – provide an account of how the restoration of 'properly basic belief' is achieved, in compensation for the damaging effects of sin. Plantinga does this through his 'extended A/C model', which will be articulated in more detail below.

In his conclusion, Hoitenga claims that the central insight that emerges from the epistemic tradition he has traced, that of direct knowledge or acquaintance of God, is what protects Reformed epistemology from the excesses of fideism on the one hand, and rationalism on the other. He writes that 'The mistake of Protestant fideism is to ignore or even deny the rationality of belief in God; the mistake of Thomistic rationalism is to locate the rationality of belief in God in the proofs of natural theology' (Hoitenga, 1991, p. 238). He points out, however, that Reformed epistemology still lacks an explicit account of Augustine's 'faith seeking understanding' – the closest to this being Nicholas Wolterstorff's account of this phenomenon in *Reason within the Bounds of Religion*. Wolterstorff's account, however, does not deal with 'faith seeking understanding' in its broad epistemic sense, but only within the field of academic scholarship.

While I have drawn here mainly from Hoitenga's reconstruction of the Reformed epistemology tradition, there are certain defects in his account. James Sennett (himself an avid supporter of Reformed epistemology) points out that 'Even if Hoitenga is right about the deep roots of the Reformed tradition, the fact remains that Plantinga explicitly credits Calvin as the primary historical influence on his doctrine. Unless Plantinga is simply ignorant about the major influences in his own work – an hypothesis with at best dubious credibility – it would seem that an extended examination of Calvin's views would be in order in any volume that purports to be a history of Reformed epistemology' (Sennett, 1994, pp. 344–5). But the account actually given of Calvin's views in Hoitenga's book is considered by Sennett to be too brief and sketchy to suffice for this purpose. An additional point worth raising here, in terms of a retrospective reading of Hoitenga's book, is Plantinga's explicit identification with Aquinas as an historical source for his epistemic model, which he labels the 'Aquinas/Calvin model' (Plantinga, 2000a, p. 170).[9] Finally, another important omission from Hoitenga's account is an explanation of the role that the 'common sense' epistemology of figures such as Thomas Reid plays in the theory espoused by contemporary Reformed epistemologists, the importance of which will become evident as we examine the specific arguments put forward by Reformed epistemology's main proponents. Nonetheless, whatever one thinks of the details of Hoitenga's analysis, it seems hard to deny that Reformed epistemologists can legitimately point back into antiquity and identify epistemological ideas that have a distinct resonance with their core notion of the immediacy of the knowledge of God.

---

9 In fairness to Hoitenga, however, it should also be pointed out that Plantinga explicitly aligns his overall approach to philosophy with Augustine in his paper 'Augustinian Christian Philosophy' (Plantinga, 1992).

Plantinga's A/C epistemological model

In the first two of his trilogy of books on epistemology, *Warrant: The Current Debate*, and *Warrant and Proper Function*, Plantinga critiques the state of contemporary epistemology and then sets about building an alternative epistemic model. His starting point is the notion of *warrant*, a refinement on the traditional epistemological concept of justification through which he aims to avoid the confusion that has resulted from differing uses of the latter term. Warrant, then, is that factor which, when added to true belief, results in knowledge.

Plantinga's own account of epistemic warrant is one that rests on the notion of proper function. That is to say, epistemic warrant only results from 'having epistemic faculties that *function properly*' (Plantinga, 1993b, p. 4). But, Plantinga argues, the notion of proper function cannot be separated from the idea of a design plan, for something operates properly if, and only if, it operates according to its design plan. Furthermore, a design plan can only be properly understood in relation to the existence of a conscious designer. Plantinga addresses several attempts at explaining the notion of proper function from a naturalist, evolutionary perspective (which must, by its very nature eschew the idea of a design plan), and concludes that they all fail, and that, indeed, any evolutionary account of properly functioning truth-directed cognitive faculties is self-defeating. He concludes that 'naturalism simpliciter is self-defeating and cannot rationally be accepted' (Plantinga 2002a, p. 12). The flip-side of his conclusion is that 'the denial of the existence of a creative deity is problematic' (Beilby, 2002, p. vii).

In *Warranted Christian Belief* Plantinga turns from arguing that warranted belief can only exist if theism is true, to arguing that belief in God, and specifically Christian belief, is (if true) warranted. Here he proposes what he calls the Aquinas/Calvin (A/C) model – so named because its central insight is articulated by both of these thinkers. Both Aquinas and Calvin draw from the biblical canon the idea of the *sensus divinitatis* – the 'sense of divinity' which, in certain circumstances, causes us to form beliefs about God. As Plantinga puts it 'The *sensus divinitatis* is a disposition or set of dispositions to form theistic beliefs in various circumstances, in response to the sorts of conditions or stimuli that trigger the working of this sense of divinity' (Plantinga, 2000a, p. 173). Plantinga argues further that beliefs produced by the *sensus divinitatis* are basic beliefs, in the same way as beliefs arising out of perception, memory beliefs, *a priori* beliefs and the like are basic. Thus the belief, 'God is great', produced by the *sensus divinitatis*, has the same epistemic status and basicality as the belief 'there is a tree in front of me', produced by visual perception. As with any cognitive faculty, however, the *sensus divinitatis* can malfunction, and it is Plantinga's understanding of Christian scripture that it teaches that the *sensus divinitatis* is damaged and compromised in its operation by *sin*. In his extended A/C model, Plantinga argues that the damage done by sin to the *sensus divinitatis* can only be undone by the work of the Holy Spirit, who enables the new believer to 'see'[10] God by faith through the medium of the Bible, the God-inspired scriptures.

As mentioned at the outset of this introduction, the purpose of the model Plantinga develops here is not to convince the unbeliever of the truth of the Christian story, but rather to defend the claim that, if true, 'full-blooded Christian belief in all its particularity is justified, rational, and warranted' (Plantinga, 2000a, p. 242). Its purpose is to refute 'the widespread idea that Christian belief is lacking in positive epistemic status, even if it happens, somehow, to be true' (Plantinga, 2000a, p. 242).

---

10 The scare quotes are important here – Plantinga does not, as Alston does, attempt to set up his model as a strictly *perceptual* model. This is an important distinction between the two theories, as will become clear in Chapters 2 and 3 below.

A Taylorian Argument for Theism

Charles Taylor is, without doubt, one of the leading philosophers of his generation. His book *Sources of the Self* has established itself as a classic of contemporary philosophy. It is the arguments presented in *Sources of the Self* that provide the basis for the reading of Taylor's work that I will present in this book. As I make clear below, the reading I am giving is a contested version of Taylor's account – one, however, that I will argue can be plausibly drawn from the material available in *Sources of the Self*, and which, further, makes good sense of the general thrust of that work. It is an argument that is phenomenological in nature, in that it begins with the claim that it is an inescapable feature of the nature of our phenomenology that we 'view' the world in moral terms. The argument continues by contending that the moral terms in which we cannot help but address the world, when articulated, reveal to us a certain structure or framework of the good which is definitive of our moral identity. This moral framework, in turn, is dominated by a good which falls into the class of what Taylor calls 'hypergoods' – 'goods which not only are incomparably more important than others but [which also] provide the standpoint from which these must be weighed, judged, decided about' (Taylor, 1989, p. 63). Finally, the argument I outline in this book goes on to make the crucial claim that the best account of that incomparably higher good, and the moral framework it defines, is one expressed in the terms of Christian theism.

There is of course a great deal here to be discussed and argued over, and I have only given the barest outline of Plantinga's theory and the account I wish to draw from Taylor's work. What I have said, however, should provide enough information to make it possible to draw some tentative links between Plantinga's epistemology, particularly the extended A/C model, and the argument for theism that I argue emerges from Charles Taylor's work. It is to that task that I now turn.

Introduction

Linking the A/C Model and the Taylorian Argument for Theism

The first obvious connection between the two models under examination is that they are both defences of Christian belief. While this is true in the broad sense, there are subtleties here. First, as we have already mentioned, Plantinga's model is not intended to settle the *de facto* question about Christian belief, but only the *de jure* question. Plantinga's arguments do not aim to present a full and complete account of the truth *and* warrant of Christian belief, but only the latter. As will become clear, the argument that I will draw from Taylor's work is also not a full and complete argument for the truth of Christian belief, but rather for the claim that this belief system provides the best account of the nature of human phenomenology. Neither approach provides a full defence or *apologia* for Christian faith, and nor will any combination of the two. Conjoining the two will, however, provide a fuller and more defensible account, particularly in response to the *de jure* challenge, as I hope to show.

The central focus of Plantinga's A/C model is, as I have already discussed, the *sensus divinitatis*. This, I believe, is the critical locus for combining the two models. Taylor's argument can, I believe, also be understood in terms of the *sensus divinitatis*, where this is understood as the resonance between our phenomenology, properly described, and the truest description of God and his greatness and glory. This seems to be what Jean Elshtain has in mind when, in her response to Taylor's paper 'A Catholic modernity?' (Taylor, 1999) she draws a parallel between Taylor's work and Augustine's writings on the Trinity. She writes that 'Augustine helps us see the way in which the *imago Dei* maps on to mind, body, and self . . . The argument works like this. Being the sorts of creatures that we are, we see the world through forms or conceptual spectacles. As beings circumscribed by bounds of time and space, we require certain fundamental categories to *see* the world at all' (Elshtain, 1999, pp. 97–8). Following this Augustinian reading of Taylor, we see

13

that the *imago Dei* is reflected in the way our phenomenology (particularly in Taylor's case, our moral phenomenology) has been 'constructed', that is, we have been wired to recognize our creator – this is the basis of the *sensus divinitatis*.

So, then, Plantinga's epistemology and the theistic argument I have drawn from Taylor's work seem to reach a natural confluence at the concept that lies at the heart of both theories, the *sensus divinitatis*. It seems, therefore, entirely possible that the two models could be drawn together. Of course, the two theories are very different in their nature, and there may well be difficulties to be overcome to make this combined model, what I will call the 'Augmented model', feasible. That aside, however, it is worth asking the question of what is to be gained from such an attempt at unifying these two models.

First, what advantage does the Augmented model have over the A/C model on its own? As I pointed out earlier, one of the criticisms raised against Reformed epistemology, of which the A/C model is a central part, is that it does little to commend Christian belief other than to establish positive epistemic status of the most minimal kind. Adding the phenomenological argument that I will outline in this book, however, adds a far more compelling element for the non-believer – it is far more difficult to respond 'So what?' to a claim about the nature of our moral phenomenology than it is to the bare rationality of a belief system. Plantinga's own, minimal, account of the functioning of the *sensus divinitatis* offers little to suggest that this faculty could account for 'full-blooded Christian belief *in all its particularity*' (Plantinga, 2000a, p. 242, italics added), but I hope to show that the Augmented model is far more compelling on this front, though certainly not conclusive. Furthermore, as I will argue, the Augmented model goes some way to responding to the challenge of religious diversity that is made against Reformed epistemology, and to which Plantinga's model offers little by way of response.

Second, what advantage does the combined model have over Taylor's argument when considered on its own? The first obvious point is that the combined model offers a more detailed and structured account of the nature of Christian belief. In addition, the extended A/C model's developed notion of the noetic effects of sin, and of the necessity of the intervention of the Holy Spirit to rectify the damage so caused, and of the role of Scripture and faith in this process, provide a defensible answer to the question, which must obviously be posed of the Taylorian argument, of why it is so difficult to reach agreement on the best account of human phenomenology. This is not to say that such an answer will be convincing to all, or even most, but rather that it fills a gap in the Taylorian argument in a way that is coherent with the overall argument and which cannot be challenged on the basis of its internal rationality.

The Way Ahead

With this general description of the thesis of this work in place, a brief outline of its overall structure is in order. Part I of this book focuses on the current state of the Reformed epistemology movement. To this end I begin, in Chapter 1, by focusing on the first of the triumvirate of philosophers whose work is central to the Reformed epistemology project, namely Nicholas Wolterstorff. William P. Alston's contribution to Reformed epistemology is considered in the second chapter, and as with Wolterstorff I conclude that his approach faces significant challenges, particularly regarding whether or not these approaches meet the *de jure* challenge. In Chapter 3 I turn to a detailed exposition of the work of Alvin Plantinga in the area of Reformed epistemology, as well as presenting an overview of the main lines of response that have been raised by Plantinga's critics. In the last chapter of Part I, I assess how Plantinga's extended A/C model fares in the face of its critics, and I conclude that it fares somewhat better than the alternatives proposed by Wolterstorff and Alston. Nonetheless, I argue that Plantinga's model, in unaltered form, falls short of fully meeting what I call the expanded *de jure* challenge.

This sets the stage for Part II of the book, in which I attempt to identify in Charles Taylor's work an argument for Christian theism which I argue can be appended to Plantinga's extended A/C model in order to block the central criticisms that that model faces. I begin in Chapter 5 by laying the groundwork for this task by articulating the central features of Taylor's thesis, which provide the building-blocks for the argument I wish to articulate and defend. I also outline the structure of that argument, following an amended version of Melissa Lane's reading of Taylor's *Sources of the Self*. Chapter 6 focuses on the primacy that Taylor gives to phenomenology, responding in part to Lane's own objections to this aspect of Taylor's argument, as well as considering those offered by Gary Gutting. I also defend Taylor's use of a transcendental argument strategy in establishing the foundation of his argument, and suggest why such a strategy has potential to bear fruit as part of a response to the *de jure* challenge to Christian belief.

Chapter 7 has as its central focus what Lane calls 'the claim of transcendence', which is roughly the idea that transcendent moral sources are required to explain the structure of our inescapable moral phenomenology. The centrepiece of the chapter is a set of objections to this claim put forward by Gary Gutting, as well as a recent argument by Taylor rejecting the general conditions in contemporary thought that seem to make the claim of transcendence so objectionable. The most important element in Taylor's argument in establishing what Lane calls 'the claim of theism' (the contention that the Best Account of our moral experience is provided by theism in general, and Christianity in particular) is his retrieval of the historical philosophical sources of the modern Western identity. Chapter 8 shows that this historical retrieval is indeed part of Taylor's argument and is not simply descriptive. The chapter goes on to assess just what can be shown in this way. The final chapter, Chapter 9, draws together the main contentions and conclusions of Parts I and II, and shows how Plantinga's extended A/C model and Taylor's theistic argument can be drawn together. Finally, an analysis is given of what the resulting 'Augmented model' can and cannot achieve.

Part I

Reformed Epistemology and the *de jure* Challenge

I

Wolterstorff's Reformed
Epistemology

Despite the distaste with which the claims and arguments of
Reformed epistemology are often received by epistemologists in
general, it is becoming ever more difficult to ignore this theory
of knowledge. Expounded by a vanguard of respected and able
philosophers – Alvin Plantinga, Nicholas Wolterstorff and
William Alston in particular – the declarations of Reformed
epistemology, while centred on the idea of knowledge of God,
nonetheless make strong claims about epistemology in general.
The idea that knowledge of God is possible, in the way that
Reformed epistemologists conceive of this knowledge, acts as a
particularly difficult test case by which to assess the conditions
under which beliefs might be considered justified, or rational, or
indeed knowledge. In this chapter I begin by giving a detailed
analysis of Nicholas Wolterstorff's contribution to the Reformed
epistemology project, and in the chapters that follow I do the
same for the work of the other two central figures of Reformed
epistemology. The goal of these expositions is to establish
which of these philosophers has put forward an epistemic
model that shows the most promise in overcoming the objections that have been levelled against Reformed epistemology in
general and the specific models that are at the heart of the
Reformed epistemology project in particular.

Wolterstorff's Theory

Nicholas Wolterstorff, until recently the Noah Porter Professor of Philosophical Theology at Yale, is widely recognized, along with William Alston and Alvin Plantinga, as one of the leading figures in the Reformed epistemology movement.[1] Wolterstorff's first foray into the area of the relation between reason and religious faith was his *Reason within the Bounds of Religion* (1976). The specific focus of that book, however, was on the bearing of Christian faith on the practice of scholarship, and while Hoitenga for one regards this book as important to the Reformed epistemology project (Hoitenga, 1991, p. 241), its claims are peripheral rather than central to that project. Wolterstorff's next incursion into this arena came in the book he co-edited with Hendrik Hart and Johan van der Hoeven, entitled *Rationality in the Calvinian Tradition*. This book, a collection of papers drawn from a conference on the theme of 'Rationality in the Calvinian Tradition' which took place in Toronto in 1981, is an interesting early step in the genesis of the Reformed epistemology project. It was the first book to include papers by all three of Reformed epistemology's leading figures – Alston, Plantinga and Wolterstorff – and the first to specifically focus on the concept of rationality within the Calvinist tradition. It did not receive wide recognition, however, and Wolterstorff's contribution, 'Thomas Reid on rationality', was again peripheral to the Reformed epistemology project.[2] It was

---

1 Terence Penelhum, for example, writes that '"Reformed epistemology" is the title often given to an influential body of apologetic arguments that have been offered in recent years by a group of Protestant Christian philosophers: in particular by William Alston, Alvin Plantinga and Nicholas Wolterstorff' (Penelhum, 'Reflections on Reformed epistemology'). While not usually identified as a member of this core group, George Mavrodes deserves at least an honourable mention.

2 Peripheral, but not unimportant. Like Wolterstorff, Plantinga identifies Reid as an important ally, in some respects, to Reformed epistemology (Plantinga, 2000a, pp. 98–9, 118). Wolterstorff picks up and develops this aspect of his philosophical work in his recent book, *Thomas Reid and the Story of Epistemology*.

not until the publication of *Faith and Rationality* in 1983, a book edited jointly by Wolterstorff and Plantinga, that Wolterstorff made his first contribution to the central ideas of Reformed epistemology.

Faith and Rationality is a landmark book in the history of contemporary Reformed epistemology. It grew out of a year-long project entitled 'Toward a Reformed View of Faith and Reason' which was supported and directed by the Centre for Christian Studies at Calvin College. While the book is not, strictly speaking, a manifesto for Reformed epistemology,[3] it comes very close to being one, and the four themes that Wolterstorff picks out (in his introduction to the book) as tying the contributions in the book together, provide a useful first framework within which to place Reformed epistemology.

The first thing that Wolterstorff sees as providing a unique context for the papers in *Faith and Rationality* is the collapse of what he calls 'classical foundationalism'. Foundationalism, broadly speaking, is the view that beliefs cannot be justified by circles of inference or by an infinite regress of reasons, but must either be justified by inference from other beliefs via a finite chain of reasons, or be intrinsically reasonable. It is the latter class of beliefs, known as 'basic' beliefs, which, provided that they are rationally held, form the proper foundation for knowledge. The classical foundationalist is that theorist who holds that

> The foundation of a rational belief-structure will . . . contain just two sorts of propositions. It will contain propositions which are *self-evident* to the person in question – proposi-tions which he just sees to be true. $1 + 1 = 2$ would be an example of something self-evident to most of us. Second, it will contain propositions about one's states of consciousness which one cannot mistakenly believe to be true (or mistakenly

---

3 Among the papers included in the book are an historical analysis of the collapse of American evangelical academia by George Marsden, a response to the theology of Wolfhart Pannenberg by David Holwerda, and two short stories (which, admittedly, reflect Reformed epistemology themes) by George I. Mavrodes.

believe to be false). That I am dizzy would be an example'.
(Wolterstorff, 1983a, pp. 2–3)

Although he does not argue the point, Wolterstorff takes it as
given that classical foundationalism has been thoroughly dis-
credited.[4] The papers in the volume (and, it seems safe to say,
Reformed epistemology in general) exist in the context of
this demise. Unlike some responses to the collapse of classical
foundationalism, epistemologists of the Reformed persuasion
have not concluded, following Richard Rorty and others, that
the project of epistemology is a futile one. Nor have they taken
the even more radical step proposed by the likes of Paul
Feyerabend of taking as meaningless any distinction between
rational and non-rational beliefs. Instead these contributors
have presented a positive exploration of post-classical foundationalist epistemology and its impact (in particular, but not
exclusively) on the centuries-old debate about the relationship
between faith – Christian faith in particular – and reason.

The second important contextual parameter Wolterstorff
identifies as defining the contributions to *Faith and Rationality*
and to Reformed epistemology in general, is the evidentialist
challenge to religious belief that emerged from the European
Enlightenment. The Enlightenment's casting off of 'the shackles
of tradition and superstition' left the voice of reason as the
essential guiding voice of the free human being.[5] It is in listening
to this voice that the evidentialist challenge emerges. 'The
challenge can be seen as consisting of two contentions. It was
insisted, in the first place, that it would be *wrong* for a person to
accept Christianity, or any other form of theism, unless it was
rational for him to do so. And it was insisted, second, that it is

---

4 Here Wolterstorff gestures at Plantinga's arguments in support of
this belief set out in his contribution to this volume. These will be considered below. There seems to be a certain amount of bravado in this
claim by Wolterstorff, for as we shall see below, he still finds it necessary
to spend a good deal of attention on refuting the Locke-inspired foundationalism that deigns to label theistic belief as 'irrational'.

5 As we shall see in Part II of this thesis, Charles Taylor calls this the
'subtraction thesis', and argues that it is fundamentally misguided.

not rational for a person to do so unless he holds his religious convictions on the basis of other beliefs of his which give to those convictions adequate evidential support. No religion is acceptable unless rational, and no religion is rational unless supported by evidence. That is the evidentialist challenge' (Wolterstorff, 1983a, p. 6). The evidentialist challenge is widely perceived, particularly in the contemporary West, to be an overwhelming one for Christian and theistic belief.

Wolterstorff's own contribution to the volume, 'Can belief in God be rational if it has no foundations?', is a direct response to the evidentialist challenge. He rejects the reaction to the challenge adopted by many proponents of Christian theism, namely the fideism in which 'the believer has thrown in his lot with revelation' and has thereby rejected the claims of rationality, viewing it as 'only a siren tempter' (Wolterstorff, 1983b, p. 136). Wolterstorff views this approach as 'profoundly misguided'. His preferred methodology is instead to re-examine the terms of the evidentialist challenge, to see whether it in fact stands up under critical rational scrutiny.

Wolterstorff begins his response to the evidentialist challenge by unveiling one if its central points of origin, in the work of John Locke.[6] He argues that Locke extended the classical foundationalist epistemology of Descartes to include not just *scientia*[7] but all beliefs in general. 'If anyone was to believe anything rationally, he had to satisfy the demands of classical foundationalism. Locke noticed that the central claims of Christianity, and of theism generally, are neither self-evident to us nor incorrigible reports of our states of consciousness. And so he insisted that to be rational in holding them we needed evidence for them. If we are to be rational in holding them, they must occur in the superstructure of our system of belief. And concerning the contention that one ought never believe what it is not rational to believe, Locke, as a good precursor of the

---

6 Wolterstorff takes his assessment of Locke's epistemology further in his recent book, *John Locke and the Ethics of Belief*.

7 i.e. science, or well-founded belief.

Enlightenment, seems to have had no doubt whatsoever' (Wolterstorff, 1983a, p. 6).

Wolterstorff's counter takes the form of an alternative criterion of rational belief. In its final form, the criterion is as follows:

> A person S is rational in his eluctable and innocently produced belief[8] Bp if and only if S does believe p, and either:
>
> (i) S neither has nor ought to have adequate reason to cease from believing p, and is not rationally obliged to believe that he does have adequate reason to cease; or
>
> (ii) S does have adequate reason to cease from believing p but does not realize that he does, and is rationally justified in that.

Wolterstorff concludes that 'S will have done as well as can rightly be demanded of him in the use of his belief-governing capacities toward the goal of getting more amply in touch with reality if and only if all of his beliefs are innocently produced and none of those is nonrational on this criterion' (Wolterstorff, 1983b, p. 168).

With this criterion in place, Wolterstorff returns to his central question – does belief in God satisfy the requirements of rationality? Or, more specifically, is *immediate* belief in God (i.e. belief not based on evidence or argument) rational? Wolterstorff can see no reason, in the light of his criterion of rational belief, to deny this, and believes that the evidentialist challenge is thus overcome.

The third defining theme of the papers in *Faith and Rationality* is one I have already discussed, namely their authors' commitment to the Reformed/Calvinist tradition of theology. In this context Wolterstorff explicitly deploys the term 'Reformed epistemology' (Wolterstorff, 1983a, p. 7). Finally,

---

8 This rather clumsy phrase seems, in the context of Wolterstorff's argument, to refer to something like a 'first impression' belief, that is, a belief not arrived at on the basis of some argument based on the available evidence.

the last defining parameter given by Wolterstorff within which Reformed epistemology fits, is that of the 'inevitable pluralism of the academy'. Articulating how Christian philosophers and other academics should respond to this pluralism within academic circles has been an important part of the work of Wolterstorff, Plantinga and others. This is not, however, central to the Reformed epistemology project when considered on its philosophical merits, and will therefore not be a focus of attention in this book.

In his subsequent philosophical career, intermingled with his work on aesthetics and political philosophy, Wolterstorff has produced a number of papers related to Reformed epistemology.[9] His most significant contribution since *Faith and Rationality* has, however, been his book *Divine Discourse*. While not at the heart of Reformed epistemology (that is, not directly concerned with 'the immediacy of our knowledge of God'), the arguments of *Divine Discourse* provide a crucial support for the Reformed epistemology project. Plantinga, for example, seems to recognize this when he takes Wolterstorff's arguments as providing underlying reinforcement for the model of basic or immediate Christian belief articulated in his *Warranted Christian Belief* (Plantinga, 2000a, 251n, 271n, 377n). Emerging out of his Wilde Lectures at Oxford University in 1993, Wolterstorff's book, as the title suggests, focuses on the cogency of the claim that God speaks. The importance of this is obvious for an epistemic project based in a theological tradition that holds a high view of Christian scripture as God's 'Word', and which is committed to the idea of God speaking to us by his Word and through his Spirit.[10] As Wolterstorff says, '. . . many if not most Jews, Christians, and Muslims, if asked to

---

9 Relevant papers include 'The migration of the theistic arguments: from natural theology to evidentialist apologetics' (1986), 'Evidentialism, entitled belief, and the gospels' (1989), and 'The assurance of faith' (1990).

10 For the centrality of this idea to the epistemological branch of this theological tradition, see, for example, Plantinga's extended A/C model below.

explain why they allow Scripture to form their beliefs – if they do – would say, sooner or later, that they do so because it is the *word* of God or the *revelation* of God. So a discussion of divine discourse, along with a discussion of divine revelation, belongs on the agenda of the epistemologist. And as for myself, I will be wanting to ask what a non-evidentialist epistemology of beliefs grounded on divine discourse might look like' (Wolterstorff, 1995, p. 15).

All of this is, as I have said, an important support to the core Reformed epistemology project, but is not at the heart of that project. The exception to this is the penultimate chapter of *Divine Discourse*, 'Are we entitled?' At first Wolterstorff suggests, somewhat misleadingly, that the question at hand in that chapter is 'Does God speak?' (Wolterstorff, 1995, p. 261). It soon becomes clear that the title of the chapter is a more apt description, and Wolterstorff confirms this later when he writes that 'The topic before us is how we are to appraise that enormous number of humanity's believings which consist of believing that God said so-and-so' (Wolterstorff, 1995, p. 266). To answer this question Wolterstorff returns again to an analysis of the epistemological model that he contends remains strongly influential in Western thought, particularly in the area of religious belief – the epistemology of John Locke. The similarity of Wolterstorff's response here with that which he put forward in 'Can belief in God be rational if it has no foundations?' twelve years earlier is, not surprisingly, very evident. In *Divine Discourse*, after gesturing towards Plantinga's notion of epistemic warrant and Alston's concept of justified belief as set out in *Perceiving God*, Wolterstorff puts the question in terms of Locke's deontic notion of epistemic entitlement – are human beings justified in believing that God speaks? The criterion introduced to assess this is as follows: 'a person S is entitled to his belief that p just in case S believes p, and there's no doxastic practice D pertaining to p such that S ought to have implemented D and S did not, or S ought to have implemented D better than S did' (Wolterstorff, 1995, p. 272).

Central to Wolterstorff's contention in favour of this criterion of entitlement is his application of it to the case of Virginia. 'Virginia' is represented by Wolterstorff as a pseudonym for an acquaintance of his, a Christian, 'who is a well-established member of the faculty of one of the old, Eastern seaboard universities of the United States' (Wolterstorff, 1995, p. 273) and who has claimed to have had the following experience and subsequent beliefs. On a particular day (12 February 1987), Virginia 'suddenly knew with certain knowledge' (Wolterstorff, 1995, p. 274) that God had given her a message, made up of seven connected statements, that she was to communicate to her pastor. This experience left her 'awe-struck and terrified' for nothing like this had ever happened to her before nor to anyone she knew (Wolterstorff is quick to point out that Virginia neither is nor was an evangelical Christian, acknowledging that claims of God speaking are commonplace in such circles). Virginia communicated the message to her pastor, as well as passing on to other members of the church a second message she also experienced as coming from God. Most importantly for Wolterstorff's purposes, though Virginia took the messages to be from God, she also considered the possibility that her experience could be the result of mental illness, and chose to consult a psychologist to ensure that this were not the case:

> I met with a psychologist at Harvard Community Health Plan and told her everything that had happened. After listening to my story, she said that these kinds of things happen all the time, and why was I surprised. She suggested a book that I might read, and thanked me profusely for sharing my experience with her. She did not feel that I required any further sessions . . . (quoted in Wolterstorff, 1995, p. 275)

Wolterstorff asks the question whether Virginia is entitled to her belief that God has spoken to her, and applies his criterion of entitlement. As one might expect, Wolterstorff concludes that '. . . yes; it is possible for an intelligent adult of the modern Western world to believe that God has spoken to him or her. I draw that conclusion because the possibility seems to me to have been actualised in the case of Virginia' (Wolterstorff 1995, 280).

Responses to Wolterstorff

Representative of the responses to Wolterstorff's argument in Chapter 15 of *Divine Discourse*, 'Are we entitled?', are those put forward by Philip L. Quinn (2001) and Michael Levine (1998), both in papers to which Wolterstorff has replied. As Quinn's arguments cover much the same ground as Levine's, and in more depth, I shall concentrate my attention here on Quinn's formulation and only draw on Levine where further insight might be gained.

Quinn focuses first on Wolterstorff's notion of entitlement, which he describes as 'part of a family of concepts of epistemic deontology whose logical structure is the same as that of the textbook concept of moral deontology' (Quinn, 2001, p. 265). Wolterstorff divides beliefs into three main categories – those that a person ought not to have, those that a person ought to have, and those 'for which it is *not* the case that he *ought not* to have them' (Wolterstorff, 1995, p. 267). These latter beliefs are beliefs that a person is *entitled* to hold – they are epistemically permissible for that person.

The second important point, from Quinn's perspective, is that Wolterstorff, in common with his fellow Reformed epistemologists, accepts the idea that our beliefs are not formed voluntarily. What are in our control, however, are our doxastic practices. Plantinga puts it well when he writes:

If you offer me $1,000,000 to believe that I am under 30, or even to stop believing that I am over 30, there is no way (short of mind-altering drugs, say) I can collect. Still, this is by no means the whole story. . . . some of my beliefs are indirectly within my control (in the way in which, for example, my weight is), even if I can't simply decide what to believe and what not to. I can train myself not to assume automatically that people in white coats know what they are talking about, I can train myself to pay more attention to the evidence, to be less credulous and gullible (or less cynical and skeptical), and so on. (Plantinga, 2000a, p. 96)

Wolterstorff argues that we often have an epistemic obligation to make use of such doxastic practices, 'so as to form beliefs on a more reliable basis' (Wolterstorff, 1995, p. 271).

It is the fact that Virginia fulfils such an epistemic obligation that, in large part, leads Wolterstorff to conclude that she was entitled to believe that God had spoken to her. Having come to believe that God had spoken to her, Virginia nonetheless set in motion a specific doxastic practice aimed at ensuring her belief was formed on a reliable basis – she consulted a psychologist. As Wolterstorff puts it, 'she seriously entertained the possibility that her experience was a symptom of mental disorder rather than a case of God inwardly appearing to her as speaking, and took steps to check it out' (Wolterstorff, 1995, p. 275).

Quinn, however, finds Wolterstorff's account to be unsatisfactory, and the case as expressed to be inconclusive. He imagines a scenario in which the psychologist consulted by Virginia concludes that she has suffered a 'mild delusory episode' but is nonetheless 'perfectly harmless', and on a par with 'all those nice people who wander into the office to report receiving communications from space aliens'. The psychologist, concerned to move on to those patients in genuine need of help, 'tries to reassure Virginia, thanks her for sharing, and then moves briskly on to a case in more urgent need of her immediate attention' (Quinn, 2001, p. 267). This scenario is quite compatible with the account that Wolterstorff has given, and so Quinn concludes that not enough detail has been given the reader to entitle her to accept Wolterstorff's claim that Virginia is entitled to her belief that God has spoken to her. Furthermore, even if it were granted that Virginia is entitled to her belief, Quinn points out that there is a difference between Virginia being 'merely entitled' to believe that God has spoken to her, and her being 'both entitled and epistemically obligated to believe as she does' (Quinn, 2001, p. 268), and he contends that Wolterstorff's approach only shows Virginia to be entitled to her belief, but not obligated to believe as she does.

Levine makes a similar, but perhaps stronger point, which raises a question about just how philosophically illuminating Wolterstorff's notion of entitlement really is. 'For all that Wolterstorff has said, the "Yorkshire Ripper" is also "entitled" to believe that God spoke to him – and may be correct in his belief. So too may Margaret Thatcher if she believes, as some others undoubtedly believe and are "entitled" to believe, that God speaks to her. They could have gone to the same Harvard Health Plan psychologist as the woman in Wolterstorff's example, believed they were being commanded by a loving God, and judged that "accepting that the experiences are veridical, have the consequences that one would expect if the experiences were indeed of God speaking"' (Levine, 1998, p. 15). Levine argues that Wolterstorff's account of entitlement, even if true, 'covertly obfuscates the real issue', which is about 'objective justification rather than entitlement' (Levine, 1998, p. 15).

In both cases the fundamental objection is the same, namely that Wolterstorff's notion of entitlement is not strong enough to achieve the degree of epistemic respectability he desires for Virginia's beliefs. For Quinn what is needed in addition to entitlement is epistemic obligation, while for Levine the missing element is that of 'objective justification'. The claim is that Wolterstorff's notion of epistemic entitlement is too thin a concept to be of real use, for though we might not want to say that Virginia has violated any epistemic duty in believing what she does and might well therefore be in some sense entitled to her belief, nonetheless this is insufficient to show that the belief is epistemically justified, as this notion of entitlement leaves open the likelihood that people holding what would generally be considered to be bizarre beliefs[11] are also epistemically entitled to those beliefs.

---

11 Quinn's reference to people who believe they have been communicated with by space aliens, and Levine's example of the 'Yorkshire Ripper', suggest this interpretation.

Even when Wolterstorff's promise of a developed theory of entitlement materializes, there is reason to doubt, on current evidence, that it will advance Reformed epistemology's position particularly far. As pointed out above, his notion of epistemic entitlement is a fundamentally deontological notion – that is, it is intended to address the question of whether a believer has fulfilled her epistemic duty in coming to believe some or other belief. Both Quinn and Levine attack Wolterstorff's notion on the same basic point – while it might be acknowledged that some believer S might be *entitled* to believe x, and therefore not be in violation of the ethics of belief, a more important question remains unanswered. That question (and here I offer an interpretation of what Quinn and Levine in fact say) is whether the conditions under which S has come to believe x are such that there is good reason to think that S *knows* x.

An important part of the background to this debate is the confusion in contemporary epistemology around the notion of justification – what Plantinga calls a 'blooming, buzzing confusion with respect to justification' (Plantinga, 1993a, p. 10). Plantinga identifies four central ideas connected to the term justification, Alston (1993) finds at least six. Most fundamentally, though, as Zagzebski (1996, pp. 29–43) points out, the confusion in the meaning of the term justification is linked to the usage thereof by internalists and externalists. Generally speaking, internalists use the term to refer to the idea of doing one's epistemic duty, while externalists use 'justification' as the label for that component which, when added to true belief, accounts[12] for knowledge. Plantinga attempts to overcome this confusion by renaming the externalist version of justification, calling it warrant, and reserving the term justification for the deontological internalist concept.

Wolterstorff is also clearly trying to avoid this confusion by deploying the term 'entitlement', but it is not difficult to see that for Wolterstorff entitlement is very closely allied to the internalist deontological idea of justification. But both Quinn

---

12 Barring Gettier problems.

and Levine make it clear that this is simply not the interesting question – their use of space aliens and the Yorkshire Ripper strongly suggests that they view this kind of justification as trivial. Put another way, the claim seems to be that Wolterstorff's standard of entitlement, even if achieved, is insufficient to the task of offering *de jure* justification for beliefs. While it is difficult to express what the *de jure* requirement is in this case (particularly as this is not a term used by Quinn and Levine), it seems that what is offered is a sort of argument by analogy which claims that it matters not if Christians are entitled to their beliefs in the way Wolterstorff is arguing, because holders of delusional and insane beliefs can be just as entitled to those beliefs, and we clearly think that the latter category of believers are not justified in holding those beliefs, regardless of whether or not those beliefs turn out to be true. If Wolterstorff's defence of Christian beliefs leaves Christians still in the company of those with obviously mad beliefs, then his notion of entitlement has not done much for the epistemic status of Christian beliefs. Quinn and Levine's arguments seem instead to show the need for something closer to a defence of *warranted* Christian belief, where warrant is 'that, whatever precisely it is, which together with truth makes the difference between knowledge and mere true belief' (Plantinga, 1993a, p. 3). Perhaps most damning for Wolterstorff's position, Plantinga seems to agree with Quinn and Levine, arguing that responding to criticism of the epistemic status of Christian belief by defending it from the basis of the internalist deontological idea of justification is unsatisfactory, simply because it is too easily answered. Whether Christians are entitled to their beliefs, in the way Wolterstorff understands that notion, simply cannot be what the *de jure* objection is about. Plantinga asks us to consider a particular Christian believer:

> as far as we can see, her cognitive faculties are functioning properly; she displays no noticeable dysfunction. She is aware of the objections people have made to Christian belief; she has read and reflected on Freud, Marx, and Nietzsche

(not to mention Flew, Mackie and Nielsen) and the other critics of Christian or theistic belief; she knows that the world contains many who do not believe as she does. She doesn't believe on the basis of propositional evidence; she therefore believes in the basic way. Can she be justified (in this broadly deontological sense) in believing in God in this way? (Plantinga, 2000a, p. 100)

Plantinga thinks that it is blatantly obvious that she can be justified (or entitled) in this sense. If she has investigated all the objections to Christian belief that she can lay her hands on, and has found none of them to be compelling, and has also considered the positive arguments for Christian belief, and has found those attractive but also not ultimately compelling, and then goes on believing in this basic way, she cannot for a moment be accused of violating her epistemic duty. 'There could be something *defective* about her, some malfunction not apparent on the surface. She could be *mistaken*, a victim of illusion or wishful thinking, despite her best efforts. She could be wrong, desperately wrong, pitiably wrong, in thinking these things; nevertheless, she isn't flouting any discernable duty. She is fulfilling her epistemic responsibilities; she is doing her level best; she is justified' (Plantinga, 2000a, pp. 100–1).

This scenario painted by Plantinga bears obvious parallels to Wolterstorff's case of Virginia. In particular both are clearly based on the central presumption of Reformed epistemology, that knowledge of God is *immediate*, rather than being the result of some kind of inference. The main difference is in what each party thinks their case study achieves – not a lot, according to Plantinga, and in this he is in clear agreement with Quinn and Levine. Immediately after setting out the above-quoted case of the very reasonable Christian believer, he compares it with the (apparently genuine) case of an inmate of Pine Rest Christian Psychiatric Hospital who expressed dissatisfaction at not receiving sufficient credit for having invented a new form of non-sexual human reproduction – primarily involving suspending a woman from a rope and spinning her around at great speed – by which he claimed to have populated Chicago. Plantinga evaluates this case in much the same way as the case of the Christian believer:

> Now there is no reason to think this unfortunate man was flouting epistemic duty, or derelict with respect to cognitive requirement, or careless about his epistemic obligations, or cognitively irresponsible. Perhaps he was doing his level best to satisfy those obligations. Indeed, we can imagine that his main goal in life is satisfying his intellectual obligations and carrying out his cognitive duties. Perhaps he was dutiful *in excelsis*. If so, he was *justified* in these mad beliefs [and therefore, in Wolterstorff's terms, 'entitled' to them], even if they are mad, and even though they result from cognitive dysfunction. (Plantinga, 2000a, pp. 101–2)

Where Plantinga's Christian believer example was close to Wolterstorff's Virginia, this second case seems to make exactly the same point as Quinn's delusional 'space aliens' believer and Levine's Yorkshire Ripper. Clearly Plantinga agrees that achieving some level of deontological justification is no great shakes, and that gaining this status offers the Christian little protection against those who object (epistemically) to her holding Christian beliefs. The 'real' question, then, seems to be, Plantinga contends, a question about warrant rather than about justification, and on this score Wolterstorff's notion of epistemic entitlement offers very little. This being so, it seems that we will need to look beyond Wolterstorff's contribution to Reformed epistemology if we are to find an epistemic model that meaningfully responds to the *de jure* challenge. We turn next to William Alston.

2

Alston's Reformed Epistemology

William P. Alston, Professor Emeritus of Philosophy at the University of Syracuse, is undoubtedly one of the leading figures of contemporary epistemology. His unquestionable impact on the field of epistemology in general has given quite some weight to his many incursions into the specific area of religious epistemology. In this chapter we continue, through an examination of Alston's contributions to Reformed epistemology, our quest to discover the epistemic model within this tradition that offers the greatest possibilities of responding to the *de jure* objection against Christian belief.[1]

Alston's Theory

Like Wolterstorff, Alston's first major contribution to the core project of Reformed epistemology came in his contribution to the book *Faith and Rationality*, in a paper entitled 'Christian experience and Christian belief'. Prior to that paper Alston had produced a number of papers in general epistemology that laid important groundwork for his contribution to Reformed epistemology.[2] Though 'Christian experience and Christian belief' was Alston's first contribution to Reformed epistemology

---

1 A version of the argument outlined in this chapter is to be published in the journal *Scriptura* in 2007, under the title 'Perceiving God? A critical analysis of William Alston's Reformed epistemology'.

2 See for example his 'Varieties of privileged access' (1971), 'Has foundationalism been refuted?' (1976a), 'Self-warrant: a neglected form of privileged access' (1976b), and 'Two types of foundationalism' (1977).

proper, in that it explicitly deals with specifically Christian belief, it must however be bracketed with a closely related paper published the preceding year, entitled 'Religious experience and religious belief'. It would in fact be quite legitimate to consider 'Christian experience and Christian belief' to be a development of 'Religious experience and religious belief', for while the title and opening gambit[3] of the latter paper suggest that it is religious belief in general that Alston is dealing with, it soon becomes clear that it is specifically Christian belief that he has in mind.

In 'Religious experience and religious belief' Alston deals broadly with what he calls 'M-beliefs' (where 'M' stands for 'manifestation'). These are 'beliefs to the effect that God, as conceived in theistic religions, is doing something that is directed to the subject of the experience – that God is speaking to him, strengthening him, enlightening him, giving him courage, guiding him, sustaining him in being, or just being present to him' (Alston, 1982, p. 4). The question on which the paper focuses is whether such beliefs might be epistemically justifiable. Alston approaches his subject by setting up a comparison between 'Christian epistemic practice' (CP), which involves 'M-beliefs', and 'the practice of forming beliefs about the physical environment on the basis of sense-experience', which he calls 'perceptual practice' (PP).

Before embarking on this mission of epistemic comparison, however, Alston adds an important rider – that he takes it that both sensory experience and religious experience could at most only provide *prima facie* justification for the beliefs that they give rise to. With regard to sense experience he writes that beliefs arising from these will only be justified under 'favourable circumstances' – 'If I am confronted with a complicated

---

3 'Can religious experience provide any ground or basis for religious belief? Can it serve to justify religious belief, or make it rational? This paper will differ from many others in the literature by virtue of looking at this question in the light of basic epistemological issues. Throughout we will be comparing the epistemology of religious experience with the religious epistemology of sense perception' (Alston, 1982, p. 3).

arrangement of mirrors, I may not be justified in believing that there is an oak tree in front of me, even though it looks for all the world as if there is. Again, it may look for all the world as if water is running uphill, but the general improbability of this greatly diminishes the justification the corresponding belief receives from that experience' (Alston, 1982, p. 5). Likewise with religious perception: 'It would seem that direct experiential justification for M-beliefs, is also, at most, *prima facie.* Beliefs about the nature and ways of God are often used to override M-beliefs, particularly beliefs concerning communications from God. If I report that God told me to kill all phenomenologists, fellow Christians will, no doubt, dismiss the report on the grounds that God would not give me any such injunction as that' (Alston, 1982, p. 6).

Alston's central argument here begins with the observation that the perceived difference in epistemic legitimacy between CP and PP, as argued by CP's detractors, exists because of certain widely recognized differences between CP and PP – differences that (as van Inwagen helpfully summarizes) 'center around the fact that PP prescribes standard ways of checking the veridicality of particular sensory episodes and the (alleged) fact that the prescriptions of PP are followed by all normal adults of every age and clime' (van Inwagen, 1982, p. 13). Alston argues, however, that the commonly cited differences between PP and CP in fact offer no reasons for taking CP not to be reliable. van Inwagen helpfully illustrates this by asking us to imagine the following entirely feasible account of God and his ways:

'God exists and is so "wholly other" that we can only dimly grasp his nature and can discover no "regularities" on the basis of religious experiences. He decrees that religious experiences will be comparatively rare, owing to the fact that they are reserved for very special people in very special circumstances. Nonetheless people who do have these experiences experience God and come to know truths about him thereby.' This story entails both that religious experiences are (sometimes) veridical and that these experiences differ from sense experience in the ways commonly cited. Since no one has ever given any good reason for supposing that this story is false, no one has any reason for supposing that the commonly cited differences between CP and PP are a compelling reason for supposing CP to be unreliable. And, therefore, CP is justified in the only sense in which PP is justified: there is no known compelling reason for supposing it to be unreliable. (van Inwagen, 1982, pp. 13–14)

This argument-trajectory is continued in 'Christian experience and Christian belief'. Having already argued that there is no relevant difference between 'perceptual practice' and 'Christian epistemic practice', Alston moves on to look more closely at the idea that one is epistemically justified in each of these practices. Going back to the famous confrontation between William Clifford and William James over the ethics of belief, Alston develops two tests for epistemic justification. From Clifford he draws the view that 'one is obliged to refrain from engaging in a practice unless one has adequate reasons for supposing it to be reliable'. James, on the other hand, provides a less demanding test – 'one is justified in engaging in a practice provided one does not have sufficient reasons for regarding it as unreliable' (Alston, 1983, p. 116). Alston assumes, without argument, that PP is justified by the Jamesian test. The Cliffordian test, not surprisingly, provides a greater challenge. Alston points out that PP is very difficult to assess in terms of the Cliffordian test, since it is not a belief or even a set of beliefs that is facing the test, but an entire practice. 'Since this practice, and what is based on it, constitutes our sole access to the subject matter, we cannot carry out a direct investigation into its reliability by comparing its deliverances with how the subject matter is, since we have no other way of determining the latter' (Alston, 1983, pp. 117–18). How then to establish a non-circular justification for PP? Alston conducts a brief survey of the main attempts at doing this. First, he points out there are those who attempt to justify PP on the basis of premises that have not been obtained from PP itself – Descartes' appeal to the goodness of God being one such case. Second, there is the attempt to justify PP on the basis of some sort of transcendental argument, in which PP is seen as inescapably necessary to the existence of experience itself (or some similar claim). Finally Alston draws his readers' attention to pragmatic arguments for the justification of PP. All of these approaches, however, fall short, in Alston's approximation. Attempts to justify PP on the basis of premises not obtained by PP are all vulnerable to scepticism. Transcendental arguments can at most show us something about the nature of our experience, but are unable to tell us about how things actually are. And finally, pragmatic arguments are just straightforwardly circular – 'We have to use PP to determine that the predictions we make on the basis of perceptual beliefs often turn out to be correct, and to determine that there is a large measure of agreement in perceptual beliefs. We do not discover this by using a crystal ball or being told by an angel' (Alston, 1983, p. 118).

From this brief survey Alston concludes that the likelihood of finding an approach that will provide a non-circular Cliffordian justification for PP is not good. But apart from the extreme sceptic, most epistemologists would take it as more or less given that PP *is* reliable. This, therefore, leaves the Jamesian test as the only viable approach to epistemic justification with regard to PP.[4] Alston states that as he is unaware of any compelling argument showing that PP ought to be regarded as unreliable, he takes it that PP is justified. Alston links his approach with the epistemology characterized by the thought of Thomas Reid. Here the Cartesian-inspired reliance on intuition and reason in establishing which beliefs are justified is taken to be a case of

---

4 From this it seems that Alston views the Cliffordian and Jamesian options as exhaustive, which seems unlikely. Perhaps a more sympathetic reading of Alston would see him claiming rather that the Clifford/James distinction is the one generally accepted by those with whom he is engaging, and so these are the only two options he is forced to take seriously.

'arbitrary partiality'. 'Why accept intuition and reason without any basis, while refusing to do the same for sense perception?' (Alston, 1983, p. 119) In avoiding this arbitrariness, Reid and like-minded thinkers are left only with the option of taking as justified beliefs gained from our normal faculties – sense perception, memory, rational intuition, reasoning, self-consciousness and the like – unless presented with reasons for believing otherwise in specific instances.[5] Here again, then, is the Jamesian epistemological test.

With this analysis in place, Alston goes back over the ground covered in 'Religious experience and religious belief' – that is to say, he moves on to assess the question of whether CP can be thought of as being justified in the same way as PP. Alston identifies four central differences between CP and PP which opponents of CP take as being important in distinguishing the justifiability of CP (which they take to be unjustified) from that of PP:

1 Within PP there are standard ways of checking the accuracy of any particular perceptual belief . . .

2 By engaging in PP we can discover regularities in the behavior of objects putatively observed, and on this basis we can, to a certain extent, effectively predict the course of events.

3 Capacity for PP, and practice of it, is found universally among normal adult human beings.

4 All normal adult human beings, whatever their culture, use basically the same conceptual scheme in objectifying their sense experience. (Alston, 1983, p. 121)

---

5 The debt to Reid is one acknowledged by all three of the central figures of Reformed epistemology. Wolterstorff's most recent book is a largely positive exposition of Reid's epistemology (Wolterstorff, 2001a), and Plantinga takes great support from Reid in his response to what he calls 'The classical package', that is classical foundationalism and classical deontologism, as well as Humean scepticism (Plantinga, 2000a, pp. 97–8 and 218–27).

As in 'Religious experience and religious belief' Alston concludes for each of these that the difference is not sufficient to show that CP is importantly different from PP for the purposes of Jamesian justification, and that therefore beliefs arising out of CP are justified where there are no compelling reasons for thinking otherwise.

The zenith of Alston's contributions to Reformed epistemology comes in his book *Perceiving God*, which Brian Hebblethwaite described as 'unquestionably one of the most important philosophy of religion books to have been published during the [preceding] fifteen years', an assessment made all the more impressive by Hebblethwaite's identification of that period as one of 'remarkable growth in both the quantity and the quality of work in this field' (Hebblethwaite, 1994, p. 116). *Perceiving God* is the culmination of 'at least fifty years' (Alston, 1991, p. xi) of work of varying degrees of intensity in this area of epistemology of religion. The ideas developed in the two papers considered above remain central to the project, and the book is also foreshadowed by a number of other papers on the subject.[6] The overall thesis is inevitably more developed than in its earliest incarnations, particularly, as George Pappas points out, in the general epistemology that lies 'behind' the Reformed epistemology (Pappas, 1994, p. 877).

One of Alston's leading critics, Richard Gale, succinctly sums up the thrust of *Perceiving God* when he writes that its aim is

> to show that we are rationally justified in believing that our apparent direct perceptions of God's presence (called 'M-experiences') are reliable and thus for the most part veridical, the objective, existentially-committed beliefs based on these experiences thereby being *prima facie* justified, subject to defeat by certain overriders supplied by some background

---

6 'The Christian language-game' (1981); 'Religious experience as a ground of religious belief' (1986); 'Is religious belief rational?' (1986); 'Perceiving God' (1986); 'Religious diversity and the perceptual knowledge of God' (1988); and 'The perception of God' (1988).

religion. It is argued that our rational justification for believing this is of both an epistemic and pragmatic (or practical) sort, in which an epistemic reason for believing a proposition is truth conducive, rendering the proposition probable, while a pragmatic one concerns the benefits which accrue from belief. (Gale, 1994, p. 135)

The concepts deployed in *Perceiving God* have developed somewhat from their starting-points in Alston's earlier papers. Foundational to his argument is what he calls 'mystical perception' (MP), which is an awareness of the presence or activity of God, which is parallel to sensory perception. It is important to Alston's argument that MP not be understood as a subjective feeling that is interpreted as being the result of the presence or activity of God – he vigorously defends the notion that MP is *perceptual*, in that it involves a presentation, 'givenness' or appearance of its object (God). It is *mystical* perception because of its object – though Alston is careful to leave open the question of whether, in any particular case, the experience in question is, in fact, caused by God.

In the second chapter of the book Alston sets up his general theory of epistemic justification, an externalist theory according to which 'To be epistemically justified in believing that *p* is for that belief to be based on an adequate ground, which could either be experiences or other things one knows or justifiably believes. A ground is adequate provided it is a sufficiently reliable indication of the truth of the belief' (Alston, 1994a, p. 864). This justification is, however, defeasible – such beliefs are subject to 'over-riding reasons' (and undercutting reasons) that may afterwards become evident. MP is treated the same way – to be taken as epistemically justified this practice must be a reliable (true-making) source of beliefs, and individual beliefs must also be considered to be subject to overriding reasons.

In an extended treatment of the argument in 'Christian experience and Christian belief' Alston goes on to show the impossibility of showing a doxastic practice like sense perception (SP)[7] to be justified in an independent, non-circular way. Alston then generalizes this conclusion to include all doxastic practices, including MP, and argues that only internal grounds can be used to assess the reliability of any doxastic practice. For MP the internal support for the practice is, in Alston's view, to be found in the spiritual development that results from MP. Alston then moves on to focus on specifically *Christian* mystical practice (CMP[8]). This part of the book is again an extended version of the argument that first appeared in 'Religious experience and religious belief' and in 'Christian experience and Christian belief'. As in those papers, Alston analyses the general reasons that are put forward to show that CMP differs from other doxastic practices in ways that disqualify it from being a justified doxastic practice, and concludes that the differences identified do not, in fact, disqualify CMP in this way.

In the latter part of the book Alston tackles two of the most central objections that have been raised against his thesis – naturalist accounts of CMP and the problem of religious pluralism. In response to the former, Alston argues that none of the arguments offered undermine CMP as a justified practice, though he does admit that CMP may not be as reliable as SP. The latter challenge presents, Alston admits, the greatest difficulty for his position. The problem lies with the internal nature of justification that he has been arguing for – if one assumes that there are no sufficient external reasons for accepting CMP over any other form of mystical practice, then on what grounds can it be rational to prefer CMP over any of its competitors? Alston deals with this by setting up the 'worst-case scenario' in which there are, indeed, no external reasons for preferring CMP (Alston does suggest that there may be, in reality, external metaphysical and historical external reasons for preferring CMP, but he does not pursue this suggestion). Alston addresses his

---

7 A slight modification of 'perceptual practice' or PP in 'Religious experience and religious belief' and 'Christian experience and Christian belief'.

8 This is basically equivalent to CP in 'Religious experience and religious belief' and 'Christian experience and Christian belief'.

worst-case scenario by examining a number of analogous practices, and concludes that 'though this is not epistemically the
best of all possible worlds, it is rational in this situation for one
to continue to participate in the (undefeated) practice in which
s/he is involved, hoping that the inter-practice contradictions
will be sorted out in due time' (Alston, 1991, p. 7). Related to
this is a discussion of the relationship between beliefs based on
perception and beliefs based on testimony about perception.

The final chapter of *Perceiving God* is dedicated to a discussion of the place of mystical experience within the 'larger pic-
ture' of religious belief. The relationship of mystical perception
to non-perceptual sources of belief like natural theology, tradition, and various kinds of revelation is examined. Alston concludes that all these sources of religious belief can be reduced to
two main types – 'perceptual presentation' and 'inference to the
best explanation'. 'It is then suggested that the different grounds
interact not only by adding up to a total case that is greater than
any of its components, but also in more intimate ways – for
example, by one source contributing to the background system
presupposed by another source, or by one source helping to
remove doubts about another' (Alston, 1991, p. 8).

Responses to Alston

Responses to Alston's *Perceiving God*[9] fall mainly into four
broad categories: challenges to his claim that no plausible non-
theistic alternative explanations of mystical experience exist or
are likely to exist; attempts to undermine his analogy between
perceptual practice and mystical practice; arguments against
Alston's contention that mystical experiences constitute a form

---

9 As stated above, *Perceiving God* represents the zenith of Alston's
Reformed epistemology-related work thus far, in that it brings together
in revised form all the central arguments of his work in Reformed epistemology preceding the publication of the book. I will take it, therefore,
that the main responses to *Perceiving God* represent the central thrust of
responses to Alston's Reformed epistemology.

of perception; and, finally, claims that the fact of religious diversity in some way undermines Alston's thesis. In what follows I will give a brief outline of each of these lines of attack as proposed by their main proponents.[10]

Non-theistic explanations of mystical experiences

The idea that there exists some alternative explanation of the experiences that religious believers accredit to an encounter with God or some other spiritual being, an explanation that does not require any departure from what Plantinga calls 'metaphysical naturalism' (the idea that there is no supernatural realm and that there are no supernatural beings), is one with a long history and one which has been put forward by such thinkers as Freud, Feuerbach and Marx. Usually some psychological explanation of the phenomenon is given – for Freud such experiences are the phenomenological product of an unconscious attempt to 're-create the world, to build up in its stead another world in which its most unbearable features are eliminated and replaced by others that are in conformity with one's own wishes', in effect a form of delusion resulting from wishfulfilment (Freud, 1961, p. 18), while for Feuerbach and Marx social alienation is the key explanatory factor.

Evan Fales has directed a response of this kind specifically against Alston's position. He claims that 'theists recognize . . . that the plausibility of [the view that mystical experiences provide perceptual contact with God] would be significantly compromised by the possibility of scientifically explaining mystical experiences – especially if a scientific explanation were incompatible with, ruled out, or made unlikely the supposition that God has anything to do with the occurrences of these

---

10 Of course it goes without saying that not all the attacks on Alston's thesis fall into these categories, and nor do those that do fit into them neatly. Ward (1994), for example, seems to be deploying the fact of religious diversity (the fourth category I outline here) as a means of undermining Alston's idea that mystical experiences can be properly considered as perception (the third category).

experiences'. Fales holds that this is particularly relevant to Alston, who argues in *Perceiving God* (pp. 228–34) that 'the various scientific disciplines do not have anything to offer by way of plausible competitors to the theistic view of mystical experience, and that there is no real prospect of their ever doing so' (Fales, 1996, p. 297).

In response to Alston's claim, Fales (1996a, 1996b) tests the theory proposed by the social anthropologist I. M. Lewis against the reported experiences of St Theresa, whom he chooses because of her prominence and the 'considerable' amount of biographical data available on her. He concludes that 'Alston's claim that mystical experience is by its very nature not amenable to scientific explanation is borne out neither by the data nor by the record of what has been achieved' (Fales, 1996b, p. 311). He claims further, in response to Alston's claim that naturalistic accounts fail to show that at least some mystical experiences can be more justifiably (or at least not less justifiably) claimed to be veridical, that 'Theism cannot hope to match the explanatory power or empirical backing of Lewis' theory' (Fales, 1996b, p. 311).

Analogy with perceptual practice

Foundational to Alston's argument for the epistemic justifiability of beliefs based on mystical practice is the analogy he draws between mystical practice and perceptual practice. As we saw above, Alston distinguishes between a strong, Cliffordian, approach to epistemic justification on the one hand, and a weaker, Jamesian approach on the other, and he concludes that the likelihood of finding an approach that will provide a noncircular Cliffordian justification for PP is not good. Alston argues that this leaves the weaker test for justification. He contends further that, on any comparison between PP and MP, no differences can be found that would make it such that PP would be justified according to the Jamesian test but MP not be justified.

Charles Daniels claims that 'all sorts of practices we deem

superstitious are free of ineradicable inconsistencies and so qualify as [justified in the Jamesian sense]', and that 'whether a practice is . . . justified in this weak sense turns out to be of very little interest' (Daniels, 1989, p. 488).[11] He contends, however, that PP *is* in fact justified in the strong sense. He then goes on to offer reasons why MP cannot be considered to be justified in the strong sense, because it is lacking in a number of areas where PP succeeds, namely the existence of agreement independent of authority and alternative explanation; success in actions explained by the sense or refinement of discriminatory power; the existence of trivial yet complex webs of beliefs due to the sense or heightened discernment; and the persistence of beliefs among the educated as more comes to be known about how things actually work in the universe (Daniels, 1989, pp. 492–4).

The overall thrust of Daniels' argument is that 'none of these reasons gives the non-religious grounds to think a religious side of reality is there to be experienced and the religious at times experience it' (Daniels, 1989, p. 487).

Matthias Steup takes on Alston's analogy between perceptual practice and mystical practice from a slightly different angle. He tackles Alston's claim that perceptual practice is justified in terms of practical rationality, a claim that arises from two central considerations: '(i) there are no alternative doxastic practices available to us, we're stuck with [PP]; (ii) even if there were alternatives to [PP] available to us, we could not possibly have any reason to prefer these practices to [PP]. Because of these two considerations, we are acting rationally when we engage in [PP]' (Steup, 1997, p. 416). Steup argues, however, that this is simply not so, even in the case of PP. In response to consideration (i) above, Steup points out that there are in fact two alternatives available – 'to suspend [PP], and to judge [PP]

---

11 While Daniels does not develop the theme, his argument here seems to presume that this fact constitutes some form of a defeater for the claim that beliefs arising from Christian mystical practice are (meaningfully) justifiable in this weak sense. This is one version of the objection that will be considered below in terms of the challenge of religious diversity.

to be unreliable' (Steup, 1997, p. 416). He argues further, in response to (ii) above, that there are in fact very good reasons for preferring the option of suspending judgement regarding the reliability of PP. As we have already seen, Alston's justification of mystical practice depends in large part on his claim that PP is practically rational, and that, by analogy, so is MP. But by Steup's argument, if there are good reasons to suspend judgement regarding the reliability of PP, then, by the same analogy that Alston is at such pains to set up, the same must be said for MP.

Mystical experiences as perception

The third main counterthrust to Alston's thesis comes as an attack on his claim that mystical experiences can be properly considered as perceptual in their nature. As George Pappas points out 'It is crucial to this argument overall that mystical experiences be *perceptual*. This is the foundation of Alston's analogical argument, without which the argument does not get started. Is Alston right about this? Are mystical experiences really *perceptions*, as he says?' (Pappas, 1994, pp. 877–8). Pappas thinks there are real doubts about this. He challenges Alston's claim that 'in mystical experiences something is presented to one's consciousness in a way analogous to what happens in perception', on two main fronts. First he points out that 'Alston's way of definitively specifying the generic concept of perception seems too broad, allowing vivid object and even memory to count as perceptions, contrary to fact'. He then argues that 'several of the sources [of MP that Alston singles out] are disanalogous with ordinary perception in a way that seems to show that, whatever those reported experiences are, they are not direct presentations of God to one's consciousness' (Pappas, 1994, p. 883).

Richard Gale makes the same attack using different weaponry. He wields the sword of subjectivity against Alston: 'In order for [mystical practices] to qualify as *objective*, not just reliable, it is necessary that their M-experience inputs really be perceptual as advertised. This requires that they admit of the veridical–unveridical distinction and take objective rather than just cognate or internal accusatives when veridical, unlike the experiential inputs for the reliable but merely subjective [doxastic practices] based on sensations and introspection, in which an objective accusative is one that exists independently of experience' (Gale, 1994, p. 869). Gale argues that there are two generic conditions for an experience being perceptual – a metaphysical requirement and an epistemological requirement. The former is the requirement that 'the object of a veridical . . . perception be perceivable by different perceivers at the same time and the same perceiver at different times' (Gale, 1994, p. 871), while the latter is the requirement that 'there must be a system of background overriders that make it possible for a belief to be shown to be epistemically unwarranted or even false' which confers on the relevant experience a 'cognitive status', 'in that it bestows a prima facie justification upon the objective belief based on it' (Gale, 1994, p. 873). Both of these requirements are fulfilled by sense experiences, thus qualifying them as objective. But, Gale argues, it is 'at least dubious' whether mystical experiences live up to the epistemological requirement, and 'it is certain that they completely fail to meet the metaphysical requirement' (Gale, 1994, p. 875). Thus Gale concludes that mystical experiences are therefore subjective and are as a result not properly considered perceptual. If Gale and Pappas are successful in their arguments, then, as Pappas puts it, 'a key premise in that argument has been lost' (Pappas, 1994, p. 883).

Religious diversity

Of all the approaches in the offensive against Alston's arguments in *Perceiving God*, the most widely deployed is what could be called 'the problem of religious diversity', or, more accurately, 'the problem of mutually incompatible forms of mystical perception across religious traditions' (Schlamm, 1993, p. 562).

Schlamm rejects Alston's argument that 'where the "fruits of the spirit" (e.g. sanctity, serenity, peace, joy, fortitude, love etc.) are realized in an individual's life, it is reasonable for that individual to claim that Christian mystical perception provides genuine cognitive access to ultimate reality, even if he cannot see how to solve the problem of religious pluralism' (Schlamm, 1993, p. 562). Schlamm bases his rejection of Alston's argument on his observation that it must be unconvincing to 'sophisticated' Christians who must of necessity recognize that the 'fruits of the spirit' may be present in believers from other religious traditions, and may, indeed, be more pronounced among non-Christian believers. 'Such a disturbing realization will hardly be reassuring to the Christian mystic, or to the mystic of any other religious tradition' (Schlamm, 1993, p. 562).

While this 'problem of religious diversity' seems to be one that resonates with many of Alston's critics, quite how the problem is seen by those critics differs. In Steup's opinion, for example, the problem is that Alston's epistemological account is too narrow to do justice to the diversity of mystical practices that exist among the range of religious traditions. He writes that 'Alston's reliability constraint is too stringent a condition to impose on epistemic justification. For if it is imposed, then, precisely because there are so many different and incompatible religious traditions, perceptual beliefs about God cannot, contrary to the book's thesis, be epistemically justified – except perhaps within the one and only one religious tradition that might be reliable' (Steup, 1997, p. 419).

Adams, on the other hand, concludes that it is the *similarity* of mystical practice among divergent religious traditions that provides the problem for Alston. He argues that across different religious traditions '[t]he ways in which people form beliefs about God's speaking to them, reproving them, forgiving them, and calling them to various tasks often remain largely the same' and concludes from this that 'there is no short or uncontroversial route from [MP] to the justification of any doctrinal system' (Adams, 1994, pp. 889–90).

Evaluation of Responses to Alston

As can be seen from the responses to Alston's thesis that we considered above, one of the biggest limiting factors of his approach to the topic is the centrality of his claim that mystical experiences constitute a form of *perception*. This is not to say that all of Alston's critics who have focused their attention on this point and the related analogy between perceptual practice and mystical practice are necessarily successful in their attacks. Alston has responded to many of his critics, often in telling ways.

Daniels (1989), for example, claims that perceptual practice is, *contra* Alston, justified in the strong, Cliffordian, sense and that mystical practice is disanalogous with perceptual practice as a result. But as Alston points out (1989, p. 501) Daniels offers no convincing argument to show that perceptual practice is, in fact, justified in the stronger (evidentialist) sense. Furthermore, some of Alston's reviewers base their criticisms on misunderstandings of his thesis. Again Daniels provides an example – he contends that he has shown that none of what Alston argues 'gives the non-religious grounds to think a religious side of reality is there to be experienced and the religious at times experience it' (Daniels, 1989, p. 487). But of course this is not Alston's purpose: 'I do not wish to argue that the non-religious have, in these kinds of considerations, a sufficient reason for supposing that some people genuinely perceive God' (Alston, 1989, p. 503). Instead, Alston's goal is more limited, namely to show that the non-religious have sufficient reason to hold that the religious are not irrational (or epistemically careless, or showing signs of malfunction, or some such), in believing that they perceive God (even if the non-religious contend that these beliefs are, in fact, false).

Still, it is hard to deny the impact of many of the criticisms levelled against Alston's Reformed epistemology. There does, for example, seem to be something clearly unsatisfactory about the central pole of Alston's theory, his attempt to account for religious epistemology solely in terms of *perception*, and it is this that lies behind many of the objections set out above.

Pappas' point that Alston's account of perception is too broad, in that it allows even phenomena such as memory to count as perceptions (Pappas, 1994, p. 883) seems hard to ignore. Indeed Alston admits that Pappas' argument 'bothers' him, and that he 'cannot claim to have the knock-down contrary argument [he] would like to deploy' (Alston, 1994a, p. 894), though he does try to respond by engaging with the specific cases that Pappas employs to back his claim.

The concern here is compounded by the fact that in *Warrant and Christian Belief* Plantinga argues that what Alston considers 'putative perception of God', by his own description, often does not involve sensory content, and therefore cannot strictly speaking be considered as perception. Plantinga grants that there have often been reported cases of non-sensory encounters with God in which nonetheless 'the presence of God is . . . palpable' (Plantinga, 2000a, p. 181), and that this, while not strictly perception, is something very like it. While Alston might be happy enough to accept 'something very like perception' as adequate to his goals, even this concession leaves concerns about the sufficiency of Alston's model – 'there is also a sort of awareness of God where it seems right to say one feels his presence, but where there is little or none of the sort of sensuous imagery that typically goes with perception' (Plantinga, 2000a, pp. 181–2). Plantinga's extended A/C model, which he does not tie to any particular form of religious experience,[12] seems, at least on this ground, to offer better prospects. Furthermore, Plantinga's model does not rely, as Alston's does, on knowledge of God resulting from a kind of perception (or any other particular belief-forming mechanism), and therefore avoids most of the difficulties Alston faces in showing this analogy to be accurate.

---

12 Though he does suggest (Plantinga, 2000a, pp. 182–3) that several different kinds of experience could, and probably do, accompany the operation of the *sensus divinitatis*, and that what he calls *doxastic experience* ('the sort of experience one has when entertaining any proposition one believes' (Plantinga, 2000a, p. 183)) is always present in the functioning thereof.

In addition to the problems linked to Alston's specific attempt to defend Christian mystical practice, there is the broader difficulty that the sort of epistemic status he is attempting to secure for Christian belief is of questionable value. As Daniels put it, 'whether a practice is . . . justified in this weak sense turns out to be of very little interest' (Daniels, 1989, p. 488). This accounts in large part for the difficulties Alston faces in dealing with the challenge of religious pluralism.

Once again we see that it is Plantinga who is among the sharpest critics of his fellow Reformed epistemologist. Among his criticisms of Alston's account is the fact that there are important kinds of belief, such as *a priori* belief and memory belief, that are obviously epistemically sound but which seemingly cannot be accounted for in Alston's schema. Another biting criticism is that Alston's account of justification is unable to fully account for what we take to be rational or reasonable beliefs:

> there are also beliefs that do have a truth-conducive ground (explained as Alston explains it) but [which] are nonetheless not sensible or reasonable. . . . So suppose I am extraordinarily gullible when it comes to set theory and believe, say, Cantor's Theorem . . ., not because I have understood a proof or been told by someone competent that it is true, but just because I picked up a comic book on the sidewalk and found therein a character who claims it is his favourite theorem. Then this belief of mine has a truth-conducive ground, but isn't rational or reasonable. (Plantinga, 2000a, p. 107)

The impact of this on the Reformed epistemologist's goal of defending belief in God is made clear when Plantinga continues as follows: 'Suppose God is indeed a necessary being; then if I believe in God just to please my friends, or because I am brainwashed or hypnotized, or because I am part of an evil social system, I will be justified in the Alston sense'[13] (Plantinga,

---

13 That is, in the broadly Jamesian sense that Alston affirms in 'Religious experience and religious belief', as discussed above.

2000a, p. 107). But this clearly will not do, and so Plantinga concludes that, like Wolterstorff, the sort of justification in terms of which Alston is defending Christian belief is too easily achieved, and that 'the *de jure* question is not the question of whether Christian belief is Alston justified' (Plantinga, 2000a, p. 107).

Enough has been said to enable us to draw our analysis of Wolterstorff's and Alston's contributions to Reformed epistemology to a close. As we have seen, both theories have drawn formidable responses, and in both cases the most telling criticisms have been echoed, and expanded upon, by their fellow Reformed epistemologist, Alvin Plantinga. In both cases the most critical weakness in their attempt to show that basic belief in God is justified has fallen short as a result of arguing for a form of justification that seems insufficient to the task of meeting the objections of Reformed epistemology's opponents. The onus therefore shifts to Plantinga's own contribution, and the obvious questions to be answered are, first, whether Christian belief meeting his notion of warrant will suffice to answer the *de jure* question, and, second, whether Plantinga's extended A/C epistemological model is able to show Christian belief to be warranted. Considering these questions, and the central objections of Plantinga's critics, is the purpose of the next two chapters.

3

Plantinga's Reformed Epistemology (I): Theory and Responses

Alvin Plantinga, John A. O'Brien Professor of Philosophy at the University of Notre Dame, is widely considered to be the leading proponent of Reformed epistemology.[1] This is in part attributable to the sheer volume of work Plantinga has produced that is related to this topic, and in part to the important role he has played in recent developments in general epistemology.[2] In this chapter I will attempt to clearly articulate Plantinga's Reformed epistemology, as well as the main lines of response that his theory has evoked. In the chapter that follows I will subject the central criticisms that have been raised against Plantinga's theory to close analysis, and draw some conclusions as to how well Plantinga's theory stands up to those criticisms.

Plantinga's Theory

One of the many reasons for Plantinga's pre-eminence in the field of Reformed epistemology is the pioneering role his work

---

1 The members of the Reformed epistemology e-group (http://groups.yahoo.com/group/reformed-epistemology/), for example, while ostensibly dedicated to discussing the work of all contemporary Reformed epistemologists and their historical predecessors, expend the vast majority of their efforts on discussions of Plantinga's work. Plantinga would, of course, be the first to acknowledge that this focus on his work unjustifiably downplays the work of Alston, Wolterstorff and others.

2 On this latter point I have in mind, in particular, his central contribution to the development of the epistemic notion of 'warrant'.

has played. His 1967 book *God and Other Minds*[3] offered the first suggestion identifiable as falling under the umbrella of Reformed epistemology, that Christian theistic belief might be justified in the absence of conclusive evidence in favour of that belief. In this work Plantinga analysed the main arguments of natural theology in favour of the existence of God. He concluded that, while there is some value in these arguments, they do not present a compelling case for God's existence. He then considered the main arguments of natural *a*theology, and again found that they do not present a compelling case, this time for God's non-existence. Plantinga next turned his attention to the case for other minds, and expounded what he considers to be the best argument for justified belief in other minds, the argument from analogy. He concludes, however, that even though this is the best argument available, it falls prey to the same problems that the teleological argument[4] succumbs to, namely that while the objections to belief in other minds 'don't seem at all formidable', at the same time, as Plantinga reasserts in a more recent work, 'there also aren't any good arguments *for* other minds – particularly if we employ the same high standards of goodness as [are] ordinarily applied to theistic arguments' (Plantinga, 2000a, p. 70). The argument is thus a parity argument based on the similarity of the dialectical structure of theistic arguments and responses to those arguments, on the one hand, and the structure of arguments for other minds and responses to those arguments on the other. The importance of all this for Reformed epistemology lies in his final conclusion – 'belief in other minds and belief in God are in the same epistemological boat; hence, if either is rational, so is the other. But obviously the former *is* rational; so, therefore, is the latter' (Plantinga, 1967, p. viii).

---

3 Which was reprinted in 1981 and 1990 – an indication of the nearly classic status this book has achieved.

4 This argument, also known as the argument from design, postulates God's existence from the claim that the universe (or living things, or human beings, or parts of living systems such as eyeballs, or capabilities such as language, etc.) shows evidence of having been designed by some or other designing agent.

While this argument offered no specific discussion of a non-evidentialist criterion for epistemic justification, it makes clear the need for such a criterion (and strongly suggests that religious belief would be justified thereby). It would thus not be unjustified to see *God and Other Minds* as the work that, more than any other, set the contemporary Reformed epistemology project in motion, though its significance only became clear even to Plantinga some time after its publication. As he writes in *Warranted Christian Belief*, 'In *God and Other Minds*, I took for granted what was then axiomatic: that belief in God is rationally justifiable only if there are good arguments for it, and only if the arguments in favour of it are stronger than the arguments against it' (Plantinga, 2000a, p. 81).

As has already been mentioned, it seems likely that it is Plantinga who should be credited with the first important use of the term 'Reformed epistemology', in his 1980 paper 'The Reformed objection to natural theology', which made more specific the underlying critique of natural theology that was present in *God and Other Minds*. Like his compatriots Alston and Wolterstorff, however, the most convenient starting-point for an investigation into the beginnings of Plantinga's contribution to Reformed epistemology proper, is in his contribution to the book *Faith and Rationality*, a chapter entitled 'Reason and belief in God'.

'Reason and belief in God' has four parts, reflecting three main 'streams of thought' relating to the topic. The first part of the paper consists of an exposition of the evidentialist objection to belief in God raised by such notable figures as W. K. Clifford, Brand Blanshard, Bertrand Russell, Michael Scriven and Anthony Flew. Plantinga unpacks just what is meant by the notion 'theistic belief', what form objections to theistic belief take, and just what the evidentialist objection amounts to. The second stream of thought that Plantinga addresses is one in which he compares Aquinas' views on faith and knowledge with evidentialism, and concludes that Aquinas' approach depends, like the evidentialist position, on classical foundationalism. Plantinga then goes on to argue the by-now-familiar general epistemological point taken as starting-point by all three of Reformed epistemology's key thinkers, 'that classical foundationalism is both false and self-referentially incoherent; it should therefore be summarily rejected' (Plantinga, 1983a, p. 17). The third stream of thought, though negatively phrased in terms of 'The Reformed objection to natural theology', sees the emergence of Plantinga's positive response – drawn from the Reformed tradition in theology and characteristic of Reformed epistemology in general – to the 'collapse' of classical foundationalism and its cognates evidentialism and natural theology. At the heart of this response is the idea that belief in God is *basic*, 'that is, such that it is rational to accept it without accepting it on the basis of any other propositions or beliefs at all' (Plantinga, 1983a, p. 72). More than that, it is *properly* basic, according to Plantinga. In *Warranted Christian Belief*, Plantinga points out that there are at least two senses in which a belief can be properly basic. First, a belief can be properly basic for a person if it is indeed a belief that is not dependent on other propositions, 'and, furthermore, he is justified in holding it in the basic way: he is within his epistemic rights, is not irresponsible, is violating no epistemic or other duties in hold-ing that belief in that way' (Plantinga, 2000a, p. 178). This is the sense of proper basicality that occupied Plantinga in 'Reason and belief in God'. The second form of proper basicality, proper basicality with respect to warrant, is only dealt with in his later work, and will be discussed below.

Plantinga's claim in 'Reason and belief in God' is that 'one can *rationally accept* belief in God as basic; . . . one can *know* that God exists even if he has no argument, even if he does not believe on the basis of other propositions' (Plantinga, 1983a, p. 73).[5] More than that, Plantinga draws from the Reformers the belief that a faith that is based, not on basic belief, but on the arguments of natural theology, is an unreliable and undesir-able faith. Quoting the nineteenth-century Dutch theologian

---

5 Plantinga attributes this notion to Calvin, but it is very clear from the context that this is also Plantinga's view.

Herman Bavinck, Plantinga writes that: 'we receive the impression that belief in the existence of God is based entirely upon these proofs. But indeed that would be "a wretched faith, which, before it invokes God, must first prove his existence"' (Plantinga, 1983a, p. 64).

This is not to say that natural theology is without any merit. To the contrary Plantinga recognizes the value of natural theology in two respects. First, he claims, if there were indeed good arguments for the existence of God, 'that would be a fact worth knowing in itself – just as it would be worth knowing (if true) that the analogical argument for other minds is successful, or that there are good arguments from self-evident and incorrigible propositions to the existence of other minds' (Plantinga, 1983a, p. 73). The other great value of natural theology that Plantinga recognizes is the role it could play in 'moving people toward' basic belief in God. As he puts it in his unpublished lecture 'Two dozen or so theistic arguments', such arguments 'can serve to bolster and confirm ("helps" a la John Calvin); perhaps to convince'.

The final part of Plantinga's essay goes on to defend this fundamental claim of the basicality of Christian belief against four objections. The first Plantinga entitles 'the Great Pumpkin Objection', which he expresses as follows: 'If belief in God is properly basic, why cannot *just any* belief be properly basic? Could we not say the same for any bizarre aberration we can think of? What about voodoo or astrology? What about the belief that the Great Pumpkin returns every Halloween? Could I properly take *that* as basic? . . . If we say that belief in God is properly basic, will we not be committed to holding that just anything, or nearly anything, can properly be taken as basic, thus throwing wide the gates to irrationalism and superstition?' (Plantinga, 1983a, p. 74). Plantinga concludes that even if the Reformed epistemologist has no fully-fledged criterion of proper basicality, she may nonetheless conclude that belief in the Great Pumpkin is not properly basic, so long as she can point to some relevant difference between the two sets of belief. Such a difference can be found, according to Plantinga, when examining the conditions that 'justify and ground belief in God'. 'Thus, for example, the Reformed epistemologist may concur with Calvin in holding that God has implanted in us a natural tendency to see his hand in the world around us; the same cannot be said for the Great Pumpkin, there being no Great Pumpkin and no natural tendency to accept beliefs about the Great Pumpkin' (Plantinga, 1983a, p. 78).

The second objection Plantinga turns his attention to is related to this last response – it is the objection that belief in God is groundless. He argues for this point by drawing an analogy with other beliefs that we take to be basic, such as perceptual beliefs and memory beliefs. These beliefs are, according to Plantinga, basic but also have some ground of justification. The same goes, he argues, for theistic beliefs. The third objection to his thesis that Plantinga anticipates is that, if belief in God is basic, it must follow that no *argument* could cause a believer to alter or give up that belief – the belief would be impervious to argument. Again Plantinga argues that such a claim is unjustified. The basicality of theistic belief, like any basic belief, entitles the believer only to *prima facie* justification of that belief. Just as the basic belief 'I see a tree' faces various defeaters,[6] so the same goes for theistic belief. The final objection Plantinga defends his basicality thesis against is the accusation of *fideism*.[7] Plantinga assesses Reformed epistemology against two grades of fideism: 'moderate fideism, according to which we must rely upon faith rather than reason in religious matters, and extreme fideism, which disparages and denigrates reason' (Plantinga, 1983a, p. 87). He contends, in response, that the Reformed epistemologist views

---

6 'I might know, for example, that I suffer from the dreaded dendrological disorder, whose victims are appeared to treely only when there are no trees present. If I do know that, then I am not within my rights in taking as basic the proposition *I see a tree* when I am appeared to treely' (Plantinga, 1983a, p. 83).

7 'According to my dictionary fideism is "exclusive or basic reliance upon faith alone, accompanied by a consequent disparagement of reason and utilized especially in the pursuit of philosophical or religious truth"' (Plantinga, 1983a, p. 87).

the central truths of Christianity as among the deliverances of reason (as the Reformed epistemologist understands that notion) and that therefore there is no essential conflict between faith and reason in the Reformed epistemologist's schema.

'Reason and Belief in God', then, can be considered as foundational to Plantinga's contribution to Reformed epistemology. To this platform he added several additional papers which extended the arguments made in 'Reason and belief in God'[8] and which also added new dimensions to his basic argument.[9] In addition to this Plantinga focused a great deal of his energy on general epistemology, culminating in the development of his theory of epistemic warrant and proper function.[10] In *Warrant: The Current Debate* Plantinga undertakes a survey of contemporary epistemology,[11] clarified by his separation of the notion of justification from that of warrant. He rejects justification as being insufficient to the task of providing a basis for knowledge, and concludes that the theories of warrant he considers also fall short of the mark. This is, in effect, a 'ground-clearing exercise', through which Plantinga opens up the field for the introduction of his own theory of warrant, in *Warrant and Proper Function*. Here Plantinga argues that the

---

8 For example in 'The Reformed objection revisited' (1983b), 'Coherentism and the evidentialist objection to theistic belief' (1986b), 'Is theism really a miracle?' (1986c), 'On taking belief in God as basic' (1986d), 'The foundations of theism: a reply' (1986e), 'Justification and theism' (1987), 'The prospects for natural theology' (1991a), and 'Pluralism: a defense of religious exclusivism' (1995a).

9 Particularly in 'Epistemic probability and evil' (1988b) and 'An evolutionary argument against naturalism' (1991b).

10 See for example 'Epistemic justification' (1986a), 'Chisholmian internalism' (1988a), 'Positive epistemic status and proper function' (1988c), 'Justification in the twentieth century' (1990), 'Warrant and designing agents: a reply to James Taylor' (1991c), 'Why we need proper function' (1993c).

11 He considers all the main theories of justification and warrant (internalism, deontologism, coherentism, and reliabilism), particularly those theories linked with the thought of Chisholm, BonJour, Bayes, Pollock, Dretske, Goldman and even Alston.

factor that turns true belief into knowledge is the proper functioning of one's cognitive faculties in the appropriate environment. 'More fully, a belief has warrant just if it is produced by cognitive processes or faculties that are functioning properly, in a cognitive environment that is propitious for that exercise of cognitive powers, according to a design plan that is successfully aimed at the production of true belief' (Plantinga, 2000a, p. xi). After a 'first approximation' of his theory of warrant and some development thereof in chapters 2 and 3, Plantinga goes on to consider the applicability of his theory to some of the central areas of knowledge – other persons and testimony, perception, *a priori* knowledge, and induction. He then considers and responds to current theories of epistemic probability, before a short chapter focused on coherence, foundations and evidentialism. The final two chapters of *Warrant and Proper Function* provide a strong clue to what probably initiated the development of Plantinga's epistemic model in the first place. He first assesses whether a successful naturalist[12] account of proper function can be given, and concludes that there are no likely candidates. Plantinga then goes on to construct his now-famous[13] evolutionary argument against naturalism, in the final chapter entitled 'Is naturalism irrational?'

The final book in Plantinga's 'warrant' trilogy, *Warranted Christian Belief* (hereafter WCB), is in one sense the culmination of all the epistemological work of Plantinga's philosophical career. It is, of course, a sequel to the two preceding books on warrant, published seven years earlier, but Plantinga points out

---

12 'As Bas van Fraassen notes, it isn't easy to say precisely what naturalism *is*; for present purposes, suppose we take it to be the view that there is no such person as God, nor anyone or anything at all like him (it isn't that you believe, for example, that there are one or more finite gods). Paradigm cases of naturalism would be the views of Daniel Dennett in *Darwin's Dangerous Idea* or Bertrand Russell in "A Free Man's Worship" . . .' (Plantinga, 2000a, p. 227).

13 Plantinga's argument has provoked a flurry of responses, including an entire book dedicated to analysing it, *Naturalism Defeated? Essays on Plantinga's Evolutionary Argument Against Naturalism* (Beilby, 2002).

that it 'is also, and in a slightly different direction, a sequel to *God and Other Minds* . . . and 'Reason and belief in God' . . .' (Plantinga, 2000a, p. xi). Thus WCB represents the confluence of the two main streams of Plantinga's epistemic thought, the specifically religious dimension thereof and the development of his general model of warranted belief. WCB is 500 pages of closely argued text, expounding ideas developed over the course of a distinguished philosophical career. It would not, I think, be unjustified to view WCB as the central text of Reformed epistemology as it has developed thus far.

The main thrust of WCB is an attempt to respond to an objection to Christian belief that has been raised by such thinkers as Nietzsche, Marx and Freud. Put in the form of a question, the objection is as follows: 'is [Christian theistic belief] intellectually acceptable? In particular, is it intellectually acceptable for *us, now*? For educated and intelligent people living in the twenty-first century, with all that has happened over the last four or five hundred years?' (Plantinga, 2000a, p. viii). This question is different from the historically more common objection raised against Christian belief, that it is simply not true. This Plantinga calls the *de facto* question. The question the book is aimed at answering, on the other hand, the question of the intellectual acceptability of Christian belief *regardless of whether it is true*, is (as we have seen) what Plantinga calls the *de jure* question.

A large part of Plantinga's project focuses on establishing just exactly what the *de jure* question amounts to. 'The conclusion of such an objection will be that there is something wrong with Christian belief – something other than falsehood – or else something wrong with the Christian believer: it or she is unjustified, or irrational, or rationally unacceptable, in some way wanting. But *what* way, exactly? Just what is it to be unjustified or irrational? No doubt it is a bad thing to hold beliefs that are rationally unjustified: but what precisely is the problem? Wherein lies the badness?' (Plantinga, 2000a, pp. ix–x).

In part II of WCB Plantinga draws out the three main candidates for the *de jure* question – the question of whether Christian belief is *justified*, whether it is *rational*, and whether it is *warranted*. It is no surprise, in the light of the previous two books of his trilogy, that Plantinga considers only the latter question to be a viable version of the *de jure* challenge. In assessing the question of justification, Plantinga turns again to his critique of classical foundationalism, particularly as espoused by Locke, and various contemporary notions of justification (including Alston's notion of justification), and concludes that all these fail to produce a viable *de jure* question. The same conclusion is reached with respect to rationality, where again Alston looms large. In chapter 5 Plantinga turns to 'the Freud-and-Marx complaint', which he interprets as being the criticism 'that religious belief is not produced by cognitive faculties that are functioning properly and aimed at the truth' (Plantinga, 2000a, p. 152). This fits clearly with Plantinga's concept of warrant as proper function, and in part III of WCB he goes on to build an epistemic model whereby, he argues, Christian belief fulfils all the requirements of his theory of warrant.

Plantinga calls his epistemic model of warranted Christian belief the 'Aquinas/Calvin model' (hereafter A/C model). At its heart is the idea that is found in the work of both Aquinas and Calvin that 'there is a kind of natural knowledge of God' (Plantinga, 2000a, p. 170), what Calvin (and Plantinga following him) calls the *sensus divinitatis*. More specifically, 'the *sensus divinitatis* is a disposition or set of dispositions to form theistic beliefs in various circumstances, in response to the sorts of conditions or stimuli that trigger the working of this sense of divinity' (Plantinga, 2000a, p. 173). As one might expect from a model at the heart of Reformed epistemology, the *sensus divinitatis* produces beliefs that are *basic* – that is, not arrived at as a result of inference or argument, but in the immediate way that beliefs arrived at through perception or memory occur. Beliefs arrived at as a result of the functioning of the *sensus divinitatis* are also *properly* basic. With respect to justification, Plantinga argues that such beliefs are properly basic in that the believer 'is within his epistemic rights, is not irresponsible, is violating no epistemic or other duties in holding that belief in that way' (Plantinga, 2000a, p. 178).[14] Such beliefs also *conceptually* fit the bill for proper basicality with respect to warrant:

> The sensus divinitatis is a belief-producing faculty (or power, or mechanism) that under the right conditions produces belief that isn't evidentially based on other beliefs. On this model, our cognitive faculties have been designed and created by God; the design plan, therefore, is a design plan in the literal and paradigmatic sense. It is a blueprint or plan for our ways of functioning, and it has been developed and instituted by a conscious, intelligent agent. The purpose of the *sensus divinitatis* is to enable us to have true beliefs about God; when it functions properly, it ordinarily *does* produce true beliefs about God. These beliefs therefore meet the conditions for warrant; if the beliefs produced are strong enough, then they constitute knowledge. (Plantinga, 2000a, p. 179)

Whether Christian beliefs are *in fact* warranted is a question Plantinga does not propose to answer, because it is dependent on the *de facto* question about Christian belief. If there is not, in fact, a God as described by Christian theism, then it is unlikely in the extreme that 'belief in God is produced by a process that is functioning properly in a congenial epistemic environment according to a design plan successfully aimed at the production of true belief' (Plantinga, 2000a, p. 188). On the other hand, if there is indeed a God as Christians have traditionally conceived him, then the likelihood seems very high that Christian belief *is* warranted. Thus, according to Plantinga, his A/C model shows that the *de jure* question is not separable from the *de facto* question. If his model succeeds, then the opponent of Christian theism can effectively only challenge the believer as to the *truth* of his or her beliefs.

True to traditional Christian doctrine, Plantinga does not stop with the basic A/C model. Quite obviously, if there is such a thing as a *sensus divinitatis* it does not function properly in

---

14 Plantinga directs his reader to 'Reason and belief in God' for his arguments in this regard.

every human being. This is explained in Christian doctrine as the cognitive effect of sin. Sin has a number of destructive consequences, in particular the ruin of relationship between humankind and their creator and the degradation of relationships between members of the human race. In the specifically epistemic sense, sin is analogous to a cognitive disease, which results in the partial or complete disabling of the *sensus divinitatis*. Of course, if this were true across the board, that is if all human beings were irremediably affected by this cognitive disease, there would be no Christian beliefs (or at least, no warranted Christian beliefs). But Plantinga, again reflecting traditional Christian doctrine, clearly believes that there are warranted Christian beliefs, and so he sets out to extend his A/C model to show how the negative cognitive effect of sin can be (and in some cases is) overcome in such a way that the requirement of proper function is still met. This overcoming, or salvation, is made possible by 'the life, atoning suffering and death, and resurrection of Jesus Christ, the incarnate second person of the Trinity' (Plantinga, 2000a, p. 243). The epistemic effect of this salvation is made possible by a three-tiered cognitive process set in place by God, involving Holy Scripture, the intervention of the Holy Spirit, and faith. Briefly, the fallen sinner, on encountering the divinely inspired Word of God (Holy Scripture), experiences the intervention of the Holy Spirit who rectifies the cognitive and moral damage sin has inflicted on the sinner, and who furthermore enables the sinner to become a believer by faith (which has both an epistemic and motivational aspect) (Plantinga, 2000a, pp. 243–4).

In sum, then, on this model warranted Christian belief in a believer infected with the cognitive disease of sin (the result of the Fall), is the product of the *sensus divinitatis* which has been repaired by what Plantinga calls 'the internal instigation of the Holy Spirit' (hereafter the IIHS) working in conjunction with what is revealed in the Christian Scriptures.

In the final chapter of part III Plantinga addresses some of the objections he foresees being raised against his extended A/C model, including what he calls 'Son of Great Pumpkin' – an extension of the 'Great Pumpkin' objection addressed in his earlier work. The final part of the book, part IV, constitutes an examination of what it would mean for something to be a defeater of Christian theistic belief, and a consideration of three of the main candidates – the challenge posed by historical biblical criticism, that posed by postmodernism and pluralism, and the problem of suffering and evil.

Responses to Plantinga

As we have seen, there are good reasons to doubt whether the theories articulated by Wolterstorff and Alston, at least as they currently stand, have the wherewithal to much advance the Reformed epistemologist cause. More specifically, it seems clear that they do not offer complete responses to the *de jure* challenge. Of the central proponents of Reformed epistemology, that leaves only Alvin Plantinga as a potential beacon of hope for those of this persuasion. In the remainder of this chapter I will rehearse the main objections levelled against Plantinga's thesis, and in the next I will assess them.

Like Alston, the culmination of Plantinga's work in the area of Reformed epistemology thus far appears in book form, in *Warranted Christian Belief* (WCB). For this reason, in articulating the main critiques of Plantinga's work, I shall focus mainly on those that have been raised in response to WCB. This book is the most recent of the central texts of Reformed epistemology to appear in print, and for this reason critiques continue to appear in print at a steady rate, making it impossible to give a definitive account of what the main responses to Plantinga's work are. Nevertheless, there have been sufficient rejoinders to WCB to enable readers thereof to identify no less than eight main axes of attack, namely: critiques of Plantinga's theory of warrant; expository and theological challenges; a reassessment of the 'defeaters' of Plantinga's theory which he assesses and rejects; challenges to the coherence of the extended A/C model; challenges to the proper basicality of Christian beliefs; a range of ethical objections; the objection that Plantinga's theory does not go far enough and that some further question(s) must be dealt with to properly deal with the rationality of Christian belief; and, finally, the problem of religious diversity. I have set out all of these lines of critique elsewhere (Baker, 2005), and there is little to be gained by repeating all of that here. In what follows I will set out only those objections that are most relevant to the purposes of this book. I set aside the objections to Plantinga's theory of warrant in general, for though his contribution to Reformed epistemology rests on the success of his theory of warrant, these objections nonetheless are more properly dealt with in a work dealing with general epistemology. I also do not assess reassessments of the 'defeaters' of Plantinga's theory which he assesses and rejects (defeaters which centre around the issues of the nature of Christian scripture, postmodernism and pluralism, and suffering and evil), partly because these topics are simply too broad in their scope to be analysable here, but more importantly because whether or not there exist genuine defeaters for Christian belief does not directly impact on the model of Christian believing that is put forward by Plantinga. The remainder of the objections shall be set out in what follows.

As indicated above, in the next chapter I will subject the objections set out below to close analysis, in order to make clear how well Plantinga's thesis withstands them. I conclude that, while some of the objections are misplaced, Plantinga's thesis nonetheless still suffers from some important weaknesses. In Part 2 of the book I will turn to resources I claim to be available in Charles Taylor's philosophy for addressing these weaknesses, and so for taking the Reformed epistemology project further than even Plantinga achieves.

Proper basicality

Since Plantinga published his 1981 paper 'Is belief in God properly basic?', there have been a slew of papers addressing this question. Perhaps most notable has been the series of skirmishes between Richard Grigg (1983 and 1990) and Mark McLeod (1987 and 1988) over Grigg's claim that there are at least three significant disanalogies between, on the one hand, properly basic beliefs such as certain kinds of perceptual beliefs, memory beliefs and beliefs about other persons, and, on the other hand, belief in God. The proclaimed disanalogies in question are, first, that there exists 'some kind of psychological benefit to belief in God, and hence a bias toward that belief, which does not exist in the case of the paradigm beliefs', second that 'there is a universality about the genesis of the paradigm beliefs that does not attach to the genesis of belief in God', and finally that whereas the 'paradigm beliefs' can usually be checked and tested against empirical evidence, the same is not true for beliefs about God (Grigg, 1990, p. 390).

Other questions raised in this vein ask whether religious belief in Plantinga's scheme is not in fact based on the evidence of testimony, rather than being, in fact, properly basic. Frank D. Schubert's 1991 paper 'Is ancestral testimony foundational evidence for God's existence?' is dedicated to this question, and Helm makes much the same point when he writes that:

> The extended model, extended to cover the 'full panoply of Christian belief', is a testimonial model. Suppose that as a result of study, thought, discussion and prayer [Plantinga, 2000a, p. 251] the Holy Trinity's place in the great things of the gospel is borne in upon me. I say, 'That's right, that's the truth of the matter; this is indeed the word of the Lord' [Plantinga, 2000a, p. 250]. It is hard to think that all these activities are, as Plantinga claims, simply the *occasion* for the grounding of the appropriate belief [Plantinga, 2000a, p. 259] and not part of the grounding. And of course doctrines such as the Trinity, which are thus borne in upon me, are themselves human and therefore fallible inferences from the Scriptures. (Helm, 2001, p. 1113)

Marcus Hester takes a slightly different tack on Plantinga's 'basic belief' position, one which challenges the usefulness of

Plantinga's doctrine as a stand-alone argument. Hester argues that 'one cannot show belief in a particular personal God to be properly basic except to those who already believe in the reality of a particular personal God'. According to Hester this does not, however, sound the death-knell for 'basic belief' arguments, but it does show the necessity of something like natural theology (something which Plantinga is eager to distance himself from) to do the work of 'defeating defeaters' of belief in a particular personal God. Hester concludes, in a very similar vein to Willard (below), that 'One cannot reasonably believe in the reality which is the object of an epistemological category, such as belief in a particular personal God, unless one believes all the defeaters of that category can be defeated' (Hester, 1990, p. 413)

The ethical objection

The next line of attack in the counter-Plantinga onslaught that must be considered for our purposes is more difficult to define, in that it is nowhere to my knowledge stated explicitly as an objection to Plantinga's model.[15] The objection is an *ethical* one (or at least something very close to an ethical objection), that somehow one ought not to accept Plantinga's model, on the grounds that it is *exclusivist* and restricts the category of rational belief to too narrow a circle.[16] In this sense, the ethical

---

15 It appears implicitly in statements like the following: '... Plantinga seems not to have much to say to those Christian believers whose beliefs are not of Plantinga's kind, and nothing to say to the adherents of other religions and of none' (Swinburne, 2001, p. 207); and '... it looks as if those who believe in God or Christianity only non-basically, i.e., only on the basis of reasons or arguments, are treated too harshly. Granted that atheists are irrational, for Plantinga, because of their failure to produce beliefs based on the *sensus divinitatis*, is it right to account also those who do believe, but do so only on the basis of arguments, irrational because they fail to believe basically?' (Hill, 2001, p. 49).

16 That these considerations provide a prima facie reason for rejecting or at least being suspicious of Plantinga's theory is generally assumed, and seldom defended.

objection often appears in the guise of an objection based on religious diversity – as Plantinga puts it, '. . . we can take some of the complaints about exclusivism as intellectual criticisms: it is irrational or unjustified to think in a exclusivistic way. And the other large body of complaint is moral: there is something morally suspect about exclusivism: it is arbitrary, or intellectually arrogant, or imperialistic. As Joseph Runzo suggests, exclusivism is "neither tolerable nor any longer intellectually honest in the context of our contemporary knowledge of other faiths"' (Plantinga, 2000b, p. 175).

As we shall see below, one interpretation of Terrence Tilley's response to Reformed epistemology fits closely with the objection being considered here – Tilley's implied assimilation of the dreaded label 'fundamentalist' to the Reformed epistemologist's approach. To accuse a belief-system of being fundamentalist is at least to accuse it of an unacceptable level of dogmatism, and at worst to make the claim that it displays ethically unacceptable levels of bigotry, where hatred of the excluded is also usually implied.

The 'further question' objection

Perhaps the most nagging question in the minds of many readers of WCB is, even granting the success of what Plantinga sets out to do, whether the book actually engages with a meaningful objection to Christian belief in general, or, at the very least, Christian belief of the sort that Plantinga and his cohorts are eager to defend.[17] At its root the frustration expressed by Plantinga's critics along these lines seems to go back to his distinction between the *de facto* and the *de jure* question. Plantinga attempts only to answer the latter question, and in the end concludes that it cannot be answered independently of the

---

17 This question is not one that is restricted to Plantinga's work. As can be seen in the exposition above, the same question has been raised against Wolterstorff's and Alston's contributions, and can thus be seen as a central challenge to the Reformed epistemology project as a whole.

former. In Plantinga's scheme Christian beliefs are probably warranted if they are true, and probably not warranted if they are false. Many critics find this conclusion unsatisfying – here Swinburne sums up the objection well: 'There is, however, a monumental issue which Plantinga does not discuss, and which a lot of people will consider needs discussing. This is whether Christian beliefs do have warrant (in Plantinga's sense). He has shown that they do, if they are true; so we might hope for discussion of whether they are true' (Swinburne, 2001, p. 206).

Evan Fales sounds like Swinburne in expressing his sense of dissatisfaction as to the incompleteness of Plantinga's response: 'Perhaps God has implanted within me a [*sensus divinitatis*] by the light of which I could come to know Him. Perhaps, even, the [Holy Spirit] is at work, labouring to break through that deep, tough encrustation of sin that overshadows and cripples my cognitive faculties. But how can I know whether this is so? How can Plantinga know it? Is Plantinga's "model" of our cognitive constitution correct, or merely a just-so story?' (Fales, 2003, p. 358). For Fales, however, it is not that Plantinga does not address the *de facto* question that is troubling (as is implied in Swinburne's point above), instead he contends that there are in fact two *de jure* questions that it is 'perfectly proper' to ask in response to Plantinga's theory: 'First, is Plantinga correct in his estimate of the likelihood, on theism, that God has granted us cognitive faculties that are warrant-producing with respect to Christian beliefs? Second, is there any independent evidence, presumably of an empirical sort, for the existence of such faculties?'[18] (Fales, 2003, p. 360). Rose Ann Christian makes a similar point when she writes that 'without some reason for accepting the keystone of Plantinga's analysis, Calvin's theological anthropology, we will not know whether the believer

---

18 It is not entirely clear that the latter is truly a *de jure* question. Certainly it is not the first-level *de facto* question that Plantinga sets aside, but nonetheless it seems to be a *de facto* question of sorts, and furthermore one that would seem to be inextricably tied to the answer of the first-level *de facto* question.

Plantinga characterizes is rational or irrational in his conduct, community practice and epistemic rights notwithstanding' (Christian, 1992, p. 572).

Like Christian, Linda Zagzebski's version of this objection revolves around her claim that Plantinga's response is not sufficient to answer the question of whether or not Christian belief is rational. She is happy enough to concede that Plantinga has responded successfully to the objectors to Christian belief he has in mind, namely 'those who, with a sneer, accuse traditional Christians of being beyond the pale of rationality while admitting that the truth status of Christian beliefs is an open question' (Zagzebski, 2002, p. 119). But this, she contends, is only part of the story, for 'some of the challenges to the rationality of Christian belief arise out of a sincere and intelligent understanding of that tradition. Some even come from Christians themselves who want a deeper understanding of how Christian belief can meet the standards of rationality in that tradition' (Zagzebski 2002, 119). Zagzebski believes that Plantinga's theory does not help these enquirers, because it falls short of two principles she identifies, one of which she calls the 'Rational Recognition Principle', which is the idea that '*If a belief is rational, its rationality is recognisable, in principle, by rational persons in other cultures*'[19] (Zagzebski, 2002, p. 120). Plantinga's model violates this principle, in Zagzebski's view, because

> It does not permit a rational observer outside the community of believers in the model to distinguish between Plantinga's model and the beliefs of any group, no matter how irrational and bizarre – sun-worshippers, cult followers, devotées of the

---

19 The other principle Zagzebski believes Plantinga's model falls foul of is her 'Need to Resolve Conflict Principle', namely, that 'It is rational to attempt to resolve putative conflicts of beliefs between cultures' (Zagzebski, 2002, p. 121). Because this principle is almost identical to 'Basinger's Rule', which I consider below, I offer no independent assessment of Zagzebski's 'Need to Resolve Conflict Principle' in this book.

Greek gods . . . assuming, of course, that they are clever enough to build their own epistemic doctrines into their models in a parallel fashion. But we do think that there are differences in the rationality of the beliefs of a cult and Christian beliefs, *even if* the cult is able to produce an exactly parallel argument for a conditional proposition to the effect that the beliefs of the cult are rational if true. Hence, the rationality of such beliefs must depend upon something other than their truth. (Zagzebski, 2002, p. 122)

Religious diversity

We come now to the objection built around the problem posed to Plantinga's model by the existence of a diverse range of religious (and non-religious) beliefs, many of them incompatible with the brand of Christian belief Plantinga sets out to defend. Or, more accurately, what we have here is a closely related family of objections stemming from the fact of religious diversity.

One such approach is to suggest that Plantinga's strategy might easily be co-opted by defenders of other religious traditions, leaving Plantinga forced to recognize a sort of epistemic pluralism which (it is implied) is something he would not wish to do. Thus Paul Helm writes that Plantinga's argument 'leaves his defence of the rationality of Christian theism not so much open to refutation as to imitation' (Helm, 2001, p. 1112), while Hill worries that 'In disposing of the traditional model of giving arguments or evidence for all one's religious beliefs, Plantinga may have disposed also of an inter-subjectively agreed standard which allows us to debate, argue, and evangelise' (Hill, 2001, p. 49). David W. Tien has arguably taken this line of attack further than any other critic. He articulates a Neo-Confucian[20] model of belief, and contends that it is probably warranted if true. Following this line of argument

---

20 Where 'Neo-Confucianism' stands for the version of Neo-Confucianism propounded by Wang Yangming.

The Neo-Confucian and the Christian would thus be on an epistemic par . . . Both parties can show how their beliefs can be warranted if their religious systems are true, but in the scenario that Plantinga has laid out, neither party can conclusively demonstrate the superiority of its position. So on the situation of religious pluralism, the Christian would be treating similar things differently if he were to continue to maintain the epistemic superiority of Christianity over Neo-Confucianism. . . . For Plantinga to escape the charge of epistemic arbitrariness, he must admit that non-Christian belief can be on an epistemic par with Christian belief. But this concession considerably weakens his argument for the rationality of Christian belief. . . . [I]f the Christian knows that other religions that contradict Christianity, such as Neo-Confucianism, can demonstrate how their beliefs can be warranted, yet she lacks a conclusive demonstration or argument for the truth of her beliefs, she has a partial defeater for her Christian belief, and by implication, for the A/C model, and hence, she is at least partially culpable in holding her Christian belief. (Tien, 2004, pp. 38–9)

Julian Willard offers a critique that explicitly straddles this 'problem of religious diversity' thrust, on the one hand, and the above-mentioned question of whether Plantinga's approach goes far enough in establishing the acceptability of religious belief, on the other. He concedes that 'true religious belief may constitute knowledge if it is produced by cognitive faculties functioning properly in an appropriate environment', but holds that 'Plantinga's religious epistemology is inadequate in another respect, for he neglects the actual intellectual and doctrinal commitments of many religious believers', and that, furthermore, 'his response to the problem of pluralism fails to account for an important intellectual obligation' (Willard, 2003, p. 279), namely that 'One who holds a given belief p, must be aware of no belief that conflicts with p, unless he has good reason for holding that p can be shown to be *more likely to be true than its rival(s)*' (Willard, 2003, p. 287, italics added).

What is suggested here is made explicit by Peter Forrest – according to this objection the fact of religious pluralism leaves Plantinga still firmly in the grip of evidentialism:

> I applaud Plantinga's robust way with those who consider that humility should make us pluralists. And he is right to note that being a pluralist on principle is self-refuting. I may have missed something but I do not think, however, that he has dealt fully with the issue. For we might be pluralists not on principle but because it so happens that some other religious or some non-religious ideology can make as good a case of being knowledge-if-true as Christianity. In that situation I fail to see why we should remain Christians unless we can give some religiously neutral grounds why Christianity is superior to other religions – which, I hold, we can. But that is to invoke reason as an aid to faith. (Forrest, 2002, p. 111)

Not surprisingly, many of Reformed epistemology's critics are less optimistic about the possibilities of finding grounds for preferring Christianity to its competitors. Here it is instructive to note the critique of the outcome of the 'properly basic beliefs' thesis given by Terrence Tilley, who argues that 'no religious discursive practice has been shown to be more reliable or justifiable than fundamentalism because the fundamentalist's basic beliefs are as reliable or justified as others' basic or derived beliefs',[21] and concludes that, depending on one's other beliefs,

---

21 David Silver offers an argument similar to this in his paper 'Religious experience and the facts of religious pluralism' (2001), in which, as Voglestein summarizes his argument, he contends that 'on Plantinga's own assumptions, if one receives testimony to the falsity of Christianity, and if one believes that the testifier is honest and that he believes that Christianity is false in the basic way, then one thereby acquires an undefeated defeater for an otherwise justified belief that Christianity is true. That is, Silver argues that even if one could rationally accept Christian belief acquired in the basic way given the absence of contra-Christian testimony, upon receiving that testimony one cannot rationally maintain Christian belief. Therefore, since there is an abun-

'The reader may take this as an argument in support either of the rationality of fundamentalism as a religious discourse, or of the irrationality of all religious discourse, or of the failure of reformed epistemology to provide any material help to theologians of any stripe' (Tilley, 1990, pp. 237–8). To rephrase Tilley's point, he is contending that Reformed epistemology is either (a) ethically objectionable because it offers legitimacy to religious fundamentalism, (b) a *reductio ad absurdum* of any and all religious belief, or (c) trivially or near-trivially true.

Finally, we would be amiss if we did not introduce David Basinger's objection to Plantinga's model. At the heart of this objection is what has become known as 'Basinger's Rule', namely the idea that, 'If a religious exclusivist wants to maximise truth and avoid error, she is under a prima facie obligation to attempt to resolve significant epistemic peer conflict' (Basinger, 2002, p. 11). This rule, while specific to the question of religious diversity, clearly also incorporates an aspect of what I called the 'further question' objection above. As Basinger describes it, the purpose of Basinger's rule is to show that the religious exclusivist (and he has Plantinga particularly in mind) must do more than simply show that he is in some minimal sense warranted in believing what he does. 'What is required of an exclusivist, as I intend it, is that she engage in belief assessment unless she can demonstrate on epistemic grounds that are (or should be) accepted by all rational people that proponents of the other perspectives *are not actually* on equal epistemic footing' (Basinger, 2002, p. 15).

Basinger opposes his 'rule' to what he calls the 'epistemic parity principle' (EPP), which he believes is at the heart of Plantinga's position and which he summarizes as follows:

---

dance of (presumably honest) testimony to the falsity of Christianity in the facts of religious pluralism, and since contra-Christian beliefs are often acquired in the basic way, Christian belief is unjustified' (Voglelstein, 2004, p. 187). Eric Voglestein offers what I believe to be a successful response to this argument in his paper 'Religious pluralism and justified Christian belief: a reply to Silver', and so I will not focus on Silver's argument here.

Even if I grant that those with whom I disagree on a given issue are justified in believing as they do, if it cannot be demonstrated that either my perspective or my explanation for why others disagree is very likely false, I remain justified in maintaining that those with whom I disagree are not actually on equal epistemic footing and, thus, in denying that belief assessment is a necessary condition for justifiably retaining my exclusive perspective. (Basinger, 2002, p. 15)

The trouble with EPP, according to Basinger, is that if the exclusivist wishes to adopt it, it must also be applied to 'intra-system disputes' (e.g. disputes between Christians over questions of Christian belief), and this surely must be undesirable. Basinger gives three main reasons for this, first that 'many exclusivists are intra-system, as well as inter-system, proselytizers' (Basinger, 2002, p. 16) and second that 'within most religious settings serious discussion of disputed doctrinal issues is encouraged' (Basinger, 2002, p. 17). The third reason Basinger points out is that 'almost all exclusivists have, as a matter of fact, modified doctrinal beliefs as the result of belief assessment triggered by the assumption that those with whom they disagree on a given intra-system issue were equally knowledgeable and sincere, that they were on equal epistemic footing' (Basinger, 2002, p. 17) and that this process of belief modification is generally viewed as both appropriate and beneficial.

Broadly, then, the basic thrust of the arguments outlined in this section is that Plantinga's model offers little to commend Christianity over any of the other religious belief systems on offer, and that this fact presents a real problem in showing Christian belief to be epistemically acceptable. The preceding sections offered related reasons to question the efficacy of Plantinga's model. In the next chapter I will turn to an analysis of what these responses achieve.

4

Plantinga's Reformed Epistemology (II): Analysis of Responses

Previously we have seen that Wolterstorff's and Alston's contributions to the Reformed epistemology project fall short of fully addressing the *de jure* challenge. We then saw that the remaining attempt by one of Reformed epistemology's central figures to address this challenge, that put forward by Alvin Plantinga, faces a wide range of objections. In this chapter we shall examine the main challenges set out above, and assess just how far Plantinga gets in responding to the *de jure* challenge.

Analysis of Responses

The main lines of response to Plantinga's work that are relevant to the project of this book, as we have seen, are those that centre around the questions of proper basicality, the ethics of belief, what I called the 'further question' objection, and the issue of religious diversity. In this section we shall consider each of these lines of response in turn. Thereafter I argue that these challenges point to a broader understanding of the *de jure* challenge, one that extends beyond the scope of Plantinga's response to what he takes to be the *de jure* challenge.

Proper basicality

I begin, as I did in the previous chapter, with a consideration of the challenges to Plantinga's theory that cluster around the claim that it does not show theistic or Christian belief to be properly basic. What is particularly interesting about these challenges is that in most cases, on analysis, it turns out they collapse into a different objection. Take for example Helm's above-mentioned objection, that it is 'hard to think' that study, thought, discussion and prayer are 'simply the occasion for the grounding of the appropriate belief' (in this case, belief in the Holy Trinity) (Helm, 2001, p. 1113) and not in fact part of the grounding of said belief.

This objection to Plantinga's basic belief thesis is, when decoded, simply an expression of the belief that Plantinga's model is not true. Put positively, Helm (and, in a more focused way, Schubert) is saying that he believes there to be a direct causal link between study, thought, discussion and prayer and the formation of theistic beliefs such as belief in the Trinitarian nature of God. The extended A/C model, on the other hand, contends that such beliefs, when formed as the result of proper functioning cognitive faculties, are arrived at through the functioning of the *sensus divinitatis* (as restored by the IIHS), which functioning is (perhaps) occasioned by study, thought, discussion and prayer. Which is correct? Certainly Helm's position has some intuitive appeal, but it is not clear that such appeal would or should faze the Reformed epistemologist. For surely, on Plantinga's model, it is entirely rational to suppose that one of the cognitive faculties that is adversely affected by sin is that of intuition. Beyond the appeal to intuition, Helm offers no argument to show why his understanding of the means by which theistic beliefs are achieved should trump that presented by Plantinga. As to his claim that 'doctrines such as the Trinity . . . are themselves human and therefore fallible inferences from the Scriptures', surely it remains open to the Reformed epistemologist to simply retort that this is not so, that such doctrines are instead the true deliverances of a properly functioning cognitive faculty (the *sensus divinitatis*) operating in its proper environment.[1]

---

1 While I do not have the space to pursue this point here, I suspect that similar responses could be made to Schubert's 1991 paper mentioned above, where Schubert takes a similar approach to Helm.

Or consider the above-mentioned objections that Richard Grigg raises against Plantinga's contention that belief in God is a properly basic belief:

1 There exists 'some kind of psychological benefit to belief in God, and hence a bias toward that belief, which does not exist in the case of the paradigm beliefs';
2 'there is a universality about the genesis of the paradigm beliefs that does not attach to the genesis of belief in God'; and
3 whereas the 'paradigm beliefs' can usually be checked and tested against empirical evidence, the same is not true for beliefs about God.

These factors, Grigg argues, show that belief in God is importantly disanalogous with other, uncontroversial, basic beliefs, and that we should therefore reject Plantinga's claim that belief in God is properly basic. Grigg's case, however, does not seem a particularly strong one. Consider the first factor. The claim that there exists some kind of psychological benefit to belief in God is, I think, often overplayed – or at least, the idea that the psychological benefit of believing in God somehow outweighs the psychological benefits of *not* believing in God, such that there is an obvious bias in favour of belief in God, seems far from obvious. Consider some of the psychological discomforts that belief in God often carries with it – the uncomfortable belief that God is aware of all my innermost thoughts and schemings, the heart-wrenching thought that many of my friends and loved ones will probably be consigned by God to an eternity in hell, the weighty idea that (as the apostle Paul puts it) the right way to understand one's life is as that of a 'slave' to the gospel of Jesus Christ,[2] and so on. Now consider some of the psychological benefits of believing that there is no God – the belief that one's destiny is one's own to shape, the idea that there is no one to whom one's life is ultimately accountable other than oneself,

---

2 Philippians 1.1, English Standard Version (footnote 1).

the comfort of knowing that the darkest recesses of one's heart are accessible only to oneself, and so on.

Even granted the dubious assumption that belief in God has psychological benefits that outweigh the psychological benefits of not believing in God to such an extent as to cause in human beings a clear bias towards the former belief, it is still not clear that this would show a significant disanalogy with other basic beliefs. Take for example memory beliefs – surely there are significant psychological benefits to believing that one's memory beliefs are, on the whole, truthful renderings of past experiences? Imagine the psychological stress if one came to doubt whether the memories you seemed to have were really memories of your own past experiences. And what about perceptual beliefs? Surely the belief that one's perceptions are truthful renderings of the world around us offers significant psychological benefits, perhaps enough so to cause us to have a significant bias towards such a belief. And doubtless the same goes for all the other beliefs that are generally accepted as uncontroversially (barring scepticism) basic. It is only the fact that these beliefs are uncontroversial that makes the psychological benefits of holding them less obvious than those that go along with belief in God.

What of the second factor, that 'there is a universality about the genesis of the paradigm beliefs that does not attach to the genesis of belief in God'? Certainly, though it might be argued that the bulk of humankind across history has held some kind of theistic (or at the very least, religious) belief, such beliefs are clearly not universal in the way that, say, memory or perceptual beliefs are. But is this point sufficient to undermine the claim that belief in God is properly basic? I do not think so. Consider this scenario, borrowed from Plantinga's response to Pollock's attempt to give a naturalistic account of proper function: 'Due to high-energy radiation from a nuclear holocaust (so we can imagine), most human beings are born with damaged optical nerves, so that they are nearly blind and nearly always in severe pain. The number of people with the new style visual system vastly exceeds the number of human beings (going all the way back to the beginning of the human race) who display the old style' (Plantinga, 1993b, p. 200). Under such conditions, beliefs formed as a result of the (undamaged) proper function-ing of visual faculties would clearly not meet any criterion of universality, at least with respect to vision-specific claims such as claims about colour, or claims about the existence of objects that cannot be known other than by visual perception (e.g. the moon and the stars). But would that therefore mean that per-ceptual beliefs formed in this way would not be properly basic? Surely not.

Of course that may just be because individual memory and later testimony has established the existence of properly basic visual perceptual beliefs in the minds of the population at large, so such a claim would be uncontentious. But let us extend the scenario as follows: The result of the nuclear holocaust was the blinding of *all* surviving human beings, and an unexpected long-term result of the radiation was that all children born thereafter were also blind. Millennia pass and the cause of the blindness disappears into the murky depths of time, and the idea that human beings could once form visual perceptual beliefs disappears from humanity's consciousness. Then one day, by some evolutionary quirk, a small number of children begin to be born with the ability to see. The bulk of the popula-tion take the claim that some people are being born with a 'new' kind of perceptual ability to be just so much poppycock, and of the media only National Enquirer Radio shows itself to be will-ing to broadcast the story of the seeing children, who report the existence of such hitherto unknown phenomena as colour and light. Clearly the perceptual beliefs formed by these children as a result of the (repaired) proper functioning of their visual faculties are not only not universal, but their having visual per-ception at all is a matter of great controversy. Does *this* now mean that their visual perceptual beliefs are not properly basic? Again it seems clear that the imagined scenario has no such consequence.

Both of these factors, while unsatisfactory in showing belief in God not to be properly basic, do however carry with them an implicit further complaint. An accusation of bias involves claiming that a certain belief or set of beliefs is out of kilter with the available evidence. Pointing to the non-universal nature of belief in God is also, in one reading, pointing out the need for something further to be said in support of such belief. This implicit thrust is made explicit in the final factor that Grigg singles out – the 'fact' that there is no way of testing or measuring belief in God against 'the evidence'. Again what is, at least in part, being expressed is a frustration at the limited nature of the Reformed epistemologist's claim – that it does not go far enough for it to be counted as weightily as the Reformed epistemologist would have us believe. Very roughly, what is implied in Grigg's argument is that *something more* must be said before the claims of Reformed epistemology can be truly taken seriously.

In this guise, Grigg's complaint about Reformed epistemology is remarkably similar to Marcus Hester's observation that 'one cannot show belief in a particular personal God to be properly basic except to those who already believe in the reality of a particular personal God' (Hester, 1990, p. 413). Hester seems here to be overstating his claim, for if what he says is true, then the philosophical debate over this issue is ultimately pointless – those who do not believe in God will never accept that belief in God is properly basic until such time (if ever) as they come to believe in God, at which point they are unlikely to be hostile to the claim that belief in God is properly basic. At best, Hester's comment consigns the question about the basicality of belief in God to the area of debate between fellow believers of different theological persuasions. But Hester cannot intend this, for one of the main points of Hester's argument is to show that Reformed epistemology still needs the arguments of natural theology. Considering that the arguments of natural theology are, on the whole, arguments for the *existence* of God, I take it as given that he does not see this need as being primarily about the theological disputes between theists.

So just what is Hester claiming? Put in more modest terms, I believe that what Hester is saying is that unbelievers are unlikely to accept belief in God to be properly basic unless they have some reason (or reasons) to think that belief in God is *true*, or at the very least *possibly true*. This makes sense of Hester's claim that 'One cannot reasonably believe in the reality which is the object of an epistemological category, such as belief in a particular personal God, unless one believes all the defeaters of that category can be defeated' (Hester, 1990, p. 413). Again this is poorly expressed – as it stands (fideism aside) it is trivially true. Of *course* if I believe that it is true that God exists I will also believe that all the defeaters of that belief can be defeated – even if, for the moment, I am at a loss to know how. If, on the other hand, I think it likely that some defeater exists for the belief that God exists, then it seems more than probable that I do not really believe that God exists.

So again it seems that a tentative restatement of Hester's claim is needed, in order for it to be at all useful. It makes better sense to phrase it, not in terms of the believer, but from the position of the unbeliever contending the claim that belief in God is properly basic. Seen this way, Hester's claim looks something like this: 'The supporter of the Reformed epistemology thesis cannot reasonably expect rational people who do not believe in God to accept that belief in God is properly basic, unless some compelling reason is given as to why the unbeliever should consider belief in God to be not just possible, but also *plausible*.'

In sum, then, the objections considered in this section turn out to be primarily challenges either to the truth of Plantinga's claims, or (more importantly for our purposes in examining the *de jure* challenge) to the plausibility of Plantinga's model. As we shall see, this latter line of objection turns out to be similar to, if not the same as, what draws together many of the other objections Plantinga's model faces.

The ethical objection

The next line of attack to be considered is what I called the ethical objection. This objection is a difficult one to pin down, as I said above, due to its largely implicit status in the writings of Plantinga's critics. At its heart, though, the ethical objection seems to focus on the *exclusivist* nature of Christian belief (or at least, that brand of Christian belief that Reformed epistemologists care to defend). It is the fact that Plantinga's model brands those who do not believe in Reformed Christianity (or something like it) as 'defective' and therefore holders of false beliefs, that troubles many of his detractors, and it is not at all difficult to understand why. The history of religious exclusivism has not been a pretty one, with the consequence that exclusivism has by and large come to be associated with intolerance, hatred and even violence.

Of course exclusivism cannot be taken to be by its nature unethical. When Plantinga presents this challenge as involving the question '. . . am I really arrogant and egoistic just by virtue of believing what I know others don't believe, where I can't show them that I am right?' (Plantinga, 2000b, p. 179), he thinks it obvious that the answer is a negative one. Certainly, anytime anyone makes some claim that some belief p is true, that statement excludes a whole range of opinions and beliefs that conflict with p. In most spheres, however, such exclusivist claims are not considered to be at all unethical – in fact, by and large, making claims of this kind is taken as a necessary component of epistemic progress. It is only really in religion (and to a lesser degree, politics) that the exclusivist is held to be morally suspect, for the historical reasons mentioned above. The historical contingency of the ethical reaction to religious exclusivism does not, however, render it irrelevant. It is only right, in the light of the excesses of the past, that exclusivist claims be treated with a healthy degree of scepticism. Of course the ethical principle does not, in itself, show that exclusivist religious claims are false – at most it tells us that in the realm of religious discourse, exclusivist claims ought only be accepted where there are strong reasons for doing so.

The ethical objection takes the challenge to Plantinga's account of warranted Christian belief a step further than those objections that simply point to the possible plurality of 'warranted-if-true' religious and non-religious positions. As we shall see below, where the plurality objections ask 'So what?' of Reformed epistemology, the ethical objection adds the rider that the exclusivist nature of Reformed-style Christian belief (and the practices associated with such belief) places an onus on the contender for this belief-system to give compelling reasons why unbelievers should give up their ethical qualms and take exclusivist Christianity seriously. Certainly, as it stands, Plantinga's model of warranted Christian belief does not meet this challenge.

The 'further question' objection

As we have seen, many, if not most, of the objections to Plantinga's thesis that are explicitly aimed at refuting his claim that religious or Christian belief can be properly basic, turn out to in fact be about something else, namely the claim that Plantinga has not done enough to show his model to be plausible or reasonably likely to be true. Swinburne's objection, as articulated in the previous chapter, may be interpreted either as something very much like this same challenge, or else as a complaint that Plantinga does not address the *de facto* question (in which case we can simply set it aside).

Evan Fales is, I think, the most articulate exponent of this line of objection when he says (as we saw): 'Perhaps God has implanted within me a [*sensus divinitatis*] by the light of which I could come to know Him. Perhaps, even, the [Holy Spirit] is at work, labouring to break through that deep, tough encrustation of sin that overshadows and cripples my cognitive faculties. But how can I know whether this is so? How can Plantinga know it? Is Plantinga's "model" of our cognitive constitution correct, or merely a just-so story?' (Fales, 2003, p. 358). Again this question does not challenge Plantinga's claim that Christian belief is warranted, instead it challenges him to provide some further reason or argument that might compel the non-believer to take seriously the claim that the extended A/C model just might be true. Likewise Rose Ann Christian and Linda

Zagzebski peg the question of the rationality of Christian belief to the ability of others to recognize its rationality, and argue that Plantinga's model does not offer sufficient motivation for the broader epistemic community to accept Christian belief to be rational.

In his response to Zagzebski's challenge, Plantinga points out that she overstates her position. In particular he takes her to task for her assumption that any set of beliefs, no matter how crazy or weird, can be defended using a model like Plantinga's A/C model. This, Plantinga argues, is manifestly untrue. While accepting that some theistic beliefs, such as those articulated in Judaism and Islam, might well be defended in this kind of way, he points out that his argument 'depends essentially upon premises about God's knowledge, intentions, and power; parallel premises about the sun or the moon or Greek gods will be manifestly false. Naturalists, furthermore, will also be unable to construct such an argument, as, indeed, will non-theists of any stripe' (Plantinga, 2002b, p. 131).

But what of the possibility of manifestly irrational theistic beliefs? Here Plantinga asks us to consider for example the belief 'that God has created rabbits that weigh 800 lbs. and live in Cleveland' and to furthermore consider that God might have created us with a *Sensus oryctolagus giganticus* to enable us to have true and properly basic beliefs about these rabbits (Plantinga, 2002, p. 131). Wouldn't such a belief, backed by this epistemic model, undermine the extended A/C model of warranted Christian belief by showing that it too would be Plantinga-warranted? Plantinga argues to the contrary:

> Zagzebski says we think such a belief irrational even if its partisans can come up with an argument like mine. Right; we do think that; and we also think that belief *false*. There aren't any rabbits of that size in Cleveland (they'd be pretty hard to miss); therefore God hasn't created any giant rabbits that live in Cleveland. This belief may be such that probably it is rational (or warranted) if and only if it is true; but the fact is it's false. So I fail to see how my strategy violates the Rational

Recognition Principle; I also fail to see that there is a problem for my strategy here. (Plantinga, 2002, pp. 131–2)

Plantinga's response here is, I believe, unsatisfactory. Implied in his response is his confidence that Christianity is true, and that this clearly sets Christian belief apart from giant-Cleveland-rabbit belief. But of course for many unbelievers Christianity seems just about as likely to be true as the existence of giant rabbits in Cleveland. As such, therefore, a model such as Plantinga's which offers no positive reason to believe that the claims of Christianity are at least plausible, does seem to fall foul of the Rational Recognition Principle. More generally, it seems clear that Plantinga's model does not meet the very reasonable requirement articulated by the thinkers whose objections fall into this 'further question' category.

Once again, therefore, as with the ethical objection, it seems a reasonable expectation of any model of Christian belief that it provide reasons for unbelievers to consider it to be plausible enough to take seriously, but again this expectation is not one that Plantinga's model satisfies.

Religious diversity

The challenge raised under the 'further question' banner is, if anything, intensified by the problem of distinguishing Christian beliefs from a multiplicity of apparently equally rational religious beliefs and practices. If Helm is right that Plantinga's argument 'leaves his defence of the rationality of Christian theism not so much open to refutation as to imitation' (Helm, 2001, p. 1112), then there's little reason to think that other religious beliefs (unless internally inconsistent, or self-undermining or something of the sort) are not also warranted if true. David Tien's attempt at showing a Neo-Confucian model of belief to be warranted-if-true, if successful, offers important support to this claim.

Before evaluating the effect of this challenge, it must be said that most of Plantinga's objectors who have taken this line of argument have overstated just what its consequences are. As a Christian himself, Daniel Hill worries that Plantinga's approach offers all religions an 'impregnable fortress', and thereby removes the grounds on which adherents of different religions can 'debate, argue, and evangelise' (Hill, 2001, p. 49). But this is quite obviously not the case – Plantinga's model only shows Christian belief to be warranted *if true*, and where the model is co-opted by other religious believers it can do no more than that. So the *de facto* question, the question of whether the beliefs one holds are in fact true, remains consciously unanswered by Plantinga-type models, and hence 'the traditional model of giving arguments or evidence for all one's religious beliefs' is in no way 'disposed of'. Nor does the existence of Plantinga's model show the *de jure* question to be a dead end – questions of internal consistency and the like can and should be asked of all belief systems, and some might well be found wanting (perhaps, say, in a manner similar to Plantinga's critique of metaphysical naturalism).

In a recent paper Michael Sudduth points out that the sort of problem that worries Hill is based on mistakenly viewing Reformed epistemology as a particular school of apologetics. He clarifies by defining the project of Reformed epistemology as follows: 'Reformed epistemology aims to clarify, defend, and – with qualification – positively support a range of second-order claims about the positive epistemic status of theistic and Christian belief' (Sudduth, 2003, p. 308). Understanding Reformed epistemology in this way helps us to see that while it is true that Reformed epistemology is in part an attempt at Christian apologetics,

> it does not follow that Reformed epistemology is itself a distinct apologetic methodology or school of apologetics. The similarities between Reformed epistemology and apologetics stem from the fact that epistemological questions are implicated in the task of apologetics. The distinctly epistemological interest of Reformed epistemology also explains why it has not focused on evidence for the truth of theistic and

Christian belief. Like other projects in general epistemology, the success and value of the project does not depend on establishing the *truth* of the beliefs the positive epistemic status of which it aims to discuss. (Sudduth, 2003, p. 308)

We saw above that Peter Forrest, David Silver and Julian Willard raise what amounts to roughly the same objection to Plantinga's model, so to avoid repetition I shall focus only on Forrest's version thereof. Forrest's statement[3] is revealing, for it shows that, like Helm, Forrest simply does not believe that belief in God is (or can be) properly basic. The manner in which Forrest speaks of Christian belief makes it clear that he thinks of Christianity as something like a theory or hypothesis, which one either assents to, or withholds assent from. But, as Plantinga points out in his response to John Mackie's similar view, there is no good reason to think that this is the best way to understand Christian belief. He asks us to consider the example of our memory beliefs – while we could of course understand and explain these beliefs in the manner of a scientific hypothesis such that 'if there were a more "economical" explanation of these phenomena that did not postulate, say, the existence of the past or of past facts, then our usual belief in the past "could not be rationally defended"'. But that this would be very obviously a false step – 'the availability of such an explanation wouldn't in any way tell against our ordinary belief that there has really been a past. Why couldn't the same hold for theism, or more broadly, for Christian belief?' (Plantinga, 2000a, p. 92)

Implicit here is Plantinga's contention that Christian belief, like memory belief, is properly basic, and can therefore not be treated in the same way as some kind of hypothesis. Here again Plantinga's case of the epistemically responsible Christian

---

3 As we saw, he claims that the fact that adherents of other religions could, at least in theory, offer as compelling a case for their beliefs being 'warranted if true' as Plantinga does for Christian belief, leaves us with no reason to remain Christians 'unless we can give some religiously neutral grounds why Christianity is superior to other religions' (Forrest, 2002, p. 111).

believer seems relevant – imagine this time, however, that not only is she aware of the philosophical objections that have been made to Christian belief, and not only has she read her Freud, Marx, Nietzsche *et al.*, but she has also undertaken a thorough investigation of other religions. She is aware that many of the religions are 'warranted-if-true' in the Plantingian sense. Nonetheless she has found that her investigation into other religions has left her unmoved, her belief in the 'great things of the gospel' remains. She has also considered the best arguments that Christian theologians have mustered to contend that Christianity is the one true faith, and while she finds much to be admired in these arguments, they are not the basis on which she 'remains a Christian'. Instead, she believes basically. Under such conditions Forrest's charge that her epistemic duty is to give up her Christian belief seems unwarranted, and, perhaps more importantly, implausible.

As with the other objectors we have considered here, however, Forrest's claim makes far more sense if the perspective is changed to that of the unbeliever. While the existence of other 'warranted-if-true' religious beliefs need not compel Christians to give up their belief, unless something further is offered beyond Plantinga's extended A/C model the fact of the plurality of religious beliefs provides a good reason why non-Christians need not give Christianity any particular credence. The charge here being levelled leaves the atheologian or the adherent of some other faith in the position of being able to shrug her shoulders and say (to borrow and adapt a phrase from Daniel Dennett) 'warranted Christian belief – so what?'

David Basinger is laudably clear-sighted about what his objection achieves. He grants that the considerations he introduces in response to what he calls Plantinga's 'epistemic parity principle' do not constitute a knock-down argument. While he restates his personal belief that religious exclusivists have an epistemic obligation to assent to 'Basinger's Rule',[4] he admits

---

4 'If a religious exclusivist wants to maximise truth and avoid error, she is under a prima facie obligation to attempt to resolve significant epistemic peer conflict' (Basinger, 2002, p. 11).

that his arguments have not proven such an obligation to exist. Instead, he believes that he has given compelling reasons why religious exclusivists should do so 'voluntarily'. In particular, he argues, in line with the other objections outlined here, that religious exclusivists need to do more than just defend the rationality of their own positions. Exclusivists 'need to see that there are good reasons to assure themselves that those religious beliefs that form the core of their exclusivity really are beliefs worthy of continued acceptance, especially in the face of epistemic peer conflict' (Basinger, 2002, p. 27). This much seems hard to deny, and again it comes to light when the focus is shifted from defending the claim that the believer is warranted in holding her beliefs, to the idea that there is value in attempting to show the unbeliever that those beliefs are warranted. As Sudduth points out, the proper basicality thesis that is at the heart of Reformed epistemology 'is a thesis about the conditions for *being* rational in holding a theistic belief, not what is permitted or for that matter required for *showing* that theistic belief is rational, much less showing it to be true' (Sudduth, 2003, p. 311). This explains why so many of the objections we have examined fail to undermine Plantinga's model – because, inarticulately, that is not their primary object. Instead, as Basinger perspicuously shows, these objections express the belief that there is a further question beyond giving a model of warranted belief for the believer, namely showing the unbeliever that there is good reason to think that the believer is in fact warranted in her belief.

Restating the Problem: The 'Expanded' *de jure* Objection

In the previous chapter I set aside the contributions to Reformed epistemology put forward by Wolterstorff and Alston, on the grounds that, for both thinkers, their attempt to show that basic belief in God is justified has fallen short as a result of arguing for a form of justification that seems insufficient to the task of meeting the objections of Reformed epistemology's opponents.

I pointed out, further, that the most damning version of this point is made, not by an opponent of Reformed epistemology, but by none other than Alvin Plantinga. In the light of what I have said in this chapter about the problems facing Plantinga's own approach to the central question of Reformed epistemology, it might be thought that Plantinga falls foul of his own criterion, and that his approach offers no advantages over the theories presented by his illustrious compatriots. But this would be too hasty a conclusion. Because of the danger of this misreading it is important to consolidate and clarify before moving on to the next chapter (and, indeed, Part 2 of the book).

First, it is important to see just what Plantinga's model does achieve, that Wolterstorff's and Alston's do not. Wolterstorff, it will be remembered, was defending Christian belief against the claim that such belief is not justified, where 'justification' is understood in the straightforward deontological sense common to many internalist theories of epistemology. But as we saw, this kind of justification could just as easily be achieved by the psychiatric patient discussed by Plantinga, who expressed dissatisfaction at not receiving sufficient credit for having invented a new form of non-sexual human reproduction by which he claimed to have populated Chicago. This illustrates Plantinga's point that Wolterstorff's notion of epistemic entitlement, with its sole focus on doing one's epistemic duty, is insufficient to the task of addressing the full range of the *de jure* challenge. Clearly, achieving this level of justification, while not unimportant,[5] falls well short of buttressing Christian belief against its objectors.

Alston seems to recognize this, and consequently adds a reliabilist element to his definition of justification (while retaining the internalism characteristic of the form of justification defended by Wolterstorff), by defining it in terms of believing on adequate *grounds*. In the light of Plantinga's psychiatric patient, Alston's approach can be seen as an attempt to shift

---

5 In that one's epistemic motives, at least, must be correct in order to achieve it.

from dealing with justification that involves only doing one's *duty*, to one that could achieve beliefs that could be considered to be *rational*. But as we saw, Plantinga argued that Alston's theory falls short of achieving this goal. Plantinga concludes that 'it is too easy to achieve justification in this sense' (Plantinga, 2000a, p. 107) – that is, Alston justification can be achieved in cases where we would wish to doubt that the belief in question counts as knowledge – and that the question that Alston answers is not really the *de jure* question directed at Christian belief.

Plantinga goes on to identify the *de jure* question as the question of whether Christian belief can be rationally considered to be (if true) *warranted*,[6] and proposes his A/C epistemological model to show that the *de jure* question can be answered in the affirmative. He concludes that, on his model, Christian belief is properly basic and therefore warranted if it is true, and not warranted if false. It seems to me that, as far as it goes, Plantinga's model achieves what he intends it to show, namely that provided Christian belief is true Christians are not irrational – or, more accurately, unwarranted – in holding the beliefs that they do hold, something that neither Wolterstorff's nor Alston's theories manage to accomplish. I take as evidence of Plantinga's success in this respect the fact that there are very few responses to Plantinga's model that take on his model directly. The vast majority of the responses (at least when decoded, as we have seen above) fall into what one could call the 'Yes, but . . .' category – that is, most take it as given that there is no internal inconsistency in Plantinga's model, but contend that this is still not a sufficient answer to the question.

So Plantinga's model does achieve more than the theories put forward by his fellow Reformed epistemologists, Wolterstorff and Alston. Nonetheless, there remain, as we have seen, real

---

6 That is, in Plantinga's terms, whether it is rationally conceivable that Christian beliefs are the product of cognitive faculties functioning in the appropriate cognitive environment according to a truth-directed design plan.

problems for Plantinga's approach. None of the arguments we have considered show (despite what some of their authors might believe) that the Christian theist ought to give up her beliefs. But many of them do give reasons to believe that there is more to be done than simply establishing that Christian beliefs, if true, are probably warranted.

So what is to be done? One possible response is to take Plantinga's model in a consciously fideist direction, as do John Bishop and Imran Aijaz in their paper 'How to answer the *de jure* question about Christian belief' (Bishop and Aijaz, 2004). But such an approach sits uncomfortably with the very reasonable position put forward by David Basinger and the many critics of Reformed epistemology who echo his position, that the Christian has a duty to at least *attempt* to offer a positive apologetic for her beliefs. From a Christian perspective, this duty arises because of the importance of *evangelism* – to be the human agents in God's quest to seek and save the lost. This is Hill's point. From an epistemological perspective, this duty arises out of the overarching goal of *discovering truth*, as Basinger reminds us. From an ethical perspective, this duty arises because of the historically contingent, but all too real, *moral wrongs* that have been carried out in the name of religious exclusivism – this point is, as I have argued, the basis of the ethical objection that seems to be implicit in the writing of many of the critics of Plantinga and his fellow Reformed epistemologists.

So it seems that the only option, other than an unattractive dogmatism, is to accept that the charge Plantinga lays at the door of his fellow Reformed epistemologists, William Alston and Nicholas Wolterstorff, that their theories are insufficient to the task of answering the *de jure* question, must also be directed at Plantinga's own response to this challenge. For Plantinga sets out to shut down the *de jure* challenge altogether, leaving only the *de facto* question to be answered. But clearly Plantinga's model leaves a gap – as we have seen, there are a range of challenges to Christian belief that still fall under the broad banner of challenges to the rationality rather than the truth of Christian belief, that are unanswered by Plantinga's model. The short-coming of Plantinga's model is not that it fails to answer the question of warrant. The problem is on a different level, namely that Plantinga is wrong to say that the *de jure* question *is* the question of warrant. Of course warrant is unquestionably part of the question, but it is not the whole question. In fact, it now seems clear that it is a mistake to think of the *de jure* challenge as being a single-faceted question. For though the Alston/Wolterstorff models are answers to 'easy' questions, it is not at all obvious that those questions are not among the cluster of questions that, setting the *de facto* question aside, are raised as challenges to the rationality of Christian belief. If we think of the *de jure* challenge as involving a number of different questions, this has the advantage that we are not forced to simply discard the theories put forward by Alston and Wolterstorff, but, instead, the option remains open to see them as partial responses to the challenge.

In order to distinguish this multi-faceted *de jure* challenge from the narrower challenge Plantinga dedicates himself to answering, I shall refer to the broad challenge as the 'expanded *de jure* challenge'. It seems clear, from what we have seen in this and preceding chapters, that the expanded *de jure* challenge has at least three facets: the question of deontic justification (addressed by Wolterstorff and Alston), the question of warrant (addressed by Plantinga), and a third question that emerges from the analysis of the responses to Plantinga's A/C model undertaken in this chapter. While this third question is difficult to formulate exactly, we will not be far off the mark if we take it to be the question of 'why should the unbeliever take Christian belief seriously enough to consider that the *de facto* question warrants attention, even granting that the Christian believer might well be both justified and warranted in her beliefs?' The plurality of other beliefs that might well also be justified and warranted raises this question, as, working in a negative direction, does the ethical challenge to Christian belief. It is a question that challenges the defender of Christian belief to offer some independent reason or reasons that might motivate her unbelieving interlocutor to take seriously the question of whether or not Christian belief is true.

Can this challenge be met? Plantinga seems to think that at least theism can be shown to be more worthy of affirmation than its competitors – this much is suggested in an unpublished but widely available lecture given by Plantinga some years ago, entitled 'Two dozen (or so) theistic arguments'. In answering the self-imposed question of what such arguments achieve, Plantinga responds: 'They can serve to bolster and confirm ("helps" a la John Calvin); perhaps to convince'.

Whether Plantinga thinks something similar can be said for specifically *Christian* apologetics can only be guessed at, though I suspect the answer is in the affirmative. If my guess is correct, then Plantinga and I are in the same boat – we both believe that positive arguments for Christian belief are possible. Where we differ is in thinking that such arguments are necessary in the face of the *de jure* question – I think they are, Plantinga seems to think they are not. C. Stephen Evans is a thinker who, like me, is sympathetic to the Reformed epistemology project but who also believes there are 'some good reasons not to break off the conversation [as] abruptly [as Plantinga does]. First, some of the atheists who find this move a little high-handed may not be hostile opponents, but sincere seekers, honestly looking for an account of the reasonableness of belief in God which they can accept. Second, some of the people who find this story of the natural tendency to believe in God dubious are not atheists at all, but believers who think one should and can have argu-ments for God's existence'[7] (Evans, 1988, p. 33).

I introduce Evans here not because his reasons for wanting to 'continue the conversation' add anything new to what the other critics of Plantinga's model that we have considered here raise,

---

7 It should be noted that Evans wrote these words in 1988, when Plantinga's full theory had yet to emerge, and they are therefore directed only at what Plantinga wrote in 'Reason and belief in God'. Nonetheless it seems clear to me, for the reasons outlined in this chapter, that these points are just as valid with regard to the fully developed A/C model of Christian belief as a response to the *de jure* challenge.

but rather because Evans offers a unique suggestion of how Plantinga's model might be augmented in order to meet this challenge. In response to the question of whether there is anything that Plantinga can do to make his argument 'more plausible', Evans expresses his belief that the answer is 'yes', and directs his reader's attention to something Plantinga himself says in this regard, namely that 'There are . . . many conditions and circumstances that call forth belief in God: guilt, gratitude, danger, a sense of God's presence, a sense that he speaks, perception of various parts of the universe. A complete job would explore the phenomenology of all these conditions and of more besides' (Plantinga, 1983a, p. 81). Evans is enthusiastic about the potential for this sort of phenomenological exploration: 'Such a phenomenology of the conditions which serve as the grounds of belief in God would be helpful in two ways. First, a fuller account would make it more understandable why the tendency is actualized in some but not others. Second, this fuller account of the ground of belief in God would provide the honest seeker with a point of contact' (Evans, 1988, pp. 32–3).

Evans dedicates the bulk of his paper to suggesting that one direction such a phenomenological exploration could take would be aided by an examination of Kierkegaard's philosophy. Evans contends that it is a central claim of Plantinga's approach that one must reject the Descartes-inspired view that we must suspend all beliefs until a criterion of rationally acceptable beliefs is established, but that instead we have no choice but to begin with 'our actual commitments, what we are subjectively willing to accept as rational, and use these commitments as examples to test hypotheses about epistemological criteria. To me it is obvious that this puts personal commitments – subjectivity in a Kierkegaardian sense – into the heart of the knowing process' (Evans, 1988, p. 31).

Evans pursues this very interesting suggestion by arguing that Kierkegaard's phenomenology offers Plantinga's project a way of 'fleshing out' his account of the proper basicality of Christian beliefs, and that the phenomenological nature of Kierkegaard's account gives it the crucial point of 'contact' with the honest enquirer that is so frustratingly absent from Plantinga's account.

The particular direction Evans takes his Kierkegaardian 'fleshing out' of Plantinga's theory is by attempting to show how Kierkegaard can give a fuller account of the action of sin in 'suppressing or overlaying this natural tendency to believe' (Evans, 1988, p. 33). I will not follow Evans any further in this regard. Instead, I want to pick up on what seems a very promising idea, namely that some phenomenological account provides a way of extending Plantinga's theory in such a way that the 'conversation' between the Christian believer and the honest enquirer can be continued. To put this in terms of the analysis of this chapter, I intend to explore whether such a phenomenological extension of Plantinga's theory might provide an answer to the question formulated above, namely, 'Why should the unbeliever take Christian belief seriously enough to consider that the *de facto* question warrants attention, even granting that the Christian believer might well be both justified and warranted in her beliefs?' The appeal to phenomenology certainly seems on the face of it to offer real potential here, for it seems to provide exactly the point of contact with the enquirer that is needed.

In what follows, in Part 2 of this book, I shall set out one such phenomenological argument, one that I believe emerges (with a little cajoling) from the philosophy of Charles Taylor. Doubtless there are other such arguments, of varying degrees of success. I have chosen to focus on this particular argument because, as I said at the beginning of this book, it seems to me to fit very neatly with the phenomenology of Plantinga's extended A/C model, and so can easily be understood as a further extension of that model. More specifically, I believe that Taylor's moral phenomenology can be seen as an expanded account of the *sensus divinitatis*, at least that part of the *sensus divinitatis* that takes moral questions as the occasion for its functioning. Another reason for attempting this fusion is that, not only does it address the shortcomings of Plantinga's model in answering the expanded *de jure* challenge, but it also goes a good way to undermining some important objections that the Taylor-inspired model faces when considered alone. These conclusions must, of course, be argued for, and there is much work yet to be done. So, without further ado, let us continue on to Part 2.

Part 2

Tayloring Reformed Epistemology

5

Charles Taylor on the Self and
the Moral

It is the goal of this part of this book, as I have said, to find some way of addressing the shortcomings of Plantinga's Reformed epistemology that were revealed in the latter stages of Part 1. It is Charles Taylor's work that I believe, and will attempt to show, offers real potential in this regard. In pursuing this argument the reader will notice that I direct my attention primarily (though not exclusively) on the analyses of Taylor's work put forward by three thinkers: Melissa Lane, Gary Gutting and Stephen Mulhall. In so doing I do not intend to suggest that Taylor's other commentators have not offered any valid critiques of his work, nor even that Lane, Gutting and Mulhall put forward the 'best' objections to Taylor's work. My reason for focusing on these three philosophers is instead that each of them offers a reading of Taylor that is in some important respect similar to mine, and therefore the concerns and criticisms they raise are of particular importance to this project.

In order to make a case for the argument I shall outline, a preliminary first step must of necessity be to set out my reading of the central elements of Taylor's work that I will be deploying in articulating that argument. That ground-laying task is the purpose of this chapter. In what follows I shall attempt to present what I believe to be the best interpretation of the relevant aspects of Taylor's work. That said, however, it must be admitted that, as will become clear, it is sometimes difficult to fix an exact definition of Taylor's concepts. In this regard we must keep in mind C. Stephen Evans' level-headed comment regarding his interpretation of the even more difficult to pin down work of Søren Kierkegaard, that 'regardless of who is right on the question of interpretation, the more interesting question is whether or not a sound point can be salvaged (or reconstructed) from [the articulated] position' (Evans, 1988, p. 30).

First Principles

Charles Taylor has been called 'the leading analytic exponent of Continental philosophy' (Smith, 2002, p. 10). Certainly his time as a student at Oxford University in the 1950s led to a genuine respect for the clarity and rigour that has long been a characteristic of the analytic tradition. Nonetheless, the strongest influences on his work have been the writings of Continental philosophers, so it comes as no surprise that among his first principles is a commitment to phenomenology.

In his book *Charles Taylor: Meaning, Morals and Modernity*, Nicholas H. Smith is perceptive in pointing out that the wide range of Taylor's philosophy, for all its diversity, is nonetheless a unified philosophical project. At the heart of that project, Smith points out, is an insight Taylor gleaned from the work of Maurice Merleau-Ponty (a crucial early influence on Taylor) namely that 'because we are in the world, we are *condemned to meaning*' (quoted in Smith 2002, p. 1). This is unpacked by Smith in the opening sentences of the first chapter of the book: 'At the core of Taylor's project is the conviction that human reality is structured, and in some sense constituted, by layers of meaning. This is the first principle of his philosophical anthropology' (Smith, 2002, p. 18).

Taylor's conviction regarding this central belief is derived at least in part from Merleau-Ponty, who, following Edmund Husserl, applied what he called 'the phenomenological method', a method aimed at producing 'an undistorted description of experience' (Smith, 2002, p. 26). The first principle of the method is the 'phenomenological reduction', also known as the 'eidetic reduction' or *epoche*. This is the principle that 'if we are to be genuinely open to the content of original experience, if we are to arrive at an undistorted or "pure" description of it, we have to be prepared to "bracket" or "suspend" the natural assumptions of ordinary reflection' (Smith, 2002, p. 26). The phenomenological reduction enables us to discover a crucial principle of the nature of consciousness, the intentionality thesis. This, in broad terms, is the idea that consciousness is always consciousness 'of' something, it is inescapably *directed*. More than that, according to Taylor, phenomenologists claim that whatever has consciousness has 'significance'. Phenomenal objects take their place in a phenomenal field, to which they refer. 'So, for instance, we perceive objects or events as "hiding" others or "bringing them into view", as being "in front of" or "behind" other things, as "the beginning of" or "end of" some object or event. Such percepts refer to or "announce" other things that are not actual or present' (Smith, 2002, p. 27). Another crucial factor of 'the significance feature' is that experience always relates to the purposes of the perceiver. 'A phenomenal object will appear, for example, as "a means to" or "in the way of" an end desired by the perceiving subject. In this sense, perception is closely tied to the way in which perceivers are "at grips" with their environment. Perception is thus intimately connected to behaviour' (Smith, 2002, p. 27)

This commitment to the primacy of the phenomenological realm is not, for Taylor, limited to perceptions of the physical world. Indeed, in his rejection of the Cartesian foundationalist project Taylor rejects any sharp division between the agent and the world she inhabits. As Taylor writes in a recent paper, 'The idea is deeply wrong that you can give a description of the agent without any reference to his/her world (or a description of the world qua world without saying a lot about the agent)' (Taylor, 2000, p. 120). The activity of knowing, for Taylor, cannot be separated from our coping with the world, a coping which depends on 'an overall sense of ourselves and our world; which sense includes and is carried by a spectrum of rather different abilities: at one end, beliefs which we hold, which may or may

not be 'in our minds' at the moment; at the other, abilities to get
around and deal intelligently with things. Intellectualism has
made us see these as very different sites; but philosophy in our
day has shown how closely akin they are, and how interlinked'
(Taylor, 2000, p. 117). It is this aspect of Taylor's thought that
accounts for his commitment to realism. As Terry Pinkard puts
it, in Taylor's view, this condition of being at grips with the
world means that 'One can be as hard-nosed about the truth-
claims of modern science as any hard-bitten naturalist and still
not be committed to philosophical naturalism; and one can
hold that there are crucial elements of human reality that defy
naturalistic accounts without being a dualist or obscurantist or
being antireason (to use a necessarily vague covering term for
all those who distrust reason while identifying it as leading to
naturalism)' (Pinkard, 2004, pp. 188–9).

One of the central aspects of our sense of ourselves, in
Taylor's account, is our sense of ourselves as intrinsically moral
beings. It is this aspect that is central for our purposes here, and
to which I therefore now turn.

Strong Evaluations

Pinkard points out that for Taylor agency is a normative
matter, and to view it this way 'is to grasp it in terms of its self-
relation, a way of assuming a stance toward ourselves, a kind of
self-conscious distance from ourselves, which realizes that even
in our most straightforward and mindless dealings with things,
we are never simply dealing with them in a way that bypasses
our interpreting our encounter with them' (Pinkard, 2004,
p. 192). For Taylor the sense of ourselves in relationship with
our world is at its base defined by what he calls 'strong evaluations'. These are assessments of ourselves and others that are
phenomenologically basic in the sense that they are 'almost like
instincts, comparable to our love of sweets, or our aversion to
nauseous substances, or our fear of falling' (Taylor, 1989, p. 5).
It is this almost visceral aspect of strong evaluations that gives

them their phenomenological primacy, but it is a second part of their description that accounts for their importance. In this second respect strong evaluations 'seem to involve claims, implicit or explicit, about the nature and status of human beings. From this second side, a moral reaction is an assent to, an affirmation of, a given ontology of the human' (Taylor, 1989, p. 5). From this angle, strong evaluations are

> discriminations of right or wrong, better or worse, higher or lower, which are not rendered valid by our own desires, inclinations, or choices, but rather stand independent of these and offer standards by which they can be judged. So while it may not be judged a moral lapse that I am living a life that is not really worthwhile or fulfilling, to describe me in these terms is nevertheless to condemn me in the name of a standard, independent of my own tastes and desires, which I ought to acknowledge. (Taylor, 1989, p. 4)

We can, according to Taylor, recognise judgements of strong evaluation if, generally speaking, they invoke in us feelings of admiration or contempt. These moral intuitions are 'uncommonly deep, powerful, and universal' (Taylor 1989, 4).

It is important here to be clear on just what Taylor understands by the term 'moral', for so doing will avoid a confusion that has led to some misguided objections to Taylor's position.[1] When Taylor speaks of morality, he paints with a broader brush than is today's convention. He is not concerned merely with what Pincoffs calls 'quandary ethics', which is the idea that 'the business of ethics is with "problems", that is, situations in which it is difficult to know *what one should do*; that the ultimate beneficiary of ethical analysis is the person who, in one of these situations, seeks rational ground for the decision he must

---

1 As Nicholas Smith points out, Owen Flanegan's objections to Taylor's argument for the claim that 'an orientation to the good is an essential feature of human subjectivity' are clearly based on this misunderstanding (Smith, 2002, p. 93).

make; often conceived of as moral rules and the principles from which they can be derived' (Pincoffs, 1983, pp. 92–3, my italics). Taylor is convinced that this approach is a dangerous narrowing of the arena of morality.

For Taylor morality involves not merely what it is good to do, but also *what it is good to be*. It is here that Taylor's debt to ancient ethics is paramount. Morality is concerned with 'what underlies our own dignity, or questions about what makes our lives meaningful or fulfilling' (Taylor, 1989, p. 4) in addition to the normal range of questions on justice, mutual respect and so on. Thus, to be moral by Taylor's definition is not merely to do what is right, but rather to live the good or meaningful life. In his more recent work, Taylor makes explicit an additional element of morality that underlies much of his account in *Sources of the Self*, the idea of love of the good:

> If we give the full range of ethical meanings their due, we can see that the fullness of ethical life involves not just doing, but also being; and not just these two but also loving (which is shorthand here for being moved by, being inspired by) what is constitutively good. It is a drastic reduction to think that we can capture the moral by focussing only on obligated action, as though it were of no ethical moment what you are and what you love. These are the essence of ethical life. (Taylor, 1996, p. 15)

Taylor contends that because we live in a world that places endless demands upon us, unless we are able to order our response to those demands in some non-arbitrary way, our lives simply cannot 'make sense'. Certain issues must weigh more heavily than others for us, or else we are, in Taylor's opinion, doomed to lives of incoherence. While strong evaluations enable us to identify what matters to us, they often conflict and on their own give no direction as to how to order our responses to the world. It is here that Taylor's notion of moral frameworks and the connected ideas of constitutive goods and hypergoods come into play.

Frameworks

Taylor believes that our identity – that which makes us who we are in a unique way – is dependent on our conception of 'the good', and it is this that defines the horizons within which we exist.[2] Put another way, Taylor's understanding of our sense of the self is as an orientation in moral space – indeed, the space metaphor is one of which Taylor is particularly fond and which he sees as having quite deep significance. Thus, when we feel moral outrage at a particular act of cruelty (for example) we are acting out of an orientation to a moral source, which with other such sources makes up a moral framework. For Taylor it is an *inescapable* part of our experience of being persons that we exist within a 'space' of moral questions, our answers to which are defined for each of us by a moral framework. As Taylor puts it, 'a framework incorporates a crucial set of qualitative distinctions. To think, feel, judge within such a framework is to function with the sense that some action, or mode of life, or mode of feeling is incomparably higher than the others which are more readily available to us' (Taylor, 1989, p. 140). Our moral frameworks are not simply constructions, but are in an important sense real: 'Taylor's rejection of that very modern epistemological worry about matching up internal representations and external facts, or linguistic utterances and that which would make them true, partially underwrites his realism about these goods. The goods toward which we orient ourselves are real, even if they depend on the existence of humans for them to be goods; they are not mere projections that we force onto the world' (Pinkard, 2004, p. 195).

In coming to an understanding of Taylor's idea of moral frameworks it is instructive to compare what Taylor says about moral frameworks to what Merleau-Ponty (at least in Taylor's reading) says about embodied agency. For Merleau-Ponty it is essential to personhood that we are embodied agents whose

---

2 'As Taylor stresses again and again in his works, to be an agent is to be oriented to a basic good or set of goods' (Pinkard, 2004, p. 195).

experience is defined by an 'orientational structure', while for Taylor it is essential to personhood that we are moral beings within a 'moral framework'. In Merleau-Ponty's vision:

> Our perceptual field has an orientational structure, a foreground and a background, an up and down. And it must have; that is, it can't lose this structure without ceasing to be a perceptual field in the full sense, our opening onto a world. In those rare moments where we lose orientation, we don't know where we are; and we don't know where or what things are either; we lose the thread of the world and our perceptual field is no longer our access to the world, but rather the confused debris into which our normal grasp on things crumbles. (Taylor, 1978, p. 23)

The similarity of Taylor's understanding of moral frameworks to Merleau-Ponty's concept of an 'orientational structure' is clear when we compare the above to the following description of moral frameworks:

> [W]e naturally tend to talk of our fundamental orientation in terms of who we are. To lose this orientation, or not to have found it, is not to know who one is. And this orientation, once attained, defines where you answer from, hence your identity. But then what emerges from all this is that we think of this fundamental moral orientation as essential to being a human interlocutor, capable of answering for oneself. But to speak of orientation is to presuppose a space-analogue within which one finds one's way. To understand our predicament in terms of finding or losing orientation in moral space is to take the space which our frameworks seek to define as ontologically basic. The issue is, through what framework-definition can I find my bearings in it? In other words, we take as basic that the human agent exists in a space of questions. And these are the questions to which our framework-definitions are answers, providing the horizon within which we know where we stand, and what meanings things have for us. (Taylor, 1989, p. 29)

Taylor's commitment to the inescapable nature of frameworks stands him in strong opposition to any naturalist point of view. For the naturalist 'the issue of what framework to adopt . . . [is] an ultimately factitious question' (Taylor, 1989, p. 31), but for Taylor one's framework is deeply entrenched, and is indeed the very source and foundation of one's self. So much so that to live without a framework and remain a person in any meaningful sense is inconceivable to Taylor. A person in this state would, in his view, experience a crisis of the utmost magnitude, the ultimate identity crisis:

> Such a person wouldn't know where he stood on issues of fundamental importance, would have no orientation in these issues whatever, wouldn't be able to answer for himself on them. If one wants to add to the portrait by saying the person doesn't suffer this absence of frameworks as a lack, isn't in other words in a crisis at all, then one rather has a picture of frightening dissociation. In practice, we should see such a person as deeply disturbed. He has gone way beyond the fringes of what we think of as shallowness: people we judge as shallow do have a sense of what is incomparably important, only we think their commitments trivial, or merely conventional, or not deeply thought out or chosen. But a person without a framework altogether would be outside our space of interlocution; he wouldn't have a stand in the space where the rest of us are. We would see this as pathological. (Taylor, 1989, p. 31)

As Klaushofer points out in her reading of *Sources*, Taylor contends that naturalism is unable to account for this aspect of human life. As she puts it, for Taylor, 'a pervasive naturalism, taking various forms from the scientific to the Nietzschean, is an evasion of the irremediably meaning-laden human condition. In seeking to establish an illusory separation of fact from value, naturalism denies the importance of frameworks, moral horizons that make up the background out of which the self is formed and which give rise to the moral judgements and intuitions governing everyday life' (Klaushofer, 1999, p. 141).

Before moving on to discuss hypergoods and constitutive goods, it is worth pausing here to consider a point regarding Taylor's account of frameworks that requires some clarification. We have seen that Taylor makes use of three interconnected terms in discussing frameworks, namely the 'space of questions' or moral space within which we exist, framework-definitions, and frameworks themselves. There is however a lack of clarity as to the relationship between these concepts when considered in the light of the comparison I have drawn with Taylor's account of Merleau-Ponty's argument regarding the 'orientational structure' that is such a fundamental part of perceptual experience. The 'space of questions' within which we (*qua* moral beings) exist is presumably analogous to the physical space within which we (*qua* embodied agents) exist. What enables us to meaningfully perceive physical space and act within it, in the Merleau-Ponty story, is an orientational structure. It makes obvious sense, then, to see moral frameworks as providing the necessary structure to enable us to meaningfully perceive and act within the space of questions. But what then of the idea of framework-definitions? In Taylor's account these seem to be open to redefinition, for how else can the question 'through what framework-definition can I find my bearings in [moral space]' make any sense? Framework-definitions, then, cannot be analogous to perception's orientational structure, for it makes no sense to ask which version of foreground/background, up/down and the like we ought to apply in order to best find our bearings in the world. So perhaps, then, framework-definitions are an attempt to describe or define something that is already inescapably there, the framework itself. Unfortunately that is not entirely obvious from Taylor's account, for he writes, as we have seen, that 'To understand our predicament in terms of finding or losing orientation in moral space is to take the space which our frameworks *seek to define* as ontologically basic' (Taylor, 1989, p. 29, italics added). This phrasing seems to suggest that frameworks and framework-definitions are perhaps the same thing – at the very least they share the characteristic of being open to redefinition with the goal of achieving a better alignment with moral space.

My view is that the best interpretation here is to view this as simply the result of ambiguous phrasing, and that we ought to stick to the understanding of a moral framework being a necessary aspect of human moral experience in the same way that an orientational structure is a necessary feature of perceptual experience. The alternative interpretation leaves no reason why frameworks (understood as descriptive accounts attempting to make sense of our strong evaluations) should be considered to be inescapable, for there clearly do exist people who have no such descriptive account. But this clearly violates what Taylor understands by frameworks.[3] Under the preferred interpretation, frameworks are the underlying structure of our inescapable moral phenomenology. Following the analogy between Merleau-Ponty's argument and Taylor's, where strong evaluations are the moral equivalent of the visual and other sensations we receive as embodied agents, frameworks are analogous to the orientational structure that allows us to make sense of those sensations and orientate ourselves in space. As Smith puts it, '. . . an orientation to the good is an essential feature of human subjectivity' (Smith, 2002, p. 93), and it is frameworks that make that orientation possible.

Following the preferred interpretation, then, the idea of a framework-definition comes to be seen as that of an account we give in an attempt to explain how our framework relates to the space of questions within which we find ourselves. This view is supported by Pinkard when he writes that 'The goods themselves . . . make their claim on us only as we interpret them and incorporate them via those interpretations into the directions in which we individually and collectively take our lives. To incorporate those goods into our ways of living, moreover, means that we must reason about them. We must see to what else such an incorporation commits us (or to what else it inclines us or for

---

3 As is obvious from the title of the first chapter of *Sources* – 'Inescapable frameworks'.

which it offers additional motivation), and we are often thereby called to evaluate and re-evaluate that orientation as it is being lived out' (Pinkard, 2004, p. 196). This reading is further supported by Taylor's notions of articulation and the Best Account thesis. According to Taylor we *do* always react because of our relation to the moral values that make up the world in which we live, but it is the fact that we are inarticulate about those values, and that we often hold conflicting values, that leaves us bewildered and without direction or deprives our moral intuitions of their power. Hence *articulation* of our goods is, to Taylor, a vital part of making sense of our lives – 'Articulating a constitutive good[4] not only helps us fine-tune what we want to be and do, it also inspires and moves us to want to be and do it. And articulating the virtues [or life goods] can have a similar effect' (Taylor, 1996, p. 14).

Articulation will, of course, result in some narrative or account of the goods that define us. The 'Best Account' is the one which best fits our phenomenology. As Taylor puts it:

> The terms we select have to make sense across the whole range of both explanatory and life uses. The terms indispensable for the latter are part of the story that makes best sense of us, unless and until we can replace them with more clairvoyant substitutes. The result of this clairvoyance yields the best account we can give at any given time, and no epistemological or metaphysical considerations of a more general kind about science or nature can justify setting this aside. The best account in the above sense trumps. (Taylor, 1989, p. 58)

From what we have seen here, then, it seems that we can justifiably say that a moral framework is the inescapable structure of our moral phenomenology, which we are made aware of by our strong evaluations. While the frameworks themselves are inescapable, the accounts that we give to explain them are open to revision and redefinition. This takes place through a

---

4 This concept will be discussed in the next section.

process of articulation, and the account that makes best sense of our moral phenomenology is, in Taylor's terminology, the 'Best Account'. Taylor's belief that investigation can yield real answers to the question of what form of life is best for us is a longstanding one, as evident in his first book, *The Explanation of Behaviour*, in which he writes that 'there is a form of life which is higher or more properly human than others, and that the dim intuition of the ordinary man to this effect can be vindicated in its substance or else corrected in its content by a deeper understanding of human nature' (Taylor, 1964, p. 4).

Hypergoods

Taylor argues that even '[t]he most comprehensive ethical theory, that which most eschews the hiving off of a special class of ends or issues as uniquely crucial, must incorporate some notion of the relative importance of goods' (Taylor, 1989, p. 64). Most ethical theories do refer to some kind of higher-order good that allows the ranking of other goods. 'Hyper-goods' are Taylor's explanation of these second-order goods. Taylor distinguishes between 'hypergoods' and 'the good' more generally, which he understands as including hypergoods as well as the contingent life goods connected with each hyper-good. Taylor explains that hypergoods are 'goods which not only are incomparably more important than others but [which also] provide the standpoint from which these must be weighed, judged, decided about' (Taylor, 1989, p. 63).

One of the difficulties in coming to grips with Taylor's notion of hypergoods is a lack of clarity of the relationship between this concept and another term used by Taylor, that of 'constitutive goods'. Perhaps the clearest definition of constitutive goods that Taylor gives comes in a post-*Sources* paper in which he describes them as invoking 'features of the universe, or God, or human beings, (i) on which the life goods depend, (ii) which command our moral awe or allegiance, and (iii) the contemplation of or contact with which empowers us to be good' (Taylor,

1991b, p. 243). Many commentators treat hypergoods and constitutive goods as distinct notions.[5] Arto Laitinen sums up this view when he offers the following taxonomy of goods as definitive of Taylor's account:

1 **Life-goods** are ordinary goods and part of a good, moral or admirable life. They include goods like authenticity, autonomy, justice, and virtues.
2 **Hypergoods** are the most important life-goods [which provide a way of ordering ordinary life-goods].
3 **Constitutive goods**, by contrast, are ontological accounts with which we try to make sense of the phenomenon of moral goodness in general. Taylor insists that the abstract question 'what constitutes the goodness of the goods' must be answered by giving an ontological account: in Plato's theory it is the Idea of Good, in the Christian tradition it is God the creator, in modern times it has often been Nature. (Laitinen, 2000, p. 155; numbering has been added)

This is, as I've said, a commonly held view. Yet nowhere in *Sources of the Self* does Taylor draw connections between these three levels of goods – indeed, hypergoods and constitutive goods are nowhere discussed together. In fact, as Abbey points out (Abbey, 2000, p. 47, footnote 38), 'constitutive goods' are mentioned only once[6] in Part I of *Sources of the Self* – yet every other major structural part of Taylor's understanding of morality is explored in depth in this section. Furthermore, it is hard to see just what the difference is between the function of hypergoods and constitutive goods. Why wouldn't an 'ontological

---

5 Greenway, for example, writes that 'Insofar as they describe the dominant frameworks against which we evaluate ourselves, our hypergoods will be significant constitutive goods. But it is critical to distinguish between a hypergood and a constitutive good, for with "constitutive good," Taylor invokes a dimension of moral intuition experienced as an external calling' (Greenway, 2000, p. 29). See also Abbey, 2000, ch. 1, and Smith, 2002, ch. 4.

6 In fact Abbey cites two mentions of constitutive goods in part I, but the second page reference she lists in fact falls into part II of the book.

account with which we try to make sense of the phenomenon of moral goodness in general' provide a means of ordering ordinary life-goods? If this is right, then it seems that adding an interim tier in the structure is an unnecessary over-elaboration. It is, therefore, my view that it makes best sense to read Taylor as simply using two terms to refer to the same idea, in the same way that he uses the terms 'strong evaluation' and 'strong qualitative discriminations' interchangeably.

Collapsing any substantive distinction between 'hypergoods' and 'constitutive goods' has the added benefit of erasing another area of uncertainty in Taylor-interpretation, namely the question of whether or not all frameworks contain a hypergood. Abbey points out that most scholars read Taylor as saying all frameworks do indeed contain a hypergood.[7] She however contends that this is not the case, claiming that '*Some* moral frameworks include what Taylor calls a hypergood', which she describes as goods which are 'supreme among strongly valued goods and provide a way of rank-ordering the other less strongly valued goods in an individual's moral framework' (Abbey, 2000, p. 35, emphasis added). While Taylor's articulation of hypergoods is certainly sometimes ambiguous in this respect, there is, however, no doubt that Taylor sees constitutive goods as an inescapable feature of our moral landscapes. In a more recent work Taylor describes constitutive goods as 'features of ourselves, or the world, or God, such that their being what they are is essential to the life goods being good' (Taylor, 1996, pp. 12–13). In the same article he is quick to quash any idea that only some kinds of frameworks require constitutive goods:

> Now it might be thought that constitutive goods figure only in theistic or metaphysical ethics, that they have no place in a

---

7 If this were not so, the framework would simply be a framework of goods which one is unable to order, and this would lead to the same outcome as Taylor recognizes in subjectivism, which, in its attempts to affirm all goods, actually makes all goods equally meaningless, and provides no reason to choose one above the other.

modern humanistic outlook. But this would be a mistake. In a modern humanistic ethic, the locus of the constitutive good is displaced onto the human being itself. In Kant, the sense of the dignity of human life, as rational agency soared above everything else in the universe, is an example of the identification of a constitutive good in a humanist ethic. My claim is that something like this sense of the dignity and value of human life, of the nobility of rational freedom, underpins the ethical consciousness of our contemporaries and plays the two roles we can see it occupying in Kant's philosophy: it defines why the human being commands our respect when she or he is the object of our action; and it sets us an ideal for our own action.

And just as defining the virtues helps us to deliberate, understanding better as we do it is good to be, so this understanding can be further aided by clarifying the constitutive goods. We help to clarify what it is good to be by getting clearer on just what is noble or admirable about the human potential. (Taylor, 1996, p. 13)

It seems, then, that it makes sense for the purposes of the argument I will be setting out in this part of the book to treat hypergoods and constitutive goods as one and the same thing. I will, therefore, refer only to hypergoods from here onwards.

Taylor's Account of the Self and Morality and his Argument for Theism

We are now in a position to pull together the main features of Taylor's account of the self and morality. It takes as its starting-point the conviction that, in understanding the self we must begin by examining the nature of our phenomenology. Such an examination reveals that we are strong evaluators, that is, beings for whom the world is inescapably experienced in broadly moral terms. Our strong evaluations point to the life goods that centrally define our identities. But as we examine our moral experience further, we realize that our life goods are not random, but instead take their places in a moral framework which defines how we live in the 'space of questions' in which we find ourselves. Frameworks are not the full story, however, for they are in turn shaped by hypergoods, which provide the ontological source for the goodness of the ordinary life goods in the frameworks. Of course not all of us are consciously aware of our frameworks or the hypergoods that define them. Articulation is necessary if we are to connect with these structures. Not all accounts are the same, however, and some framework- and hypergood-descriptions better account for our actual moral commitments than others. The goal, in the end, is to discover the Best Account, that description which most comprehensively accounts for the full range of moral issues that insinuate themselves in our moral experience.

Of all Taylor's commentators, Melissa Lane has thus far best articulated how Taylor's account of the self and morality also forms the foundation for an argument for theism that seems to be implicit in his work. In her paper 'God or orienteering? A critical study of Taylor's *Sources of the Self*' Melissa Lane identifies three claims as central to Taylor's project:

 (i) that we must have a morality ('the claim of morality');
 (ii) that we must have a morality with a certain structure, such that particular values are connected to conceptions of the good, or 'sources' ('the claim of structure');
(iii) that we must have a morality based on an incomparably higher good ('the claim of transcendence'). (Lane, 1992, p. 46)

Lane identifies four discrete argument strategies that she contends Taylor makes use of in attempting to establish these claims, which she labels Phenomenological; Transcendental; Best Account; and Historical. She adds that Taylor mentions, but defers to a later work, a fifth argument – 'a normative argument that only theism is an adequate moral source' (Lane, 1992, p. 46). While Lane provides no textual reference in this

regard, it seems clear that she is thinking of Taylor's acknowl-
edgement that 'articulation' has multiple aspects:

> It is not merely formulating what people already implicitly
> but unproblematically acknowledge; nor is it showing what
> people really rely on in the teeth of their ideological denials.
> Rather it could only be carried forward by showing that one
> or another ontology is in fact the only adequate basis for our
> moral responses, whether we recognize this or not. A thesis of
> this kind was invoked by Dostoyevsky and discussed by
> Leszek Kołakowski in a recent work: 'If God does not exist,
> then everything is permitted'. But this level of argument, con-
> cerning what our commitments really amount to, is even more
> difficult than the previous one, which tries to show, in the face
> of naturalist suppression, what they already are. I will prob-
> ably not be able to venture very far out on this terrain in the
> following. It would be sufficient, and very valuable, to be able
> to show something about the tentative, hesitating, and fuzzy
> commitments that we moderns actually rely on. The map of
> our moral world, however full of gaps, erasures, and blur-
> rings, is interesting enough. (Taylor, 1989, p. 10)

This passage suggests that, though Taylor does not explicitly set
out this normative argument for theism, he has something in
mind. In fact, it would not be too much of a stretch of the
imagination to attribute this passage to an excessive modesty on
Taylor's part, for, as already mentioned, a good number of
those who have read *Sources of the Self* have seen in it an argument for Christian theism.[8] Quentin Skinner, for example, no
friend of theism, concludes that the 'final message' of *Sources of
the Self* is that 'we cannot hope to realise our fullest human
potentialities in the absence of God' (Skinner, 1991, p. 133).

---

8 I have argued elsewhere (Baker, 2000) that a close reading of
Sources of the Self reveals that only this interpretation prevents Taylor's
arguments against those he calls 'naturalists' from falling short of their
mark. Since writing that paper I have changed my position on the value
of transcendental arguments, as will become apparent below.

William Connolly also articulates this view when he writes that 'In *Sources of the Self* Taylor contends that "high standards need strong sources" [Taylor, 1989, p. 516]. Although evincing respect for some alternative orientations, he suggests that the grace of a Christian God is the strongest source to appeal to in Western life.' (Connolly, 2004, p. 172) I will argue in what follows that this normative argument for theism is the natural conclusion of the combined effects of the other argument strategies that Lane identifies. It is thus better to view this argument for theism as a fourth claim rather than as an argument strategy.

So then, following Lane with a few amendments, we can understand Taylor as making four claims – the claim of morality, the claim of structure, the claim of transcendence and the claim of theism. I will argue that those claims each form a part of an overall argument aimed at establishing the latter claim. As such, the structure of the argument is as follows, where the key concepts in Taylor's account that are connected with each claim are listed in brackets:

 (i) we must have a morality (strong evaluations and life goods);
 (ii) we must have a morality with a certain structure, such that particular values are connected to conceptions of the good, or 'sources' (frameworks);
(iii) we must have a morality based on an incomparably higher good (hypergoods); and
(iv) we must understand the structure of our morality and the incomparably higher good on which our morality must be based in the terms of Christian theism (Best Account).

Greenway recognizes the power of this argument when he writes,

> Taylor can remain calm regarding questions over the precise contours of his moral realism because they arise at the end of the discussion. This is the absolutely critical philosophical realignment missed by incredulous critics: the theological or ontotheological realism question is consequent, not

antecedent, to concrete ethical intuitions and debate. This is not to say, of course, that the love of God qua creator, for instance, is not the ultimate source of the love we share for one another (indeed, this may be Taylor's conviction). But this understanding is consonant with the contention that our love for others is a reaction to the other and not the consequence of some internalized, prior theory regarding the nature and will of God or the categorical imperatives of reason. (Greenway, 2000, p. 32)

As I see it, this argument can unproblematically be construed as a phenomenological account of the functioning of the *sensus divinitatis*, at least to the extent that the functioning of the *sensus divinitatis* is occasioned by the individual facing broadly moral (in Taylor's sense) questions. When functioning properly, the responses our moral structures generate to the 'space of questions' in which we inescapably exist produce in us true beliefs that correspond with the moral parts of Christian theism, beliefs that can only be properly made sense of in the terms of Christian theism.

If this argument turns out to be successful, then it seems to offer a way to bridge the gap that Plantinga's commentators point out exists between the limited response his extended A/C model provides to the expanded *de jure* challenge, and the *de facto* question. Put another way, if successful this argument provides one answer to the question 'why should the unbeliever take Christian belief seriously enough to consider that the *de facto* question warrants attention, even granting that the Christian believer might well be both justified and warranted in her beliefs?' In the next three chapters, whose titles and focus loosely reflect three of the key terms of art that Melissa Lane uses in evaluating Taylor's argument, I will further articulate and defend this argument, as well as evaluate just what it achieves. I begin in the next chapter by considering Taylor's phenomenological starting-point and the transcendental argument strategy that is embedded in Taylor's phenomenological account.

6

Phenomenology

As we saw in the previous chapter, at the heart of Charles Taylor's philosophical project is an idea that he draws from Maurice Merleau-Ponty, the idea that 'because we are in the world, we are condemned to meaning' (Smith, 2002, p. 1). This insight is one that is inescapably *phenomenological* in its nature. Fergus Kerr points out that Taylor's central purpose in *Sources of the Self* 'is, as the title signals, precisely to locate "moral sources outside the subject" – but to do so, not in terms of a person's submission to some cosmic order of meanings, but "through languages which resonate within him or her, a grasping of an order which is inseparably indexed to a personal vision" [Taylor, 1989, p. 510]' (Kerr, 2004, p. 90). That is to say, human life has an unavoidable experiential dimension, and any account of human living that leaves this dimension out of the explanation is one that is fundamentally flawed. We have also seen that our experience of the world is also unavoidably *moral*, in the broad sense that Taylor uses that term. As Taylor puts it, 'we should treat our deepest moral instincts, our ineradicable sense that human life is to be respected, as our mode of access to the world in which ontological claims are discernable and can be rationally argued about and sifted' (Taylor, 1989, p. 8).

It is not surprising, then, that the argument for theism that Melissa Lane identifies in *Sources of the Self* is at its foundation built on claims about morality and phenomenology. Indeed, the first step in the argument is the claim 'that we must have a morality' (Lane, 1992, p. 46), and the first argument strategy that she credits Taylor with using in his drive to establish his argument for theism is one that she labels 'Phenomenological'. The second argument strategy that Lane credits Taylor with using is the deployment of transcendental arguments. In this chapter I will focus on this phenomenological dimension of Taylor's theory and its connection with morality, and, because I argue that what Lane calls the phenomenological strategy is indistinguishable from what she calls Taylor's transcendental strategy, I will also give due consideration to this latter aspect of his argument for theism. I will begin by responding to Lane's criticisms of Taylor in this regard, and then go on to examine some further implications of these aspects for the greater project of this book.

The Primacy of Phenomenology

Lane explains that the Phenomenological argument, at least in as far as it is directed in support of claim (i), that we must have a morality, 'proceeds by reflecting on our actual moral experience, to find that we always do have moral values. If someone claims to do without morality altogether, the Phenomenologist is consistently able to show up that claim as parasitically reliant on the morality it denies' (Lane, 1992, p. 47). The claim, then, is that it is an inescapable part of the experience of human persons that the world be viewed in moral terms.

Lane, however, is unconvinced that reflection on our actual moral experience can lead us to this conclusion. She contends that 'The reductionist could admit all the Phenomenologist's findings, but argue that the seeming inescapability of morality is in fact explicable as the inescapability of a will to power or a projection of emotions, or any other such claim' (Lane, 1992, p. 47).

This dismissal of Taylor's argument is, I think, too quick. It seems, first, to rest on an inadequate grasp of what Taylor means by morality. For, if the description of Taylor's position that I gave in the previous chapter is correct, and morality is for him everything that our strong evaluations identify, then it is clear that even the will to power falls under this heading. For in Taylor's terms even the will to power represents some discrimination of better and worse (if not necessarily right or wrong), for the will to power must be *directed*.

More importantly, Lane seems to have underestimated the force inherent in Taylor's claims about the nature of our phenomenology.[1] In fairness, this is perhaps because that force is partially occluded by the complexity and density of *Sources of the Self*. In his more recent writings, however, particularly his contribution to a symposium in honour of Bernard Williams in the *Journal of Philosophy*, Taylor has clarified this aspect of his work admirably. In this paper, entitled 'Ethics and ontology' (Taylor, 2003b), Taylor sets out to answer the question 'What are we committed to ontologically by our ethical views and commitments?' (Taylor, 2003b, p. 305). His response to this question is one that we will see is pertinent in many ways for our project here – for the moment, however, I will focus on its relevance to Lane's objection.

Central to Taylor's position is his claim that 'Ethics involves a range of "values" that are essentially understood to be on a different level, to be in some way special, higher, or incommensurable with our other goals and desires. We would not have a category like the ethical or the moral, unless this were so' (Taylor 2003b, p. 308). It is clear from Taylor's account that this understanding of the moral is based in our phenomenology, it is somehow inescapable to us. Lane does not challenge this higher status of the moral in our experience, and nor is it clear how such a challenge could be mounted. Her challenge lies instead in questioning the weight that should be given to this phenomenology when it comes to ethical theory. She rightly points out that opponents can, and do, attempt to explain our

---

1 Kerr is more insightful in recognizing that Taylor makes a case for the claim 'that if we can suspend respect for recent philosophical theories, we shall find ourselves just as inclined to acknowledge the sovereignty of the good as a moral resource which we do not create as our ancestors ever were, simply by attending to the evidence of our everyday practice' (Kerr, 2004, p. 91).

'higher' experience of the moral in reductive terms, as subjective projections onto a neutral world and the like. The source of this resistance to the deliverances of our moral phenomenology is identified by Taylor as the rift between fact and value that is so cherished a feature of our post-Galilean world. We now view the universe in neutral terms, and as a result, 'Value comes into the world with us, the human agents who evaluate. Hence the easy step to theories like emotivism, or views that see value as residing in our reactions to what is in itself neutral reality' (Taylor, 2003b, p. 306).

Such a step might be easy to make, but it is, Taylor argues, a misstep. Such accounts of morality are plagued with a serious problem, a failure of explanation. Our phenomenology, Taylor argues, if 'properly and honestly carried through, seems to show that values of this higher status, like *to kallon* for Aristotle, are ineradicable from our deliberations of how to live'. But this cannot be accounted for in reductivist terms, which leaves this property of our moral phenomenology 'ineradicably "queer", in Mackie's celebrated expression' (Taylor, 2003b, p. 310). As Taylor sees it, the difficulty here arises because of a tension between phenomenology and ontology. One approach to dealing with this tension is to try to resolve it – that is, to try to give an account of the phenomenology that is compatible with a naturalist ontology. Sociobiological explanations are the most prominent examples of this strategy. These approaches, however, 'plainly fail' in Taylor's view. 'If we try to track our sense of the incommensurably higher through our responses of admiration and its opposite, we can see that whatever the ultimate links with survival and group flourishing, the admirable is never simply defined in terms of them, and sometimes even runs athwart them (*fiat justitia ruat coelum*). . . . That admiration and its opposites are such an ineradicable part of the human life form testifies to the centrality of values that are seen as essentially higher, more worthy' (Taylor, 2003b, p. 310).

The other prominent strategy in dealing with this tension between phenomenology and ontology is simply to deny the phenomenology its force. Characteristic here are the moral theories of Mackie and Blackburn. On this approach, 'You accept that this is how it looks, but you insist that it is not really like this in the objective world. The difficulty is that this begins to pose epistemological problems for the naturalist ontology. . . . It leaves values standing in our real-life deliberations, but then makes a global, marginal comment to the effect that they are not really real. This is a strange claim, not least because it is hard to see where the warrant comes from' (Taylor, 2003b, p. 311).

And it is not only the question of warrant[2] that makes Taylor view this kind of view as problematic. For while this kind of 'projectivist' position is by its nature one that is 'external' to ethical life, in that it is not about actual ethical choices and deliberations, nevertheless it seems inextricably connected[3] to claims that are 'internal' to morality, like the claim that our primary moral directive ought to be a focus on life and happiness. The trouble with this, Taylor thinks, is that 'It is not always clear where the argument for one flips over into an argument for the other – or whether the two ultimately conflict. If you play the game internally with such vigor, how seriously can we take your claim that it is all a kind of shadow play?' (Taylor, 2003b, pp. 311–12).

That these reductionist and projectionist attempts to address the mismatch between our moral phenomenology and naturalist ontology run into a great deal of trouble, makes it clear that it is not as easy as Lane seems to think to 'admit all the Phenomenologist's findings, but argue that the seeming

---

2 It must be noted here that Taylor uses the word 'warrant' more broadly than Plantinga's specific usage, to simply mean justification in the everyday sense of that word.

3 Elsewhere Taylor unpacks the reason for this inextricable connection, namely that the naturalist view has arisen largely as a result of *moral* rather than scientific forces, and that the widely held 'subtraction story' in which naturalism and the humanism that is so closely associated with it are viewed as the result of a process of stripping away the unjustified constraints of theism is false (see Taylor, 2003a).

inescapability of morality is in fact explicable as the inescapability of a will to power or a projection of emotions, or any other such claim' (Lane, 1992, p. 47). The trouble remains that there is a tension 'between the phenomenology of the incommensurably higher and a naturalist ontology which has difficulty finding a place for this' (Taylor, 2003b, p. 316).

Before moving on to the next part of Lane's critique, it is worth pausing here to consider a specific ethical naturalist critique of the priority of moral phenomenology, one that is directly aimed at Taylor's own position. The critique to which I refer is that raised by Gary Gutting in his book *Pragmatic Liberalism and the Critique of Modernity*[4] in response to Taylor's notion of strong evaluations. Gutting's claim is that the ethical naturalist can accept the inescapability of moral intuitions (indeed he finds it impossible to deny 'our simple inability to disengage ourselves from moral sentiments' (Gutting, 1999, p. 128)), but that this need not force acceptance of Taylor's claim that 'we are discriminating real properties, with criteria independent of our de facto reactions' (Taylor, 1989, p. 6). Gutting offers no positive argument to support his position here, but instead focuses on rebutting Taylor's arguments against the feasibility of an ethical naturalist explanation of strong evaluations. Gutting first addresses Taylor's claim that ethical naturalism, because it lacks the independent standpoint that is characteristic of his account of strong evaluation, in fact renders moral argument impossible. Gutting responds by pointing out that 'we frequently argue even about claims that we think are ultimately matters of just personal taste' (Gutting, 1999, p. 139).

Gutting backs this point up by giving an example of an imaginary argument between himself and the reader over the relative merits or demerits of a particular wine. But in so doing, he plays directly into Taylor's hands. For a central feature of Taylor's

---

4 As mentioned earlier, Gutting's response to Plantinga is particularly relevant for this book because his reading of Taylor's work is importantly similar to mine, as will become clear in the chapters that follow.

objection to ethical naturalism is the phenomenological force of his claim that 'what has been left out is precisely the *mattering*' (Taylor, 1989, p. 49). By drawing a parallel between moral decision-making and one's personal wine preference, Gutting shows that his ethical account suffers from precisely the lack that Taylor is pointing to. Taylor's notion of strong evaluations is intended to account for our intuition that, for example, rejecting a wine and rejecting paedophilia or the torture of innocents are qualitatively different distinctions, something that Gutting is unable to account for. Attempting to reason with someone over some moral issue, where that someone simply did not grasp the moral weight of the question at hand, and who instead treated the discussion as she would a discussion about wine preference, would be fruitless and pointless. This is what Taylor means when he says that ethical naturalism renders moral argument impossible.[5]

Gutting continues his rebuttal as follows:

> In a similar vein, Taylor attacks ethical naturalism on the grounds that it can make no sense of the fact that we demand consistency of one another in ethical discussions. Even naturalists make this demand, 'but the issue of consistency presupposes intrinsic description. How could anyone be accused of being inconsistently nauseated?' [Taylor, 1989, p. 7]. Inconsistency, however, is a matter of the relation of two statements to one another. I cannot be 'inconsistently nauseated' because 'This is nauseating' is a single simple sentence, lacking the internal complexity needed to admit of contradiction. But it is entirely possible for two different affective expressions to contradict one another, as is the case with 'This is nauseating' and 'This is delicious'. (Gutting, 1999, p. 139)

---

5 Of course, in reality, professing ethical naturalists *do* contribute to moral arguments, and do seem to grasp the weight of the issues at hand. But this is a consequence of an inconsistency between moral intuitions and moral theory, rather than because of the power of ethical naturalism.

Gutting seems to miss Taylor's point here, treating his statement as if he were referring to inconsistency in any one particular instance. But that is not at all what Taylor is saying, he in
fact fully endorses Gutting's point that 'inconsistency . . . is a
matter of the relation of two statements to one another'.
Taylor's point is that we expect people to be consistent in their
moral judgements in *relevantly similar situations* – and we
expect an account for differing moral judgements in situations
that appear to be relevantly similar. So, for example, we
demand an explanation from the animal rights activist who is
discovered wearing a fur coat at a cocktail party. We expect no
such account for why a pregnant woman loves chocolate on one
day and is nauseated by it on another. Thus, Gutting's response
is a response to a misunderstanding of the point posed, and
therefore offers no meaningful critique.

More positively, there remains a great deal of intuitive appeal
to Taylor's claim about strong evaluations, which Gutting's
response does not seem to undermine. In 'Ethics and ontology'
Taylor offers a particular intuition, that humans are worthy of
respect, as an example of a moral intuition that seems inescapable for us and which also seems dependent on a sense of
the incommensurably higher. He points out that, though the
recipients of this respect have often been limited to a small
group in certain cultures, this sense has nonetheless been
present in all human cultures. It has been articulated in various
ways, such as 'the logos that resides in human beings and which
is close to the divine in the Universe (some Stoics), or more
recently, as our being made in the image of God. Recently,
Vaclav Havel has pointed to some such basis for universal
human rights' (Taylor, 2003b, p. 317). Taylor contends that
'these articulations of the "respect worthiness" of the human
did not just offer extra incentives or an extra rhetorical impulse
to our inclination to act rightly towards our fellows. They were
meant to articulate what respect worthiness consisted in. In
other words, they offer further specifications of the concept that
is in play here, the one that we can apply rightly or wrongly, and
that we therefore cannot see as a simple projection' (Taylor,

2003b, p. 317). In much the same way Taylor points to the importance we place on notions like nobility,[6] and challenges the naturalist to account for this.

Though Taylor does not claim to have settled the issue in this paper, he believes he has shown 'that the hoped-for reconciliation between moral phenomenology and naturalist ontology is, to say the least, somewhat premature' (Taylor, 2003b, p. 320), and that the key question in this debate is 'whether the values we espouse can be supported on the basis of the ontology to which we subscribe' (Taylor, 2003b, p. 318). Establishing this requires giving some account of those values in the terms of that ontology, which is what I claim Taylor's historical retrieval is intended to do. In the paper we are considering here Taylor hints again that his position is in line with Havel's belief 'that human rights, human freedoms, and human dignity have their deepest roots somewhere outside the perceptible world' (quoted in Taylor, 2003, p. 317, n. 10). Evaluating Taylor's historical argument which seems aimed at establishing, or at least strongly suggesting this position, is the purpose of Chapter 8.

Lane continues her critique of Taylor's phenomenological strategy when she argues further that

claim (ii) of structure cannot be established by Phenomenology. For we may experience an occlusion of our moral sources. We may feel morality to be optional or irrelevant precisely because we have lost access to those sources of moral motivation. And indeed part of Taylor's project is to say that this is not only possible but, for modern selves, actual: modern philosophy suffers an 'eclipse of our whole awareness of qualitative distinctions,' and this prevents us

---

6 'We give a special importance to nobility. People have been known to risk their lives, their prosperity, their ordinary happiness and fulfilment in its name. It is a powerful ideal. (Of course it is not for everybody, but for many who espouse it.) How can we explain its rise as a major motivation among this lately developed simian species we belong to? This would seem a legitimate question, although terribly difficult, perhaps unanswerable' (Taylor, 2003b, pp. 318–19).

from articulating the sources that are buried within us [Taylor, 1989, p. 95]. But if this is so, then appeal to our experience cannot establish necessarily that morality must have sources – for from our experience alone, we may even see reason to deny this. (Lane, 1992, p. 50)

This criticism, however, rests on a misreading of Taylor. Taylor's point about the occlusion of our awareness of the sources of our strong evaluations in modern philosophy is *not* that we do not make qualitative distinctions – he expends a good deal of ink in convincing us that these are inescapable for us – but rather that modern philosophy's neglect of this phenomenological dimension of morality leaves no *explanation* for these reactions. The misreading lies in part in the fact that Lane has quoted Taylor out of context here. In the passage she refers to, Taylor is pointing out the cost of allowing immanent humanist ontology to overwhelm moral phenomenology, where the result is that we suppress our qualitative distinctions to the point that we lose conscious awareness of them. But in such a case the point is not that the qualitative distinctions cease occurring – this is impossible in Taylor's account – but rather that they are suppressed and unaccounted for. Terry Pinkard recognizes this aspect of Taylor's account when he draws a parallel between Taylor's theory and one interpretation of Wittgenstein's notion of 'following a rule' which holds that

the 'background' against which we determine what counts as a deviant following of the rule really does incorporate understanding, but it is an unarticulated, prereflective grasp of what the rule means. Such an unarticulated, prereflective grasp of the sense of the rule not only does not rule out giving reasons when they are demanded, it is actually the condition that puts us in the position of being able to formulate such reasons in the first place. Not acting for explicit reasons (as representations to be entertained) is not to act without reason; and often the reasons for our action can only emerge when we are challenged to come up with them. (Pinkard, 2004, p. 193)

It is here that Taylor's thought comes perhaps closest to Alasdair MacIntyre's moral theory, in which he argues that modernity has left us with only 'the fragments of a conceptual scheme, parts which now lack those contexts from which their significance derived' (MacIntyre, 1981, p. 2). Taylor's phenomenology is intended to show us that we do make qualitative distinctions, but we have largely lost comprehension of the conceptual scheme or schemes that make sense of the distinctions we make. So we are left in the strange position of being committed to certain modes of life as being 'right or wrong, better or worse, higher or lower,' but at the same time having our commitments lack force or power because we have lost touch with the 'conceptual scheme' (or, in Taylor's terminology, moral framework) that makes sense of those commitments. It is *articulation* that is needed to overcome this malady – articulation allows us to reconnect our strong evaluations to the moral sources that make sense of and give power to them.

So this second critique offered by Lane also seems to fall short of the mark. She is, however, correct in pointing out that Taylor's argument is incomplete if understood merely as a phenomenological one. She quotes Taylor as saying that 'this is not only a phenomenological account, but an explanation of the limits of the conceivable in human life, an account of its transcendental conditions' (Taylor, 1989, p. 32) and uses this as a stepping-stone to an analysis of Taylor's transcendental argument strategy,[7] which I turn to consider next.

Taylor's Transcendental Argument

Transcendental arguments are most famously associated with the work of Kant, though they have been deployed by a wide range of philosophers. In a recent book on transcendental

---

7 As Nicholas Smith has pointed out to me, this makes Lane's insistence on treating the phenomenological and the transcendental argument strategies as (even analytically) separable strategies particularly strange.

arguments, Robert Stern offers one of the more comprehensive definitions of transcendental arguments when he writes that 'As standardly presented, transcendental arguments are usually said to be distinctive in involving a certain sort of claim, namely that "For Y to be possible, X must be the case", where Y is some indisputable fact about us and our mental life (e.g. that we have experiences, use language, make certain judgements, have certain concepts, perform certain actions, etc.), but where it is left open at this stage exactly what is substituted for X' (Stern, 2000, p. 5).

This description seems to fit well with Taylor's own account of transcendental arguments. Taylor writes that 'the arguments I want to call "transcendental" start from some feature of our experience which they claim to be indubitable and beyond cavil. They then move to a stronger conclusion, one concerning the nature of the subject or the subject's position in the world. They make this move by a regressive argument, to the effect that the stronger conclusion must be so if the indubitable fact about experience is to be possible (and being so, it must be possible)' (Taylor, 1978, p. 20).

In her reading of *Sources of the Self*, Lane, as we have seen, identifies the use of a transcendental argument as one of Taylor's key strategies. She is not alone in this respect – Timothy O'Hagan contends that in *Sources* 'Taylor follows the master, Hegel, in two respects: starting with the modern, he seeks an *Erinnerung* of its preconditions through a massive historical-transcendental argument, and at the same time he mounts a complex polemic against rival positions' (O'Hagan, 1993, p. 74).[8] In the previous chapter I drew the reader's attention to the striking similarity between the way Taylor describes parts of his argument and how he describes Merleau-Ponty's argument for the conclusion that we are inescapably embodied agents. That Taylor articulates Merleau-Ponty's argument to illustrate

---

8 Later in this book we shall see that O'Hagan is perceptive in seeing Taylor's historical account as being inextricably tied up with the transcendental argument.

his discussion of transcendental arguments, strongly suggests that Taylor understands his own argument as a transcendental argument.

Lane identifies the transcendental argument in *Sources* as one

> based on orientation within a community as part of the necessary conditions of human identity. The argument is developed by way of an analogy with spatial orientation. . . . The suggestion is that just as being surrounded by space requires us to orient ourselves as physical beings in relation to points in it, so being surrounded by other human beings requires us to orient ourselves as interlocutors in relation to them. The common requirement of orientation is taken to project a moral space with fixed questions, to correspond to the physical space of fixed points. Plurality forces us to stand in moral space just as depth forces us to stand in physical space. (Lane, 1992, p. 50)

Lane argues against Taylor's transcendental argument strategy, thus understood, on the grounds that

> we do not achieve our spatial orientation by appeal to one fundamental and grounding capacity; we locate ourselves in space by means of a spectrum of data, senses, and abilities, deprivation of some of which can be compensated for by increased stress on others. Second, moral questions do not form a unity in the way that questions about spatial location do. The answers we could give to questions about our spatial orientation would serve together to specify our location. But the privileging of some moral questions over others, as more central to our identity – a privilege crucial to the claim of structure – would be like treating up/down as always and fundamentally more important than left/right. So the analogy alone gives us no support for the claim of structure by sources. (Lane, 1992, p. 51)

It is here, I think, that Lane's analysis is at its weakest. While she is correct in identifying in Taylor's work a transcendental argument strategy, her reading of Taylor's transcendental argument falls down on two crucial points – treating the phenomenological argument and the transcendental argument as distinct, stand-alone strategies; and not recognising Taylor's notions of 'webs of interlocution' and 'moral frameworks' as discrete concepts.

The first error becomes clear when we consider that transcendental arguments, at least as Taylor understands them, have as their first step a phenomenological argument – an argument for the inescapability of some aspect of the nature of our experience. By ignoring this, Lane's understanding of Taylor's transcendental argument is reduced to a much weaker argument by analogy. I shall return to this link between the phenomenological argument and the transcendental argument shortly.

The second problem with Lane's critique lies in her treating as synonymous Taylor's notions of 'webs of interlocution' and 'moral frameworks'. Taylor believes that we are never outside of some social context, and that we each live continually within a 'web of interlocution', a network of others with whom we relate. Even those who shun human contact are not exempt – 'In the case of the hermit the interlocutor is God. In the case of the solitary artist, the work itself is addressed to a future audience, perhaps still to be created by the work itself. The very form of a work of art shows its character as *addressed*' (Taylor, 1991a, pp. 34–5). It is from these webs of interlocution that we acquire the commitments and values that define us. As Taylor puts it, 'No one acquires the languages needed for self definition on their own. We are introduced to them through exchanges with others who matter to us – what George Herbert Mead called "significant others"' (Taylor, 1991a, p. 33).

If webs of interlocution are the means by which we acquire our value descriptions, then, as described in the previous chapter, moral frameworks are the structures of interrelated goods that those descriptions fit to a better or worse extent. Put in other terms, the web of interlocution is the delivery system for the account that describes the moral framework, but it is not *itself* the moral framework.

The impact of this distinction on Lane's critique is marked. Lane understands Taylor's transcendental argument as being about our orientation to our interlocutors. But in reality, the 'space' that Taylor wishes to define by analogue with physical space is existential rather than social. It is about our orientation ('where do we stand') in relation to the 'space of questions' in which we inescapably find ourselves.

These two misunderstandings mean that Lane's criticisms miss the mark – the 'critique by comparison to physical space' only makes sense if the transcendental argument is reduced to an argument by analogy, and if that analogy is taken as an intended literal link between physical and social 'space'.[9]

It seems then, that Taylor's Phenomenological argument and his Transcendental argument, if properly understood, withstand Lane's criticisms. None of what Lane argues undermines Taylor's strategy of employing a phenomenologically based transcendental argument to establish claim (i), the claim of morality, by moving from the observation that we always experience the world in moral terms, to the more contentious ontological claim that such an outlook is indispensable to us as human beings. That said, however, it is worth keeping in mind that transcendental arguments are not uncontentious or without limitation, and while Lane does not herself raise the question of the value of transcendental arguments, we would be remiss if we did not address this question, particularly in the light of our focus on addressing the expanded *de jure* challenge to Christian belief.

---

9 Lane also identifies what she considers to be another transcendental argument 'buried in the text' (Lane, 1992, p. 51) of *Sources of the Self*, one relating to role of narrativity in Taylor's work. While this is an important part of Taylor's theory, it is not, I believe, crucial to the argument for theism that we are drawing from his work in these pages. I have therefore not dealt with this 'implicit' transcendental argument here, though I have considered it elsewhere (Baker, 2003).

Transcendental Arguments and the Expanded *de jure* Challenge

The question here, then, is how, if at all, transcendental arguments might contribute to answering the expanded *de jure* challenge that is directed at Christian belief. Certainly, if we considered transcendental arguments in their traditional form, they would be of no use at all in responding to the expanded *de jure* challenge. For as Stern points out, the traditional view is that transcendental arguments are supposed to give a complete answer to the sceptic about the way things are in the world. In Stern's taxonomy,[10] this approach is known as a *truth-directed*[11] transcendental argument, which he defines as follows:

> A is a *truth-directed* transcendental argument, where X is specified as some non-psychological fact or state of affairs which is claimed to be a necessary condition for experience, language, etc. [For example, for] experience to be possible, there must be physical objects. (Stern, 2000, p. 10)

Even setting aside the difficulties that are widely accepted as being inherent in this kind of transcendental argument,[12] it is clear that this approach offers nothing by way of help in answering the expanded *de jure* challenge. This is simply because the

---

10 Stern identifies four general types of transcendental arguments: *truth-directed* transcendental arguments, *belief-directed* transcendental arguments, *experience-directed* transcendental arguments, and *concept-directed* transcendental arguments (Stern, 2000, p. 10).

11 Cassam calls these arguments 'world-directed' (Cassam, 1999, p. 85).

12 This pessimism is mostly a result of Barry Stroud's 1968 paper on transcendental arguments. In a recent book Robert Stern summarizes the impact of Stroud's critique: 'Stroud convinced many that the proponent of transcendental arguments faces an unattractive dilemma: either to dispense with the verificationist assumption, and fall short of the required anti-sceptical conclusion concerning how things are, or to accept verificationism and render the use of transcendental arguments redundant' (Stern, 2000, p. 46).

truth-directed transcendental argument engages solely with the *de facto* question, which sets aside issues surrounding the rational status of the belief in question, and focuses on whether or not the belief is true.

As Stern points out, however, there is another, more modest approach to the deployment of transcendental arguments. Where truth-directed transcendental arguments are aimed at responding to what Stern calls epistemic scepticism ('which denies that we have knowledge'), modest transcendental arguments are directed at justificatory scepticism, 'which denies that we have "justified opinions" or rationally held beliefs' (Stern, 2000, p. 15). To rephrase this in the terms that are by now familiar from the first part of this book, modest transcendental arguments are aimed at those whose challenge is not directed at the truth-status of the beliefs in question, but at the claim that there is something wrong with holding such beliefs, regardless of their truth status.[13] It is clear that the expanded *de jure* challenge is just this sort of question. Stern could almost be quoting Plantinga when he writes that the justificatory sceptic's claim is that 'we are epistemically irresponsible, governed by caprice, wishful thinking, or habit, rather than reason and rational principle' (Stern, 2000, p. 18).

---

13 Two important recent papers, Quassim Cassam's 'Self-directed transcendental arguments' and one from Stroud himself entitled 'The goal of transcendental arguments', as well as Stern's book, have offered broad support for this type of 'modest' transcendental argument. Importantly, it is an approach that broadly follows a hint Taylor gives in his 1978 paper 'The validity of transcendental arguments' of how to deal with Stern's dilemma. There he claims that, while it is true that we cannot rely on a transcendental argument to tell us anything about the way things are, it does, importantly, tell us about 'the nature of our life as subjects. It says, for instance [in the case of Merleau-Ponty's transcendental argument that human beings are inescapably embodied agents], that our experience is constituted by our sense of ourselves as embodied agents. So we are inescapably to ourselves embodied subjects. Put in other terms, we can't effectively exercise subjectivity, and be aware of a world, without a sense of ourselves as embodied subjects; for this sense is constitutive of our awareness' (Taylor, 1978, p. 26).

Just precisely what role is the modest transcendental argument supposed to play in responding to the challenge of justificatory scepticism (and, therefore, the *de jure* question)? Stern points out that the answer to this question depends on what sort of epistemic account is on offer, whether it is broadly speaking a deontological normativist account (in Plantinga's terms, a justification-centred account) or a reliabilist account (what Plantinga might call a warrant-centred account). It is clearly the latter category that is of interest in our context.

What modest transcendental arguments are supposed to do in defence of broadly reliabilist epistemic accounts depends, of course, on the nature of the objection being raised by the sceptic. Stern articulates the general thrust of this objection as follows:

> The sceptic will . . . argue that, while certain methods we use might actually *be* truth-conducive (and hence while we might actually *have* justified beliefs), it is not possible for us to *show* or *properly claim* we do, as it is not possible for us to have any non-circular reason for making any such claim, since we must rely on other beliefs of the same sort as grounds for supposing this to be the case . . . [thereby] rendering this legitimating move empty, and leaving us with no reason to take our . . . beliefs to be justified. The justificatory sceptic is thus here raising what I will call the *circularity objection.* (Stern, 2000, p. 23)

While it is at this point in the book premature to attempt to bring transcendental arguments to the aid of Plantinga's extended A/C model, it is noteworthy that Stern's general description of the sceptic's challenge to reliabilist epistemic accounts resonates strongly with many of the objections that have been raised against Plantinga's account. For where Plantinga is happy to accept, on the *de jure* level, a degree of circularity in his account ('if God exists then it is highly likely that he has created us with the means to know him, and therefore, if God exists, belief in God is warranted'), his critics are not.

The question remains of just what work modest transcendental arguments are intended to do in response to the *de jure* question. Stern contends that the purpose of transcendental arguments in this context is to provide *independent* reasons for taking some belief-forming method (or, more specifically, some reliabilist epistemic model) to be reliable. By thereby giving reasons for the reliability of the method in question that are not dependent on the exercise of that method, the circularity problem is avoided.

While it seems that Plantinga does not believe there to be a real difficulty that needs solving in his Reformed epistemology, it is clear from the analysis of the first part of this book that there is indeed such a difficulty. It follows then, that a successful modest transcendental argument may well have an important role to play in responding to Plantinga's critics. To apply Stern's analysis directly to Plantinga's model, such a transcendental argument would need to provide independent reasons for thinking that Christian beliefs might be the product of a proper functioning *sensus divinitatis*, reasons that are not dependent on the presumption of a functioning *sensus divinitatis* or its precondition, the existence of God.

It remains to be seen whether the full argument for theism that we are excavating from within Charles Taylor's philosophy, based (as we have seen) on a transcendental argument, goes some way to offering such independent reasons. What has been established thus far is threefold:

1 that we have good reason to accept the primacy and weight of claim (i) of Taylor's argument for theism, 'that we must have a morality';
2 that a modest transcendental argument is an appropriate means by which to advance this crucial first step in Taylor's argument; and
3 that a transcendental argument strategy is an appropriate means of addressing the *de jure* question.

In the next chapter we shall consider the second and third

claims of Taylor's argument for theism, that we must have a morality with a certain structure (the claim of structure), and that we must have a morality based on an incomparably higher good (the claim of transcendence).

7

Transcendence

To recap, the argument that we are considering here, following Melissa Lane's reading of *Sources of the Self* (with some amendments), consists of the following cumulative claims:

 (i) we must have a morality;
 (ii) we must have a morality with a certain structure, such that particular values are connected to conceptions of the good, or 'sources';
(iii) we must have a morality based on an incomparably higher good; and
(iv) we must understand the structure of our morality and the incomparably higher good on which our morality must be based in the terms of (Christian) theism.

In the previous chapter I defended claim (i) and, to a lesser extent, claim (ii), as well as the means used to establish them, against Lane's criticisms. As we shall see, Lane's main objection to claim (ii) is fundamentally an objection to Taylor's use of History, something we will consider in the next chapter, as the objection merges with her objection to the claim of theism. In this chapter, we will focus on claim (iii), the claim of transcendence, but as will become clear claim (ii) is inextricably intertwined here too. Chapter 8 will focus on claim (iv), and then in the final chapter we will see how this argument relates to Plantinga's Reformed epistemology project.

The claim of transcendence[1] is articulated well by William Connolly when he writes that:

---

1 The 'claim of transcendence' must not be confused with the tran-

Taylor also wants, understandably enough, to speak of better and worse articulations. The best articulations, he contends, are those that draw close to a transcendent source beyond human representation. A transcendent source is the highest source. Taylor uses cautious language in discussing transcendence as a source. He generally invests presumptive priority in it by suggesting that attempts to articulate other sources either implode through performative contradiction or give insufficient recognition to a demand built so deeply into the human being as to locate a ground of morality strong and authoritative enough for the critical role we ask morality to play. So he speaks of articulations that 'bring the source closer,' that 'recognise' something inchoate that precedes them, and that are 'attuned' to a fundamental 'bent of being.' A transcendent source is thought to be the only one that really has the qualities needed. (Connolly, 2004, p. 168)

Before moving on to an examination of the arguments for and against this claim of transcendence, it is important that we define just what is meant by this term. This is no simple task, for as Taylor himself points out, it is a 'notoriously difficult and slippery' term (Taylor, 2001, p. 386). As we have seen, Lane takes the 'claim of transcendence' she finds in Taylor's work to be the claim that 'we must have a morality based on an incomparably higher good', which she connects both with Taylor's concept of hypergoods and his theism. Gary Gutting, as we shall see, wishes (also by contesting, among other things, the idea of hypergoods) to challenge Taylor's commitment to 'an irreducibility of values to human desires', which he sees as linked to 'the classical transcendent sources of morality' (Gutting, 1999, pp. 123–4) and which precludes the ethical naturalism to which Gutting is committed. Certainly this understanding seems broadly to reflect a major focus of Taylor's work, but the

---

scendental argument strategy. The former is a claim about the nature of our moral sources, while the latter is a particular argument strategy as described in the previous chapter.

difficulty of pinning down a meaning for this already slippery term is exacerbated by the fact that, despite its use by commentators on *Sources of the Self* like Lane and Gutting, it is not a word that Taylor himself makes much use of in that book. Thankfully it is now possible to turn to some of Taylor's more recent work for clarification.

In his 2001 paper, 'The immanent counter-Enlightenment', Taylor claims that the dominant trend of Enlightenment thought and post-Enlightenment culture has been 'towards the denial of transcendence'. Recognizing the opacity of this term, he identifies at least three 'dimensions' of the notion of transcendence. One is the idea that there exists 'something that transcends nature and the world' (Taylor, 2001, p. 387), by which, presumably, he means something like the traditional theological notion of a transcendent God, or its rough equivalent in other belief systems. For our purposes here, and for want of a better term, I will call this 'vertical' transcendence, as a way of capturing the idea of something 'up there', beyond our physical universe. Another dimension of the notion of transcendence that Taylor recognizes is the idea that 'life goes on after death, there is a continuation, our life doesn't totally end in our deaths' (Taylor, 2001, p. 387). Again imperfectly, I label this 'horizontal' transcendence. While he recognizes both these 'dimensions' of transcendence, and seems to be positively disposed to the idea that they are interconnected to one another and the remaining 'dimension' of transcendence he discusses, neither of these is what Taylor is primarily getting at in his use of the term. In the context of the *Sources of the Self* project (for it is arguable that 'The immanent counter-Enlightenment' is an extension of that project), what Gutting calls Taylor's *Geistesgeschichte* of modern thought, Taylor takes transcendence to mean that there is 'a point [to] life that is "beyond life"'. He articulates this further when he says that 'the point of things isn't exhausted by life, the fullness of life, even the goodness of life. This is not meant to be just a repudiation of egoism, the idea that the fullness of my life (and perhaps the lives of people I love) should be my concern. Let us agree with John

Stuart Mill that a full life must involve striving for the benefit of humankind. Then acknowledging the transcendence means seeing a point beyond that' (Taylor, 2001, p. 387).

Despite this explanation, it must be admitted that there remains an element of 'slipperiness' to this idea of transcendence, one that makes it difficult to label, even in the imperfect way I am doing here. Part of the slipperiness comes from the fact that Taylor seems to link this dimension of transcendence with religious belief,[2] seemingly tying it to 'vertical' transcendence. Setting this aside (for now), we could say that Taylor seems to be talking about a kind of 'meaning-of-life' transcendence, though of course that term won't do. We can do better, however, if we keep in mind that for Taylor meaning-of-life issues all come under the idea of the moral, and so we can perhaps label this dimension of transcendence 'moral' transcendence, with the proviso that 'moral' here is used in the broad way that Taylor uses that term. This label has the virtue of capturing the sense of the 'incomparably higher' in claim (iii), thereby justifying Lane's calling this 'the claim of transcendence'.[3] Furthermore, this label fits fairly comfortably with the idea in claim (ii) that our moral frameworks are connected to 'sources', as Taylor seems to view sources in this morally transcendent way. 'Moral' transcendence also provides a fitting counterweight to the ethical naturalism that Gutting is contending for, *contra* Taylor, which seems paradigmatic of the 'exclusive humanism' Taylor opposes, a standpoint 'based exclusively on a notion of human flourishing, which recognizes no valid aim beyond that' (Taylor, 2001, p. 387).

---

2 'I am trying to get at something that is essential not only in Christianity but in a number of other faiths, such as Buddhism. Although it enters different faiths in very different forms, the fundamental idea that they share might be grasped in the claim that life isn't the whole story' (Taylor, 2001, p. 387).

3 Lane's linking of the 'claim of transcendence' to Taylor's theism is, however, shown to be less justified, at least without further elaboration than she gives.

For our purposes here, then, it is 'moral' transcendence that is the focus of this chapter. As we shall see in the next chapter, 'vertical' transcendence – in this case theism – is nonetheless not far away. Taylor's *Geistesgeschichte* also includes an unveiling of 'horizontal' transcendence as it appears in the evolution of modern thought,[4] and it could be argued that the purpose of this is to suggest the inescapability of this dimension of transcendence. It would however take us too far from the central arguments of this book if we were also to try to follow this path.

Gutting on Taylor and Transcendence

In the course of developing his theory of pragmatic liberalism[5] Gutting appropriates aspects of Taylor's philosophy, while at the same time critiquing other aspects thereof. Of particular interest to our project here is Gutting's attempt to reject features of Taylor's account that are integral to claim (ii), the claim of structure, particularly insofar as they seem to support claim (iii) the claim of transcendence. Specifically, Gutting's critique of Taylor's explanation of moral frameworks and hypergoods are relevant here. For while we have seen that ethical naturalism faces serious difficulties in dealing with our moral phenomenology, this point is of little consequence to our goal of addressing the expanded *de jure* objection if Gutting is right that these elements of Taylor's specific argument are in fact better suited to supporting an ethical naturalist account than supporting the claim of transcendence. In what follows I will consider Gutting's response to these aspects of Taylor's theory, and show that in each case the outcome of the discussion rests on the historical argument that we shall consider in the next chapter.

---

4 He quotes, for example, Baron d'Holbach as saying 'And so, wise men . . . you are not men of your times; you are men of the future, the precursors of future reason. It is not wealth, nor honour, nor vulgar applause you should aim for: it is immortality' (Taylor, 1989, p. 353).

5 In his book *Pragmatic Liberalism and the Critique of Modernity*.

Thereafter I will turn to a discussion of some of Taylor's more recent work which I believe strengthens his general case in favour of transcendence.

Moral frameworks

Regarding moral frameworks, Gutting explains Taylor's position as follows:

> For the naturalist 'frameworks are things we invent, not answers to questions which inescapably pre-exist for us, independent of our answer or inability to answer' [Taylor, 1989, p. 30]. Taylor rejects this suggestion on the grounds that our very identity as person requires a moral orientation that, in turn, requires a moral framework. . . . Further, this orientation must occur in a 'moral space' that is not my own creation.

To put that in the terms we are using here, Taylor is putting the claims of morality and structure up against the idea of ethical naturalism. Gutting responds to this as follows:

> We may, however, wonder why naturalists must reject such claims. They certainly could agree that my identity as a person requires that I have an orientation in the sense of an overall view of what is good and bad, important and un-important. At a minimum, they could maintain that I achieve an identity by inventing a framework that provides such an orientation. Taylor, of course, insists that it makes no sense for me to invent such a framework out of whole cloth. But even here naturalists need not disagree. They can, for exam-ple, allow (with a bow to MacIntyre) that I have no choice but to begin from the moral orientation of the community into which I have been born. The naturalist is committed to understanding morality solely in terms of human attitudes, but surely these can be the attitudes an individual has in virtue of membership in a community. As I have often

emphasized, there is no reason that a naturalist has to view moral agents as isolated atoms. (Gutting, 1999, pp. 140–1)

Certainly Gutting's approach is a more sophisticated one than that offered by, say, Mackie, and it allows for an account of ethical naturalism which views morality as real rather than illusory, but where the reality of the moral is found entirely within the bounds of the social world. Warming to his Humean theme, Gutting contends that this sort of ethical naturalism 'accepts values as part of the furniture of the world' (Gutting, 1999, p. 141), an approach which avoids ethical reductionism but which does not amount to 'the foundationalist project of deriving ethics from an Archimedean point from which we could exert compelling argumentative force on any rational agent' (Gutting, 1999, pp. 142–3).

A sophisticated account of this kind clearly carries a great deal of potential explanatory power, so the question must be asked of what grounds remain on which Taylor might retain his insistence on the non-naturalism of the moral frameworks that inescapably define us? Gutting is perceptive in discussing, in connection with Taylor's project, Pascal's approach to defending the Christian faith:

Pascal planned to begin his *Apology* for the Christian religion with a description of the human condition as a combination of *grandeur et misure* – the wealth of thought and the poverty of frailty and sin. The first step in winning over nonbelievers was to get them to realize that Christianity, with its teaching about our Fall from a heavenly destiny, offers an excellent sense of what it means to be human. The second step was to have nonbelievers see that the Christian doctrine of redemption through grace should be the hope of anyone who appreciates the human condition. Through these two steps, non-believers would be prepared for faith by coming to see that Christianity was a teaching that might be true and that they hoped was true. (Gutting, 1999, pp. 129–30)

Gutting describes this approach as Pascal's phenomenology, and he correctly recognizes that something akin to this is taking place in Taylor's argument. Certainly the first step in Pascal's strategy bears a strong resemblance to what, on the reading I am offering, Taylor's approach to the idea of moral frameworks is. The idea is that, as we analyse our moral phenomenology – that is, that moral experience of the world that is inescapable for us – we discover that there are certain particular commitments (perhaps we might call them moral intuitions) that are also inescapable for us, and together these commitments form our moral framework. These commitments might, of course, be simply the result of the inevitable orientation we have to the communities into which we have been born, and if so would be entirely explicable in the terms of a sophisticated ethical naturalism. In order to decide whether naturalism or transcendence is superior here, the investigator must assess the account given by each against those inescapable commitments.

For Taylor, it is his account of the genesis of the modern Western self that supports his claim that naturalist accounts fall short of accounting for our moral phenomenology. This is what is supposed to give Taylor's non-naturalism the status of, as Gutting puts it, 'phenomenological objectivity' (Gutting, 1999, p. 149), or in the phrase we have defined above, moral transcendence. Gutting himself accepts this mode of argument when he claims that his own approach to establishing his ethical naturalism as superior to Taylor's position is not 'conceptual' in nature, but 'motivational'. Taylor's position here, then, depends on the effectiveness of his historical account, something we shall consider in the next chapter. Whether or not we accept Gutting's rejection of transcendent sources of morality as an explanation for moral frameworks will depend on whether the account he offers is more compelling than Taylor's. This we shall evaluate in the next chapter. For now, however, it is clear that Gutting's response to frameworks offers no reason to reject Taylor's view that is distinct from some historical account.

Hypergoods

Gutting's reading of Taylor's work concurs with mine in that he views the superstructure of Taylor's moral phenomenology as reaching its zenith with hypergoods, and our phenomenology thus described leaves us inescapably confronted with 'values independent not only of our individual beliefs and desires but also of the constituting beliefs of our own and others' cultures' (Gutting, 1999, pp. 149–50). Once again the claim here is one of moral transcendence. Gutting is not, however, convinced by this. He contends instead that 'even if we grant the ultimately privileged place of our moral experience over theoretical re-interpretations of it, there is still the question of whether we really require hypergoods in order to make sense of this experience' (Gutting, 1999, p. 151).

The first obvious point to make here is that it seems that Gutting has no choice but to grant the privileged place of our moral experience, considering his own commitment to the 'humdrum' realism of ethical values that he draws from Hume (Gutting, 1999, pp. 163–4). That being so, Gutting still thinks that he can avoid taking on board Taylor's notion of tran-scendent hypergoods. He argues that the modern awareness of alternative moral perspectives leads people to 'an unwillingness to absolutize moral claims. They say that certain actions are right or wrong, but they seem to find no sense in the idea that morality expresses anything other than the contingent attitudes of their social group. Why should we expect that their descrip-tions but not those given in traditional terms will turn out to be self-deceptive?' (Gutting, 1999, p. 151).

It is hard to agree with Gutting here, for it seems far more common for moderns to intuit that things like rape, paedo-philia, and female circumcision are wrong *regardless* of in which social group they take place and *regardless* of the attitude of any particular social group to those practices. Moderns may of course lack the resources to account for this intuition, and this may account for our hesitation to take firm stands on less straightforward issues, but this would only support Taylor's claim that modernity has left us largely inarticulate about our moral frameworks and hypergoods. Still, the empirical facts of how moderns view their moral commitments is perhaps something best left to sociologists to discover, and Gutting is surely right that 'even among those who do conclude something definite, we should expect that some will endorse hypergoods and some will not, and that, even among the former, there will be disagreement about which values are hypergoods.' Gutting thinks that this proves that we cannot look upon hypergoods as some kind of firm truth, but rather 'as an opinion some of us are entitled to hold on the basis of our own personal experience'. He concludes, therefore, that it is 'unlikely that we will find that hypergoods are phenomenologically objective' (Gutting, 1999, p. 152).

Gutting has, however, misunderstood Taylor's account if he takes it as contending that all people will on basic reflection simply agree with the idea of hypergoods. A key feature of Taylor's argument is the need for articulation, a means by which we can come to grips with the goods that really do motivate us. Taylor's point is not that hypergoods are *obvious* but rather that once properly understood they are *inescapable*.

The role of articulation here shows again the importance of Taylor's historical account. It is on this that Taylor's claims about hypergoods stand or fall. Once again, then, it seems that Gutting's direct response to hypergoods is, on its own, inconclusive, and does not in itself establish his claim that there is 'no reason to think that hypergoods are essential for understanding our moral experience' (Gutting, 1999, p. 157). In the next chapter we will go on to examine Taylor's historical account, and there we shall have an opportunity to evaluate its success. Before moving on, however, there remains an important strand of Taylor's recent work that demands our attention, for it offers significant reasons for taking the claim of transcendence seriously.

Closed-World Structures and 'the Death of God'

As I mentioned at the beginning of this chapter, it is in his more recent work that Taylor has focused on the issue of transcendence. As we have seen, he defines what he means by transcendence in 'The immanent counter-Enlightenment' (2001), though his purpose there is primarily to track the emergence of a transcendence-denying strand of modernity. The most direct discussion of transcendence has come in two papers that appeared in 2003, 'Closed world structures' and 'Ethics and ontology'. We have yet to consider the former paper, and it is the purpose of this section to do so.

Taylor's central purpose in 'Closed world structures' is to explore the nature of conceptual 'worlds' (or worldviews) that are closed to the transcendent. The motivation for this exploration is to make sense of the 'remarkable historical fact' that, 'say five hundred years ago in our Western civilisation, non-belief in God was close to unthinkable for the vast majority; whereas today this is not at all the case' (Taylor, 2003a, p. 47). Taylor argues that this situation has arisen in the West as a result of the development, in Latin Christendom and the secular culture that emerged from it, of the conceptual binary between the 'natural' and the 'supernatural'. This distinction is one that is, Taylor claims, 'foreign to any other civilization in history' (Taylor, 2003a, p. 48). Indeed, as Taylor points out, the very notion of the transcendent only fully makes sense in a world in which this distinction is accepted. Closed world structures, those that deny the transcendent, are therefore also the offspring of this demarcation between the natural and the supernatural, for 'The "supernatural" can be denied only from a firm footing in the "natural" as an autonomous order' (Taylor, 2003a, p. 48).

One of the closed world structures that Taylor considers is one that has obvious bearing on Gutting's position, and one that is of particular relevance to the overall project of this book. The closed world system I am referring to is one that Taylor links to the expression 'the death of God'. He acknowledges that this phrase is used in a myriad of ways, and so clarifies his usage thereof by defining it in terms of the idea that 'conditions have arisen in the modern world in which it is no longer possible, honestly, rationally, without confusions, fudging, or mental reservation, to believe in God. These conditions leave us nothing we can believe in beyond the human – human happiness, potentialities, or heroism' (Taylor, 2003a, p. 52). It is immediately striking that this description is fundamentally an ethical/epistemic one, and further that this is remarkably close to being a general description of the expanded *de jure* objection to religious belief. If we pull these two accounts together, then, we can understand the expanded *de jure* objection as expressing the central belief of the 'death of God' closed world system. For simplicity of expression, I shall from here on refer only to the expanded *de jure* objection in this context.

Taylor identifies the conditions that are singled out as the reasons for the *de jure* objection as being twofold: first, 'the deliverances of science'; and second, 'the shape of contemporary moral experience' (Taylor, 2003a, p. 52). The first of these conditions refers to the widespread belief that the success of modern science has firmly established materialism, thereby necessarily excluding the possibility of the transcendent. Adherents to this view explain the continued faith of the religious in terms very similar to the 'Freud-and-Marx complaint' we encountered in the first part of the book: faced with a cold indifferent universe, devoid of meaning or comfort, some find themselves unable to accept this reality. And so, in order to cope, 'we project a world which is providential, created by a benign God. Or at least, we see the world as meaningful in terms of the ultimate human good. Not only is the providential world soothing, but it also takes the burden of evaluating things off our shoulders' (Taylor, 2003a, p. 53). In this view religious beliefs are explained and then condemned in virtue terms – that is, that religious beliefs are the product of a lack of courage.

This version of the *de jure* question is entirely dependent on the idea that the 'closure' of the world to transcendence is a straightforward product of scientific progress, and involves no moral presuppositions. Moral accounts only come in when trying to explain the failure of some people to accept the deliverances of science. But it is exactly this foundational claim to neutrality that Taylor wishes to challenge. Instead he presents an alternative account of the historical shift to unbelief, one driven fundamentally by a moral outlook derived (ironically) from the affirmation of ordinary life that had its roots in Protestant Christianity. Once again we see the centrality of Taylor's historical account, which we shall consider in the next chapter. But Taylor does offer additional reasons for resisting this strand of the expanded *de jure* challenge. Taylor's argument here is an important one for our purposes, and is worth quoting at length:

I may leave the house without an umbrella because I believe the radio forecast to be reliable, and it predicted fair weather. But the difference between this kind of case and the issue we're dealing with here is first, that the weather, beyond the inconvenience of getting wet today, doesn't matter to me in anything like the same way; and second, that I have no alternative access to this afternoon's weather than the forecast.

The latter is simply not true in the question of belief in God. Of course, as a layperson, I have to take on authority the findings of palaeontology. But I am not similarly without resources on the issue whether what science has shown about the material world denies the existence of God. This is because I can also have a religious life, a sense of God and how he impinges on my existence, against which I can check the supposed claims to refutation.

I want to draw the Desdemona analogy. What makes *Othello* a tragedy, and not just a tale of misfortune, is that we hold its protagonist culpable in his too-ready belief in the evidence fabricated by Iago. He had an alternative mode of access to her innocence in Desdemona herself, if he could only have opened his heart/mind to her love and devotion. The fatal flaw in the tragic hero Othello is his inability to do this, partly induced by his outsider's status and sudden promotion.

The reason why I can't accept the arguments that 'science has refuted God', without any supplement, as an explanation of the rise of unbelief is that we are on this issue like Othello, rather than a person listening to the forecast as he hesitates before the umbrella stand. We can't just explain what we do on the basis of the information we received from external sources, without seeing what we made of the internal ones. (Taylor, 2003a, pp. 56–7)

What is remarkable here is how close Taylor comes to Plantinga. The tragedy, in Taylor's view, would result if we were to accept the 'authoritative' view of science on the topic of God without taking into account what our phenomenology tells us. In the terms we have used earlier in this chapter, the tension is between ontology and phenomenology. But it is much more than this, for here Taylor speaks of a 'sense of God' that gives us 'access' to him, if only we can open our hearts/minds to him. Taylor, it seems, is also a proponent of the *sensus divinitatis*, and like Plantinga he is willing to deploy it as a counter to the *de jure* challenge. But where Plantinga's use of the *sensus divinitatis* is, predominantly, part of a theoretical response to the *de jure* challenge, Taylor is here appealing to our deep-seated intuitions, those strong evaluations that are for us inescapable. Of course, as Taylor himself is the first to admit, this does not settle the issue of the existence of God. It does, however, offer significant motivation to consider the issue to be open until such time as a sufficiently careful consideration of the account given of the rise of unbelief has been made. The 'death of God', Taylor argues, doesn't help us here, 'rather it blocks the way with a pseudo-solution' (Taylor, 2003a, p. 58).

The second of the two conditions that Taylor identifies as having resulted in the 'death of God' closed world structure is one which has its starting-point in one view of our contemporary moral predicament. The idea is that religion calls for 'terrible self-mutilation', and is also a source of the infliction of suffering on others, both of which run painfully counter to the affirmation of modern humanism, with its commitment above all to human flourishing. Again this line of objection against religion fits closely with Gutting's critique of Taylor's position, indeed this is one of the key points that Gutting raises with which to oppose transcendence, in his discussion of the affirmation of ordinary life (which we shall consider in the next chapter). Also reflected here is what I have called the ethical challenge to religious belief, which, as we saw in Part 1 of this book, is one of the key objections that is raised against Plantinga's A/C model of religious belief.

Taylor describes this view as being based on what he calls a 'subtraction story', in which the stripping away of misguided commitments to serving God or some other transcendent reality is understood as revealing the true basis of human goodness, and it is this that is the basis of modern humanism. Taylor believes, however, that this account is deeply misguided, and simply cannot account for the actual commitments that are central to modern humanism:

> That I am left [after the stripping away of commitments to the transcendent] with only human goals doesn't tell me to take universal human welfare as my goal; nor does it tell me that freedom is important, or fulfilment, or equality. Just being confined to human goods could just as well find expression in my concerning myself exclusively with my own material welfare, or that of my family or immediate milieu. The, in fact, very exigent demands of universal justice and benevolence which characterize modern humanism can't be explained just by the subtraction of earlier goals and allegiances. (Taylor, 2003a, p. 61)

Put another way, Taylor's claim here is that the transcendence-denying account given by supporters of exclusive humanism is simply inadequate for the task of making sense of the actual moral commitments moderns have. Taylor also rejects the conclusion that religion must be an enemy of modern humanism, a conclusion based on the view that religious belief arises as a desperate coping response to conditions that militate against human flourishing. In this view, religion is 'the obverse of the human desire for flourishing' and 'where we are driven by our despair at the frustration of this desire' (Taylor, 2003a, p. 61). Thus where human flourishing lives and is promoted, religious ways of thinking only act as obstacles to its progress. Taylor contends that this belief is unwarranted, and is based on 'a quite inadequate account of modernity' (Taylor, 2003a, p. 60), something he claims to have shown 'elsewhere' – referring quite obviously to his historical retrieval in *Sources of the Self*.

Once again it seems that much rests on the success of the account given of our modern moral commitments, and, more fundamentally, our moral phenomenology. We have, nonetheless, already achieved something by way of defending the claim of transcendence, for we have seen that Gutting's arguments against Taylor's account of moral frameworks and hypergoods, at least when considered on their own, are no threat to the claim of transcendence. Furthermore, we have seen that there exist good reasons for at least maintaining an openness to the possibility of the transcendent, at least until the competing accounts of our moral phenomenology are properly weighed up. In the end, however, it has become clear that the claim of transcendence cannot be properly considered until those accounts are in fact weighed up, and so it is to that task we now turn.

8

History

Thus far we have defended claim (i), the claim of morality, and offered some considerations in favour of claims (ii) and (iii), the claims of structure and transcendence respectively. We saw, however, that the persuasiveness of these claims depends a good deal on whether an account can be given of these points that fits well with our moral phenomenology. It is primarily what Lane calls the 'History' argument strategy that plays this role in Taylor's work, and it is on this that we shall focus in this chapter. While Lane is correct on this point, her analysis of the History strategy is somewhat lacking. The first part of this chapter is dedicated to showing, largely through an appropriation of Stephen Mulhall's reading of Taylor's historical retrieval, that Lane's criticisms fall short of the mark. I then consider the alternative reading of the modern identity offered by Gary Gutting, which represents the best naturalist account thereof that has been raised in response to Taylor's historical account. I conclude that a certain reading of Taylor withstands all of these challenges, and that this reading supports the claims of structure and transcendence addressed in previous chapters, as well as claim (iv), the claim of theism.

Lane on the Historical and Best Account Argument Strategies

Taylor claims that his historical sketch in *Sources* is intended to capture what certain conceptions of agency meant to those people living through crucial transitions and developments in our conception of selfhood. That question is, as he argues, not causally explanatory but interpretive, and 'answering it involves giving an account of the new identity which makes clear what its appeal was' [Taylor, 1989, p. 203]. This interpretive approach is not so much an alternative to the explanatory approach to history as it is a complement to it, indeed, one that is necessary for a successful historical explanation in the first place. (Pinkard, 2004, pp. 190–1)

This much is uncontroversial. What is far more controversial is the claim that Taylor's historical account plays a role in a larger argument for theism. As I have shown previously, Lane is laudable in her recognition of this function of Taylor's historical account. Nonetheless her analysis falls short, as I intend to show in this section.

Lane correctly recognizes that Taylor understands the march of time to have the effect of making moral sources less available. Here she compares Taylor with MacIntyre, both of whom recognize that the occluding influence of history has left moderns with a range of values, not all of which are easily reconcilable. 'But whereas for MacIntyre these values, in the absence of the moral assumptions which give them meaning, are moral shards, for Taylor they are worthwhile and important values which are inextricably bound up with the modern self-concept. What they have lost, in losing their connection with the original sources, is the full force of moral power that they should possess . . . Articulation is meant to hook up these values to sources and so to restore to us the full motivating force they should have, and once possessed' (Lane, 1992, p. 54).

Here is an occasion where Taylor's now-familiar 'Best Account' principle has a role to play. As we have seen, Taylor describes this principle when he writes that:

The terms we select have to make sense across the whole range of both explanatory and life uses. The terms indispensable for the latter are part of the story that makes best sense of us, unless and until we can replace them with more clairvoyant substitutes. The result of this clairvoyance yields the best account we can give at any given time, and no epistemological or metaphysical considerations of a more general kind about science or nature can justify setting this aside. The best account in the above sense trumps. (Taylor, 1989, p. 58)

So where historical articulation is a process of seeking out the sources that empower the values that moderns find themselves inarticulately committed to, the Best Account principle provides the litmus test for what is discovered by that process. If what is discovered through the process of articulation leads to terms that 'make best sense of us' and cannot be replaced with 'more clairvoyant substitutes', then the moral sources thus discovered provide the Best Account of our moral experience. As Taylor puts it, 'To understand our predicament in terms of finding or losing orientation in moral space is to take the space which our frameworks seek to define as ontologically basic. The issue is, through what framework-definition can I find my bearings in it?' (Taylor, 1989, p. 29).

Lane, however, is unconvinced that these strategies interact as successfully as Taylor would have us believe. She sets up her criticism by pointing out how Taylor's narrative shows that moral sources like the Romantic source of nature and the Homeric warrior ethic 'lose their grip' and 'fade away' as the 'archaic culture' that spawned them recedes into history (Lane, 1992, pp. 54–5). History, then, leaves sources less available. On the other hand, according to Lane, Taylor is 'emphatic' that the work of historical articulation tightens the grip 'standards' (or, probably better, commitments or values) have on us. She uses this point to establish a tension between

the idea that a source can lose its power for . . . external historical reasons, and the idea that the most adequate source can always be identified by the Best Account. The question is in what sense articulation depends on availability. Taylor's attempt to defeat relativism implies that the Best Account should not be handicapped by availability in the immediate culture, if it can find a source which is analytically adequate. But what if this most adequate and worthy source is an idea several centuries old, already fallen into disuse for Historical reasons of social change? The best Account must be able to resurrect such sources if it is to be truly the best; but if it can do so, then History must be deprived of its role in determination of sources, if potential sources are not to be debarred due to accidental social unavailability. (Lane, 1992, pp. 54–5)

The problem here is twofold: Lane's understanding of 'standards' and their relationship to articulation, and her misreading of the nature of Taylor's historical account. I will deal with the latter first.

Although Taylor's historical retrieval in *Sources of the Self* begins with an account of the unification or 'centring' of the moral self as it is articulated in Plato's work (which itself emerges from the Homeric warrior ethos), he describes this as the 'prehistory of the story I want to tell' (Taylor, 1989, p. 120). Taylor's 'true' starting-point is the work of Augustine, which he discusses in the chapter entitled 'In interiore homine'. As Hundert puts it, 'Augustine presides over Taylor's discussion of the making of modern identity . . .' (Hundert, 1992, p. 87). This being so, using the diminishing impact of the Homeric warrior ethic to illustrate her argument is a non-starter for Lane, for to use it thus is to ignore the shape and intent of Taylor's historical retrieval.

A better candidate, though ultimately unsuccessful, for establishing Lane's understanding of Taylor's historical account is the Romantic source of nature, which has clearly receded into history and no longer provides a clear-cut moral source for moderns. Romanticism is but one of the steps between Taylor's 'true' starting-point of Augustine and the contemporary Western self. Lane is correct to recognize that Taylor's historical retrieval depicts the emergence and then recession of the Romantic source of nature as part of what was, at the time, perceived as an error-reducing transition away from theism and towards contemporary secular morality. Lane has, however, missed the crucial argument that underlies Taylor's account. As Mulhall points out, Taylor's historical narrative

> is also intended to establish that this perception [that 'the cultural transition away from theism and towards secular moral sources occurred because it was perceived to be an emancipatory, illusion-destroying and so an error-reducing one'], however understandable it might have been at the time, was itself illusory – that this secularising transition really resulted in a variety of epistemic losses. This second strand of argument is manifest in Taylor's repeated emphasis upon the theistic roots of each of the three aspects of the modern identity that he delineates, and each of the two new frontiers of moral exploration that he identifies. *Indeed, it is not too much to say that the ground-plan of his entire historical narrative is subordinate to establishing these points.* (Mulhall, 1996, pp. 142–3, italics added)

If Mulhall is right in this – and as I will argue below, I believe that he is – then Lane has crucially misunderstood the nature of Taylor's historical articulation. Far from merely showing how moral sources have become occluded by the unfolding of history, Taylor's account is in fact a systematic counter to the epistemic loss that has occurred though time. In this sense, *Sources of the Self* is best read backwards. As Alexandra Klaushofer puts it, Taylor's account is a 'counter-history', a 'retrieval' of theism (Klaushofer, 1999, p. 136).

It is at this point we need to deal with the other misunderstanding that leads to Lane's critique, her understanding of 'standards' and their relationship to articulation. Her claim is that a problematic tension arises in Taylor's argument, in part due to the fact that he portrays standards as gaining an increasing grip on us as a result of articulation. On the other hand, in Lane's understanding, Taylor depicts History as denying access to the sources that originally made sense of the standards we have been bequeathed. But there is a false separation in Lane's thought between 'standards' (which, tellingly, is not a term

Taylor uses in describing any part of his theory) and 'sources'. The intensification in commitment that Taylor argues emerges from articulation results *because* doing so 'reconnects' us with our moral sources. So the tension between 'intensification' and 'connection' in Lane's argument does not exist. Indeed, the very fact that Taylor's historical articulation *is* a retrieval defeats Lane's objection about the relevant moral sources being unavailable to us.

Lane's failed arguments lead her to conclude that History is insufficient to establish the claims of structure and transcendence. Significantly, however, Lane neglects the role that Taylor's historical retrieval plays in establishing the inescapability of hypergoods to moral frameworks. Hypergoods, as we have seen, are 'goods which not only are incomparably more important than others but [which also] provide the standpoint from which these must be weighed, judged, decided about' (Taylor, 1989, p. 63). As I will argue below, having started with the assertion that as human beings it is part of our makeup that we view the world through morality-coloured spectacles, Taylor then tries, through his historical retrieval, to show that 'we cannot make sense of our moral life without something like a hypergood perspective' (Taylor, 1989, p. 71). In other words, not only is a moral outlook on life inescapable, but a hypergood perspective is inescapably part of any moral outlook.

I have claimed, above, that Lane has misjudged the effectiveness of Taylor's argument in part because she has not properly understood the role his historical retrieval plays. I claimed also that Stephen Mulhall offers a superior understanding of that retrieval, and it is to that account we now turn.

Stephen Mulhall's Theistic Reading of *Sources of the Self*

Ruth Abbey points out that one of the biggest puzzles for scholars of Charles Taylor's work is what to make of the historical retrieval that is such a large part of his magisterial work *Sources of the Self*, and which also surfaces elsewhere in his work.[1] As we have seen, however, Melissa Lane's paper, with its focus on the structural features of Taylor's book, offers little by way of analysis of that retrieval. By contrast, in a paper entitled '*Sources of the Self*'s senses of itself: a theistic reading of modernity', Stephen Mulhall puts forward what is to date one of the most in-depth analyses of the historical retrieval that makes up the bulk of *Sources of the Self*. As I have already stated, it is also the analysis that comes closest to my own reading of Taylor's historical argument.

Mulhall rejects Taylor's claim in the Preface to the book that 'those who are utterly bored by modern philosophy' can happily skip Part I – in which Taylor primarily sets out the structural features of his theory – while '[t]hose who are bored by history' can read only the theory and, unprejudiced, ignore the remainder of the book. Mulhall contends instead that 'the business of Parts II–V of *Sources of the Self* is continuous with the concerns of Part I' (Mulhall, 1996, p. 136). This recognition enables Mulhall to get a clearer grasp on the nature of the argument in the historical section of *Sources of the Self* than is available to those who might take Taylor's claim of the independence of the two parts at face value.

However, as excellent as Mulhall's account is, my reading differs from his in one important respect. Where Mulhall reads Taylor as offering a theistic 'Best Account' of the contingent modern identity, on my reading Taylor's account is a work of philosophical anthropology, one that makes strong claims about the nature of human reality. Certainly this reading is one that seems to fit better with the broad epistemological movement into which Taylor fits most comfortably, what Nicholas Smith calls 'strong hermeneutics'. In Smith's words, 'Strong hermeneutics marks a departure from the thesis of [the radical contingency of moral identity] in that it considers human existence to be intelligible on the assumption of certain limits to contingency' (Smith, 1997, p. 3). As I have been reading Taylor in this book, those limits are defined phenomenologically.

---

1 See Abbey, 2000, pp. 52–3 for a good account of this.

Veritas: Tayloring Reformed Epistemology

In what follows I will first set out Mulhall's description of Taylor's historical account, then I will articulate the main points of Mulhall's analysis. This exercise is intended to show that Taylor's historical argument does indeed provide strong support for claims (iii) and (iv) of Taylor's theistic argument, the claims that we must have a morality based on an incomparably higher good, and that we must understand the incomparably higher good on which our morality must be based in the terms of (Christian) theism.

Mulhall's account of Taylor's history

Taylor's historical account, according to Mulhall, 'offers one possible genealogy of our culture, a biography which will inevitably present some of the transitions it has experienced as error-reducing and some as error-enhancing; but any such biography must itself be told from a particular moral perspective, and its representation of the epistemic worth of any given transition will inevitably be contestable, arguable. To present any such transition in this narrative form amounts to making a judgement on its epistemic worth; and to make such a judgement is . . . full-bloodedly to engage in moral argument'[2] (Mulhall, 1996, p. 136).

Drawing from Taylor's articulation of the structure of the nature of our identities and the moral frameworks that define them, Mulhall points out that justifying any particular moral stance requires articulation of 'a particular conception of the status and nature of human beings' (Mulhall, 1996, p. 136),

---

2 I made a similar, though less well supported claim (I was at that time unaware of the existence of Mulhall's analysis) in an earlier article where I expressed 'my belief that there may be more to Taylor's moral archaeology than meets the eye, and that on one reading of *Sources* we could see him as in fact arguing for a particular [theistic] ontology which he believes to be "the only adequate basis for our moral responses, whether we recognize this or not" [Taylor, 1989, p. 10], and which is an extension of what he has done in the first section of his book' (Baker, 2000, p. 164).

thereby revealing the moral sources underpinning that stance. But, argues Mulhall, this is exactly the sort of articulation that Taylor gives in the historical sections of *Sources of the Self*.

Taylor's genealogy begins by identifying a particular group of 'universal' moral commitments that the Enlightenment has bequeathed to moderns. The universality of these commitments is reflected not only in the fact that no modern can meaningfully attempt to deny their moral weight, but also in the fact that they are held to apply to everyone everywhere. The commitments singled out include 'a moral imperative to reduce, alleviate and even to end suffering; a recognition of the centrality of freedom to human well-being; a commitment to justice, typically understood as the protection of human rights; and a concern for democratic equality' (Mulhall, 1996, pp. 136–7).

Again following Taylor's meta-ethic in the first part of *Sources of the Self*, Mulhall points out that these moral commitments require a specific ontology of the human for their power. Taylor's historical account tracks the development of that ontology, which Mulhall describes as 'a very specific conception of human beings as selves, as individuals whose sense of their own identity has three fundamental facets: inwardness, an affirmation of ordinary life and an expressivist conception of nature as manifest within as well as around them' (Mulhall, 1996, pp. 136–7).[3]

---

3 Klaushofer's analysis, though much shorter, offers a very similar understanding of Taylor's historical argument: 'Despite the diversity of contemporary values, Taylor notes, there is in fact a great deal of consensus about the important ones; the ideals of justice and universal human rights have gained acceptance across the world. Yet his worry is that without adequate grounding, these ideals may prove unsustainable; Nietzsche's unmasking of benevolence provides a powerful illustration of what "happens" to a value deprived of a positive source: it collapses under the weight of postmodern moral scepticism. The lesson drawn from this, that "high standards need strong sources", elicits the suggestion that maybe only theism carries sufficient resources and resonance to withstand the new contestation from competing sources . . . [Taylor, 1989, p. 520]' (Klaushofer, 1999, p. 144).

The facet of 'inwardness' described by Taylor might be described as the phenomenological turn – it involves shifting our focus from the world of our experience and instead considering our experiences themselves. Taylor identifies the origin of this inward turn in the work of Augustine, and it is in turn picked up and intensified by Descartes. This shift away from the *ontic logos* and towards the self as moral source has bequeathed to moderns an understanding of the self as something radically disengaged – 'for Descartes, rational self-mastery means abstracting from our ordinary embodied way of experiencing reality, taking an external perspective on our bodies as well as the material universe, and thereby viewing both as domains of potential control by instrumental reason' (Mulhall, 1996, p. 137). The paradoxical result of this prioritizing of the first-person perspective is, then, the rise of the modern ideal of viewing the self from some ideal third-person perspective, in Thomas Nagel's celebrated phrase, 'the view from nowhere' (Nagel, 1989).

The second facet of the modern conception of the self discussed by Taylor, the affirmation of ordinary life, is identified in his account as originating in the Reformation. One of the central points of conflict between the Protestant Reformers and the medieval Catholic Church lay in the Reformers' rejection of the Church's view of the sacred. 'Protestants denied that sacramental rites or membership of a clerical or monastic order brought individuals closer to the divine . . . ordinary human realms of production and reproduction were seen as sacred to just the degree that their participants engaged in them with the correct attitude' (Mulhall, 1996, p. 138). The 'weaned affections' with which the reformers (and the Puritans in particular) urged their followers to view the world, kept the affirmation of ordinary life neatly in line with the disengaged inwardness that originated with Augustine and Descartes.

This did not, however, remain unchanged. The expressivist conception of nature has its beginnings – according to Taylor's account – in the decline and then demise of the Puritan idea of original sin. This notion lay behind the importance of one's

affections for ordinary life being weaned, for central to this doctrine was the idea that both our normal desires and the world
itself are corrupted as a consequence of the Fall. With the
decline of this notion, ordinary life and the human desires that
go along with it were affirmed unreservedly, and the maximiza-
tion of happiness and minimization of pleasure for all people
became central to the resulting morality. Key figures in this shift
were the Deists Shaftesbury and Hutcheson. Hot on their heels
were the first utilitarians, who rejected any belief in a providential order set in motion by God, but who nonetheless
retained the Deist's emphasis on maximizing utility.

Utilitarianism, however, retains the disengaged stance to the
self in its morality – the very idea of a utilitarian calculus reflects
this instrumental view. It is the other line of thought to emerge
from Deism that lies behind the third facet of the modern
identity that Taylor details. The Deists placed a great deal of
emphasis on moral sentiments – these were understood to be
our normative guide to moral behaviour. Being 'in touch' with
the natural world came to be seen as the best way to discover
our truest moral sentiments, which are the voice of nature
speaking within us. It is in this stream that Rousseau and the
Romantics who followed on after him lie. 'Simultaneously,
however, Romantic expressivism adds a new depth of inwardness to the human self; for if we can only fully know ourselves
by articulating and so realizing that depth of feeling, then our
individuality is definable only through creative self-expression.
According to Taylor, it is this which underlies contemporary
fascination with the artist, and our tendency to assign spiritual
worth to her work; the artwork has become an epiphanic locus
of the manifestation of something of the ultimate spiritual
significance' (Mulhall, 1996, pp. 138–9).

These, then, are the three facets of the modern identity that
Taylor believes lie behind the moral commitments that moderns
feel so pressingly. But, as Mulhall points out, they also lead to
diverse possible moral sources that moderns could draw on.
The most obvious source is the one that Taylor begins with in
his discussion of Augustine – God. Despite repeated claims of

the 'death' of God in modern times, 'love of Him plainly remains a constitutive and empowering idea in the lives of millions' (Mulhall, 1996, p. 139). Taylor's historical account also points to the emergence, in the modern era, of two 'new' moral sources, what he calls 'frontiers of exploration'. 'The first lies within the agent's own powers, those of rational order and control initially, but later . . . it will also be a question of powers of expression and articulation. The second lies in the depths of nature, in the order of things, but also as it is reflected within, in what wells up from my own nature, desires, sentiments, affinities' (Taylor, 1989, p. 314; quoted in Mulhall, 1996, p. 139).

The boundaries between these three moral 'frontiers' are not impenetrable – Taylor points to attempts by various thinkers to draw together two or more of them. Nor are they fixed and static, hence the description of them as frontiers of exploration. Nonetheless, these broad streams are what Taylor identifies as lying at the heart of the contemporary Western moral identity.

Mulhall's analysis

As I have already mentioned, Mulhall reads Taylor's historical retrieval as a case of 'full-blooded' moral argument. He rejects as misleading or worse Taylor's claim that the question of what our best moral self-interpretation requires is not part of the purpose of the book and 'remains to be argued out' (Taylor, 1989, p. 342). Mulhall believes that it is clear that Taylor is committed to a theistic account as the best account of what underpins the demanding moral values of modernity:

> For example, when asking whether a non-theistic explanation of the significance of human life is tenable, he says that his 'hunch is that the answer . . . is "no". It all depends on what the most illusion-free moral sources are, and they seem to me to involve a God' [Taylor, 1989, p. 342]. And in his concluding pages, when expressing the hope that the highest of our spiritual aspirations need not lead either to mutilation

or destruction, he writes: 'It is a hope that I see implicit in Judeo-Christian theism . . . and in its central promise of a divine affirmation of the human, more total than humans can ever attain unaided' [Taylor, 1989, p. 521]. My question, therefore, becomes: What, if any, aspects of Taylor's portrait of modernity actually contribute to, rather than simply preparing the ground for, the claim that our best self-interpretation must involve God? (Mulhall, 1996, pp. 141–2)

Mulhall begins to answer his own question by pointing out the nature of Taylor's understanding of practical reasoning. For Taylor, practical reasoning is a 'reasoning in transitions' between competing accounts. This involves showing that a move from one account to another involves either epistemic loss or epistemic gain, through the resolving of some contradiction, or clearing up some confusion, or something of the sort. Following this methodology in defence of a theistic account of the values of the contemporary West, argues Mulhall, must then involve showing that such an account is superior to its competitors – that is, that a move from any competing position to theism would constitute an 'error-reducing' move. Mulhall claims to see exactly this methodology in Taylor's historical retrieval, with an epistemic argument running in parallel with Taylor's account of the development of the Western self. Certainly some of Taylor's recent work suggests support of Mulhall's reading in this respect. In his paper 'The immanent counter-Enlightenment: Christianity and morality', for instance, Taylor writes that 'Immanent humanism is not simply the result of the decline of religion, but rather the product of a chain of constructions whose first links were forged by Christianity itself' (Taylor, 2005, p. 225).

Taylor's account, in *Sources of the Self*, of the emergence of secularism through and after the Enlightenment is such that it is clear that as this change occurred it was viewed as progress – a move *away* from the superstition and illusion that held humanity back, and *towards* truth. In other words, it was perceived as a process of epistemic gain. Mulhall maintains, however, that

Taylor carefully and subtly also argues that this perception was in fact false, and that the real outcome of this process was 'a variety of epistemic losses'. Mulhall claims to see in Taylor's historical argument two epistemic challenges to modern secularism. First, Taylor's account implies that the central elements of secular modern understandings of the self and the moral are all already present and accounted for in theism, and that the move to secularism therefore offers no meaningful epistemic gain over theism. The flip-side of this challenge is that Taylor's account foregrounds the worrying (for secularists, at least) possibility that the two secular frontiers of the Western moral identity and their derivatives *depend* on theism for their moral force.[4] A particularly stark example of this line of argument comes in chapter 19 of *Sources of the Self*, where Taylor describes the emergence of utilitarian thought. As Mulhall puts it, in Taylor's account 'the utilitarian combination of reductive ontology and moral impetus compels such naturalism to be parasitic on that which it most violently opposes, at once deriving its affirmation through the rejection of an alleged theistic negation of nature (its words of power mainly consisting of polemical passages in which religion is denounced as erroneous, superstitious and fraudulent) and modelling that affirmation upon the Christian notion of *agape*' (Mulhall, 1996, p. 144).[5]

---

4 As Nicholas Smith has rightly pointed out to me, even accepting this point does not necessarily force a return to theism – the option is open to take this, as Nietzsche did, as a reason to reject modern secularism while continuing to reject theism. Within the context of a reading of Taylor's work however, this does not seem to be an option that is open to us, for as Mulhall points out, Taylor's 'brief description of the Nietzschean perspective makes it clear that, for him, its power depends ultimately on a paradox' (Mulhall, 1996, pp. 149–50).

5 Taylor himself reaffirms this reading in a more recent work when he contends that

Utilitarianism articulates our sense of the importance of what I will call 'benevolence', using the eighteenth-century term – the call we feel to help our fellow creatures live and flourish, to prolong life and reduce suffering. But it does not seem to have place for the goals of personal fulfilment or for our aspirations to realize in our lives other

Taylor pushes home this line of argument on a general level by raising the question of whether we moderns are not living 'beyond our moral means in continuing allegiance to our standards of justice and benevolence' (Taylor, 1989, p. 517). The implied threat here is one of inadequacy – that the secular modern moral sources might not be up to the task of giving power to our moral commitments. In fact, this question of inadequacy is the basis of what Taylor sees as a crucial difference between theistic and non-theistic moral sources. While theism might be challenged on the grounds of being factually untrue, Taylor contends that 'no one doubts that those who embrace it will find a fully adequate moral source in it. The other two sources suffer a contestation on this score. The question is whether, even granted we fully recognize the dignity of disengaged reason, or the goodness of nature, this is in fact enough to justify the importance we put on it, the moral store we set by it, the ideals we erect on it' (Taylor, 1989, p. 317).

This question hangs over the remainder of Taylor's historical account, and by its end Mulhall sees little evidence that the secular moral sources are, in fact, adequate to this task. It therefore comes as no surprise that Taylor expresses his 'hunch' that 'the most illusion-free moral sources ... involve a God' (Taylor, 1989, p. 342). Mulhall sums up his reading of the nature of Taylor's argument strategy when he writes: 'If secular moral sources are parasitic on theistic ones and incapable of bearing the burden of empowering the full range of modern moral ideas, whereas theistic sources can bear this burden and can also acknowledge versions of the sources on which secular moral visions exclusively rely, then we have strong reason for thinking that the cultural transition away from theistic sources amounted to a significant epistemic loss. In short, theism is our best available moral account' (Mulhall, 1996, p. 146).

---

goods than benevolence; to be people of integrity, sensitivity, feeling, and love (except insofar as this instrumentally serves benevolence). This is why the demands of, say, integrity, can be taken as a challenge for utilitarianism. (Taylor, 1997, p. 171)

If Taylor's historical account is understood in this way, the full force of the relationship between Taylor's historical account and his explicit meta-ethic can be seen. The historical account is intended as an argument in the sense that it both reveals the inadequacy of the major competing moral accounts available to those of us living in the contemporary West, and is also intended to provoke in the reader a resonance[6] between her moral intuitions and the theistic account put forward by Taylor. Such an understanding seems to me to best capture the force of Taylor's historical retrieval, particularly in the light of Mulhall's articulation of that account.

It is of course insufficient to simply draw out the central argument of Taylor's historical retrieval, important as that is. For as Mulhall points out, this is but 'one possible genealogy of our culture'. With the work of exegesis now completed, what remains is to evaluate the success of this argument. Put another way, the question that must still be answered is that of just how convincing Taylor's historical argument is.[7] This is a difficult question to answer, for such arguments do not respond well to the usual tools of the analytic philosopher. It is the nature of historical accounts like Taylor's that they be always incomplete, always open to reinterpretation, such that it is difficult to

---

6 As Nicholas Smith has rightly pointed out to me, some caution is needed here with regard to this notion of 'resonance'. Taylor's use of the term singles out the subjective experiencing of a work of art as communicating some otherwise hidden feature of reality – in other words, it is connected with his notion of epiphanic art (cf. Taylor, 1989, ch. 24). Mulhall, on the other hand, uses the word to describe the experience of some moral account, or some feature thereof, 'ringing true' in a previously unrecognized way. While there are obvious parallels between the two usages, they are not the same.

7 Mulhall himself, while broadly supportive of Taylor's account, nonetheless offers his own critique of Taylor's historical argument. Mulhall's critique, however, is not directed at Taylor's support of theism per se, but rather at the *type* of theism that emerges from Taylor's account. Because our focus in this thesis is the expanded *de jure* challenge, Mulhall's critique is not of direct relevance, and shall not be considered here.

know when one has a good account in hand. Were our goal here to find the truth of the matter, this would indeed be a serious obstacle to progress. But that is not our purpose. Instead, as is by now familiar, our goal is to deploy Taylor's historical argument as part of an argument aimed at showing that there is good reason to take the truth claims of Christian belief seriously. Arguments in service of this goal need not, therefore, achieve some high standard of proof, but instead must aim to show themselves to be sufficiently compelling, such that Christian beliefs cannot be dismissed without a consideration of whether or not they are true. That said, however, even achieving this less stringent goal in this particular case requires more than simply setting out Taylor's historical argument. As Alasdair MacIntyre rightly pointed out in his review of *Sources of the Self*, 'we only have good reason to endorse Taylor's interpretation of the relevant histories if we have matched its claims against those made for at least some rival interpretation of the same subject-matter' (MacIntyre, 1994, p. 189). Here again Gutting's critique of Taylor turns out to be of value, and it is to this that we now turn.

An Alternative History: Gutting's Critique of Taylor's *Geistesgeschichte*

Gutting's response to Taylor's historical argument is not a full-blown alternative naturalist account of the development of the Western self, and to my knowledge there as yet exists no account of this kind that is consciously intended as a refutation of Taylor's retrieval. What Gutting does do is to critique central aspects of Taylor's account in such a way as to suggest that a naturalist ontology tied to a naturalist reading of history is better suited to accounting for our modern moral intuitions, and that such a history is motivationally superior to Taylor's account. As we saw in the previous chapter, much of the weight of Gutting's response to Taylor rests on this aspect of his critique. Gutting's counter therefore represents the best available competitor to Taylor's account, and as such must be addressed if we are to show Taylor's account to be successful. Once again it must be stressed that 'success' in this context is not showing that Taylor's account is the one and only true interpretation of the historical data, but rather that Taylor's history is at least as convincing as its main naturalist rival, as represented here by Gutting. In order to achieve this, in what follows I consider the two central lines of critique that Gutting directs against Taylor's *Geistesgeschichte*.

The affirmation of ordinary life

Arguably most central to Gutting's rebuttal of Taylor's *Geistesgeschichte* are his arguments regarding the affirmation of ordinary life. Gutting's challenge to Taylor's reading of the affirmation of ordinary life is based on his claim that, though this affirmation is certainly a central feature of the Christian belief system, 'in the long run, it supports the secular tendencies of modernity and poses problems for traditional Christianity' (Gutting, 1999, p. 125). Gutting's challenge is not, in his view, a conceptual one. He concedes that Christianity 'has the intellectual resources' to account for the affirmation of ordinary life. His claim, however, is that 'a Christian emphasis on the intrinsic value of ordinary life will always risk colliding with the more central claim that our ultimate goal is not in this world' (Gutting, 1999, p. 126), and this reduces the motivational force of the Christian view in comparison to Gutting's own pragmatic liberalism. He argues that 'whatever the force of Protestant arguments against monastic vows, it is very hard to deny that Christian perfection required renunciation of some intrinsically innocent goods. Otherwise, there was no way to make sense of key biblical injunctions to "sell all you have and give it to the poor", "leave mother and father for my sake", and "take up your cross"' (Gutting, 1999, pp. 125–6).

This criticism, however, ignores Taylor's discussion of the idea of sacrifice in his exposition of the roots of the affirmation of ordinary life. As Taylor points out, the very idea that the above injunctions are a call to *sacrifice* and thus involve a loss of something good, is an affirmation of their value, unlike, for example, the Stoic call to eschew the world. Thus Gutting is somewhat off the mark in his comment, which he takes to show that the affirmation of ordinary life sits most easily with the secular tendencies of modernity, that

> For Christians . . . any affirmation of ordinary life will require careful qualification. Our mundane life is good, but it cannot be our ultimate good. Moreover, there is always the very real possibility of conflict between worldly goods and our ulti- mate supernatural good. Heaven is not just icing on the cake of a life entirely fulfilling in purely natural terms. The life we lead in hope of everlasting reward is not the life we would, even at our best, lead without such hope. (Gutting, 1999, p. 126)

While there is truth in this statement, it seems to ignore the very significant fact that Christians do not view the lives we live now as *ordinary*. Human life, since humankind's fall from grace that is depicted in the biblical story of Adam and Eve's disobedience towards God and subsequent expulsion from the Garden of Eden, is *extraordinary* in the Christian story. That is to say that, since the Fall, the whole of existence is not what it was created to be, though the created order still reflects, in the manner of a broken mirror, the good cosmos that God originally created. Thus ordinary life is still affirmed insofar as it corresponds to that which God created and saw was good, but sometimes these now-distorted goods of ordinary life must be sacrificed in the interests of the new world that God will create once the fall is reversed. Still, even granted this point, Gutting's challenge remains to be fully answered. His claim is that as ordinary life is affirmed we become 'impressed with mundane values and become content with the life they define', and that this content- ment robs Christianity of its power, by removing the motiva- tional force of 'the Christian call to something better' (Gutting, 1999, pp. 126–8). Is this really so?

In a recent paper Taylor goes to considerable lengths to show that the view Gutting here articulates reaches an unwarranted conclusion. As Taylor explains it, this view takes the unquestionable uniqueness of our contemporary concern with human goods as the fundamental starting-point, and argues from there that in such a world there is no place for belief in God. 'A faith of this kind would have to make one an outsider, an enemy of this world, in unrelenting combat with it. Thus one is either thoroughly in this world, living by its premises, and then one cannot really believe in God; or one believes, and is in some sense living like a resident alien in modernity. Since we find ourselves more and more inducted into it, belief becomes harder and harder; the horizon of faith steadily recedes' (Taylor, 2003a, p. 58). It is remarkable how closely this description fits Gutting's own account, and one wonders whether Taylor might have had Gutting's arguments in view. Taylor explains the genesis of this position as follows:

> This moral version of the 'death of God' account seems plausible to many people, because they make an assumption about the rise of modernity which helps to screen from them how complex and difficult this quest is. The assumption is what I have called 'the view from Dover Beach': The transition to modernity comes about though the loss of traditional beliefs and allegiances. . . . old views and loyalties are eroded. Old horizons are washed away, in Nietzsche's image. The sea of faith recedes, to follow Arnold. . . . In other words, we moderns behave as we do because we have 'come to see' that certain claims were false . . . (Taylor, 2003a, pp. 59–60)

This 'subtraction' view, as Taylor also refers to it, is one he views as an inadequate account of modernity. It neglects, in a way that he believes his own account in *Source of the Self* does not, 'the possibility that Western modernity might be sustained by its own original spiritual vision' (Taylor, 2003a, p. 60). In the very next sentence Taylor betrays his belief (which supports Mulhall's reading of Taylor's historical retrieval) that this is more than merely a 'possibility', it is the reality. Taylor directs readers to his historical account in *Sources of the Self* in order that they may consider for themselves which account is more clairvoyant. This, of course, is not something we can pursue here. Taylor does, however, offer an additional line of attack against the sort of position that Gutting contends for, and at least two other arguments of this kind can be distilled from Taylor's recent papers. I shall consider each of these in turn.

Response 1: Radical under-description

The first line of response I want to consider here is one that Taylor directs explicitly against the 'subtraction' story favoured by the likes of Gutting. In his paper 'Closed world structures', Taylor accuses this account of 'radically under-describing' the moral position of modern humanism. What's missing from this account, Taylor contends, is any explanation of the 'very exigent demands of universal justice and benevolence'. As we have already seen, Taylor explains his point as follows: 'That I am left with only human concerns doesn't tell me to take universal human welfare as my goal; nor does it tell me that freedom is important, or fulfilment, or equality. Just being confined to human goods could just as well find expression in my concerning myself exclusively with my own material welfare, or that of my family or immediate milieu' (Taylor, 2003a, p. 61). This is a similar point to the one that Taylor raised in *Sources of the Self* against the position held by the utilitarians, with their inability to account, in the terms of their theory, for benevolence (Taylor, 1989, p. 332). And he raises the spectre of the Marquis de Sade as an illustration of where a whole-hearted commitment to human good can lead (Taylor, 1989, p. 336).

There can be no doubt that Gutting is committed to the values of 'freedom, benevolence, and the affirmation of ordinary life' (cf. Gutting, 1999, p. 114), but Taylor's general critique is exactly correct with respect to Gutting's specific position, for he offers nothing by way of explanation of the source of the first two of those values, and simply assumes that they are part of the same bundle as the affirmation of ordinary life. This is, quite clearly, not so.[8]

Response 2: A nuanced account of religion's affirmation of ordinary life

A second response to Gutting's challenge that can be extracted from Taylor's work is one that questions the adequacy of the account given of the role and understanding of the affirmation of ordinary life in religion. In 'The immanent counter-Enlightenment' Taylor offers this explanation of the basis for the secular attack on religion's ability to properly commit to the affirmation of ordinary life:

> This affirmation, which constitutes a major component of our modern ethical outlook, was originally inspired by a mode of Christian piety. It exalted practical *agape*, and was polemically directed against the pride, elitism, one might say, self-absorption of those who believed in 'higher' activities or spiritualities. . . .
>
> This earthly, one might say, earthy critique of the allegedly 'higher' was later transposed and used as a secular critique of Christianity and, indeed, religion in general. Something of the same rhetorical stance adopted by Reformers against monks and nuns was taken up by secularists and unbelievers against Christian faith itself, a faith that in their view scorns the real, sensual, earthly human good for some purely imaginary higher end, the pursuit of which can only lead to the frustration of the real, earthly good, to suffering, mortification, repression, and so forth. The motivations of those

---

8 Taylor also points to another shortcoming that he believes views of Gutting's sort face. As Taylor points out in 'The immanent counter-Enlightenment', this pervasive and uncritical outlook is also characterized by 'the widespread inability to give any human meaning to suffering and death, other than as dangers and enemies to be avoided or combated' (Taylor, 2001, pp. 391–2).

who espouse this 'higher' path are thus, indeed, suspect. Pride, elitism, and the desire to dominate all play a part in this story too, along with fear and timidity (also present in the earlier Reformers' story, but less prominently). (Taylor, 2001, p. 389)

The problem with this sort of critique (which quite clearly includes Gutting among its proponents), Taylor argues, is that it is based on an insufficiently nuanced grasp of religion's relationship with the affirmation of ordinary life. In response, Taylor outlines three stances among which religious adherents have divided themselves. The first is what he identifies as the 'symbiotic' or 'superstitious' stance, in which the key idea is that 'the supreme achievements of those who went beyond life have served to nourish the fullness of life of those who remain on this side of the barrier' (Taylor, 2001, p. 338). An obvious example of this would be the ancestor worship that is a central feature of African traditional religion, and a similar combination of the concern for flourishing and transcendence can be found, as Taylor points out, in certain strands of Christianity, Islam and Theravada Buddhism. The second stance is often a reaction to the first outlined above. This Taylor labels the purist stance. This is frequently the credo of self-declared reformers in all religions who have renounced this symbiotic approach and have instead pursued a 'pure' religion, in which concern for flourishing is almost totally driven out in favour of 'true commitment' to the transcendent.

Taylor points out that the critique of religion based on the affirmation of ordinary life crudely reduces religion to the purist stance, or in some cases a combination of the purist stance and the symbiotic stance. What this excludes from view, however, is the third stance, that of *agape/karuna*, which Taylor describes as follows:

Renouncing, aiming beyond life, not only takes you away, but also brings you back to flourishing. In Christian terms, if renunciation decentres you in relation with God, God's will is that humans flourish, and so you are taken back to an affirmation of this flourishing, which is biblically called *agape*. In Buddhist terms, Enlightenment doesn't just turn you from the world, but also opens the flood-gates of *metta* (loving kindness) and *karuna* (compassion). There is the Theravada concept of the Paccekabuddha, concerned only for his own salvation, but he is ranked below the highest Buddha, who acts for the liberation of all beings. (Taylor, 2001, p. 388)

The reason the critique of religion on the grounds of the affirmation of ordinary life does not engage with this stance of *agape/karuna*, is because, in Taylor's words, it 'becomes invisible'. 'The reason is that a transformed variant of it has in fact been assumed by the secularist critics' (Taylor, 2001, p. 389). In other words, the stance of *agape/karuna* posits a very similar (albeit differently construed) commitment to human good. Once this stance becomes visible, however, it becomes clear that it is not susceptible to the charges of elitism and the rejection of ordinary life – indeed, it becomes clear that it is the very source of the commitment to ordinary life that is the basis of the criticism that is now levelled at religious belief by those in Gutting's camp.

Response 3: The testimony of the immanent counter-Enlightenment

A final response to Gutting's 'ordinary life' critique that can be extracted from Taylor's recent work relates to what Taylor calls the immanent counter-Enlightenment. This movement, united in its opposition to Enlightenment values, is 'immanent' in two senses. It shares with the Enlightenment the denial of transcendence, leaving it firmly based in the realm of the immanent. As we shall see, however, a crucial source of this counter-Enlightenment is a frustration with the limits of immanence which gives rise to attempts to breach those limits while still rejecting the transcendent, something that leads to an uncomfortable paradox. The second sense in which this counter-Enlightenment is 'immanent' is that, because of its shared rejection of transcendence, this movement is a rebellion from within the bounds of the Enlightenment itself.

Taylor tracks the origins of this 'revolt from within unbelief' to Romanticism. As he explains:

> The Romantic movement was one of the important loci of the counter-Enlightenment, even if it was also always much more than this. Protest against a world that had been flattened, denuded of meaning, was a recurring theme of Romantic writers and artists, and this attitude blended easily with counter-Enlightenment commitments, although it didn't have to. At least such a stance made it impossible to align itself with the crasser variants of Enlightenment secularism, such as Utilitarianism.
>
> The immanent counter-Enlightenment comes to existence within this domain of Western culture. From the beginning, it has been linked with a primacy of the aesthetic. Even where it rejects the category and speaks of an 'aesthetic illusion' (as with Paul de Man), it remains centrally concerned with art, and especially modern, post-Romantic art. Its big battalions within the modern academy are found in literature departments. (Taylor, 2001, p. 394)

In Taylor's account, Mallarmé is a paradigmatic figure in this aesthetic-driven rebellion against the values of the Enlightenment. Taylor describes Mallarmé as 'the first great modern poet of absence' (Taylor, 2001, p. 395). This absence is the absence of the object, but that can only be achieved through the absence or death of the subject. This is in sharp contrast with the affirmation of life – 'What emerges is something like a counter-primacy of death' (Taylor, 2001, p. 395). The effect of this is, in a strange sense, to once again affirm transcendence, at least in terms of Taylor's definition thereof as 'a point to life beyond life'. But of course transcendence is vehemently denied, resulting in a paradox, which Taylor calls 'immanent transcendence' and which is a central aspect of the immanent counter-Enlightenment:

> Death offers in some sense the privileged perspective, the paradigm gathering-point for life. This idea recurs again and again in our culture, and not necessarily by way of Mallarmé. Heidegger's 'Sein-zum-Tode' is a famous example, but the theme is taken up in rather different forms in Sartre, Camus and Foucault, was echoed in the 'death of man' fad propagated by the latter, and so on. And in the variant that spoke of the 'death of the subject', the paradoxical affinities with certain religious outlooks – perhaps most obviously Buddhism – were patent. (Taylor, 2001, p. 396)

A related strand of the immanent counter-Enlightenment is one that receives part of its impetus from the warrior ethic, with its exaltation of heroism. This is again an expression of frustration at the levelling effects of modern humanism. The key figure in this strand of the rebellion is Nietzsche, and following him Bataille, Foucault and Derrida. Common to both of these strands of the immanent counter-Enlightenment is an enthralment with death and, sometimes, violence.

The testimony of the immanent counter-Enlightenment challenges Gutting's account in two main ways. First, it casts further doubt on the 'subtraction' story of the emergence of exclusive humanism, with its 'us versus them' view of religion. For here, now, is a third option, one that has emerged from within, and in reaction to, exclusive humanism. Second, and perhaps most importantly, the existence of the immanent counter-Enlightenment casts real doubt on whether a view like pragmatic liberalism can truly account for the values that emerge from our moral phenomenology. In particular, the testimony of the immanent counter-Enlightenment casts considerable doubt on Gutting's confident assertion that 'an appreciation of the intrinsic value of ordinary life' offers greater moral force than Christianity because it 'can readily lead to a contentment with this value as an adequate aspiration for human life. A heart fulfilled by human labor and love may lose its Augustinian restlessness' (Gutting, 1999, p. 127). As Taylor points out, from this sort of perspective it is extremely difficult to explain the emergence of anti-humanism from within the bosom of the Enlightenment. 'Why this throwback, on the part of people who are "liberated" from religion and tradition?' (Taylor, 2001, p. 398). Supporters of transcendence, on the other hand, can account for this easily by pointing to human beings' 'ineradicable bent to respond to something beyond life' (Taylor, 2001, p. 399). On this view, 'the perennial human susceptibility to be fascinated by death and violence is at base a manifestation of our nature as *homo religiosus*. From the point of view of someone who acknowledges transcendence, this fascination is one of the places where the aspiration to something beyond most easily goes when it fails to take us there' (Taylor, 2001, p. 399).

Explaining evil

The other main engagement between Taylor's *Geistesgeschichte* and Gutting's position, at least as is of relevance to our project, is that over the question of explaining evil. Gutting confesses that on this issue he begins on the back foot, for 'Where, in our secular vision can we find anything like the profundity of the Christian dialectic of sin and redemption?' (Gutting, 1999, p. 130). While Gutting is prepared to admit the power of the Christian position, he believes that a superior account can be gleaned from sources within the Romantic tradition, in particular from Rousseau's account of evil. Gutting bases his challenge primarily on the notion that sets Rousseau's account of evil most clearly apart from the orthodox Christian account, namely Rousseau's insistence that human nature is essentially innocent, and that humans have the resources to free themselves from the evil that we find ourselves entangled in. In dismissing the Christian account of evil Gutting argues that it is

very hard to see how truths about the nature and amount of

187

moral evil perpetrated by humans support the conclusion that we are beyond self-redemption. This conclusion would require evidence that, appearances to the contrary, we all lead wicked lives; or at least that we all would lead wicked lives if given the opportunity. Despite all the evils, from the monstrous to the petty, perpetrated by humans, there is no such evidence. Believers will, of course, maintain that the evidence is not there only because God has intervened to save us from what we would otherwise do. But where is the evidence of such intervention? It is hard enough to make a plausible case for the overall positive moral effect of religion, let alone for the claim that all instances of human virtue are due to its influence. (Gutting, 1999, p. 132)

Gutting takes this response to show that 'a naturalist account of evil – an account that finds the source of evil in deviations from nature and its remedy in a return to what we "really" are – need not be inferior to the Christian as an account of the Pascalian phenomenology' (Gutting, 1999, p. 132). There are, however, good reasons to doubt this conclusion. For one thing, Gutting's account of sin does not take into account the full story of the fall, in which we are also blinded to our sinful nature – one of the consequences of what we could, following Plantinga, call the epistemic problem of sin. Thus Christianity has the resources to account for the supposed problem that Gutting raises. For if the Christian account is true, then it comes as no surprise that sinful human beings like Gutting, standing as their own judges, discover no evidence that 'we all live wicked lives'. But where the biblical account of good and evil is held to be true, there is no shortage of evidence to be found that the apostle Paul does not exaggerate when he writes that 'all have sinned, and fall short of the glory of God' (Romans 3.23).

Furthermore, while Gutting demands evidence for the fact that humans are beyond self-redemption, the obvious rejoinder is to demand evidence from Gutting of humanity redeeming itself. The burden of proof seems to be on Gutting's shoulders, and there seems little cause for optimism. Despite an unprecedented acceptance of Enlightenment values, the previous century, as Jonathan Glover points out, was arguably the most brutal in history (Glover, 1999), and our century has hardly begun any better.

A final point on this subject is that it is hard to see how Gutting can fall back on an account of evil that sees this as deviations from what we 'really' are, when pragmatic liberalism rejects any substantive account of human nature. This is not a point I can pursue here, but it seems questionable how, if there are no objective values as Gutting contends, any account can be given for the very concept of 'evil' in the strong sense of the word.

Concluding Remarks on Taylor's Historical Argument

In this chapter I have been defending the thesis that Charles Taylor's historical retrieval in *Sources of the Self* successfully supports the claim that our moral phenomenology has an inescapable structure, a structure which in turn cannot be properly understood without reference to the transcendent, which reference turns out to be best accounted for by Christian theism. I began by arguing that Melissa Lane has, because of misunderstandings of how Taylor's concepts interact, mis-judged the effectiveness of Taylor's 'Historical' and 'Best Account' argument strategies. I based much of the weight of my rejection of Lane's arguments on what I believe to be a superior account of the nature of Taylor's historical retrieval, that set out by Stephen Mulhall. After setting out Mulhall's account and showing how this account generally supports my reading of Taylor's argument as contending for Christian theism as the 'Best Account' of our moral phenomenology, I turned to a con-sideration of Gary Gutting's critique of this aspect of Taylor's argument. We saw that Gutting's critique primarily focused around his claim that the affirmation of ordinary life makes best sense in a naturalist account of reality and his argument that Christian theism holds no major advantage over his pragmatic naturalism in explaining evil. In both cases I argued, drawing on Taylor's recent writing, that Gutting fails to establish that his transcendence-denying reading of history offers a superior account and that, to the contrary, Christian theism emerges from this engagement holding the higher ground.

As Taylor rightly points out, the question that we must ask of any account of our moral phenomenology is 'Who is right? . . . Who can make more sense of the life all of us are living?' (Taylor, 2001, p. 399). From what we have seen here, though this argument must of necessity always be an open one, when Taylor's theistic account is compared with its closest non-theistic competitor, the upper hand remains with the transcendent, and more specifically the Christian theistic, view. The force of Taylor's historical argument does, I believe, make it difficult, particularly when combined with the other parts of his overall theistic argument, to dismiss such a Christian-theistic reading of history without first rejecting the truth claims on which Christian theism are based.

To recap, at the beginning of Part 2 of this book I set out the following argument structure, drawn from Melissa Lane's reading of *Sources of the Self*, which I claim reflects an underlying argument for Christian theism that is implicit in *Sources* and which has become more explicit in Taylor's more recent work:

(i)   we must have a morality;
(ii) we must have a morality with a certain structure, such that particular values are connected to 'sources';
(iii) we must have a morality based on an incomparably higher good; and
(iv) we must understand the structure of our morality and the incomparably higher good on which our morality must be based in the terms of Christian theism.

In this chapter and the two preceding it, I have considered a range of arguments levelled against various parts of this argument, as well as the general suitability of the transcendental argument strategy for establishing the foundation of an argument of this kind. If my arguments have been successful, then I believe that I have shown that the claims listed above withstand the objections that have been considered in this part of the book. What remains is to consider in what way and to what degree this argument might be deployed in response to the difficulties faced by Plantinga's model of warranted Christian belief. That is the business of the next, and final chapter.

9

Conclusion

The preceding chapters have seen many a tactical skirmish both with the opponents of Reformed epistemology and with Taylor's moral epistemology. The time has now come to see whether those battles have contributed to a successful strategy. To do this, it is first necessary to plot out the main lines of the campaign, after which it will be possible to offer an assessment of its overall effect.

Reformed Epistemology and its Limitations

Reformed epistemology, as we saw, has as its central tenet the proper basicality of Christian theistic beliefs. While this is a commitment that Reformed epistemology's proponents draw from within the central texts of their theology, and most fundamentally from the Bible itself, their explicit stand on this topic is occasioned by what Plantinga calls the *de jure* challenge to Christian theistic belief. This label distinguishes the challenge from the traditional challenge to theistic and Christian beliefs, which focuses on the claim that such beliefs are false (the *de facto* challenge). Just what the *de jure* challenge amounts to, however, is difficult to pin down. As Plantinga puts it, 'The conclusion of such an objection will be that there is something wrong with Christian belief – something other than falsehood – or else something wrong with the Christian believer: it or she is unjustified, or irrational, or rationally unacceptable, in some way wanting. But *what* way, exactly? Just what is it to be unjustified or irrational? No doubt it is a bad thing to hold beliefs that are rationally unjustified: but what precisely is the problem? Wherein lies the badness?' (Plantinga, 2000a, pp. ix–x).

Different proponents of Reformed epistemology have implicitly, through their responses to the *de jure* challenge, understood the challenge differently. So who is right? Plantinga seems right when he says that the test of a good answer to the *de jure* question (and we can take it that this is also the test of a good definition of the *de jure* question), is that said response shows that, in the end, 'everything really depends on the *truth* of Christian belief' (Plantinga, 2000a, p. xiii). That said, there is something a little misleading about the way that *de jure* question is sometimes expressed, that it is the claim that Christian believers are irrational/unjustified/unwarranted etc. in their beliefs, *regardless* of the truth of the matter. For it is not really the case that those who level the many variants of this challenge think that Christianity might well be true, but that unfortunately some other factor means that we ought not to believe it to be true. Instead the challengers are almost uniformly of the opinion that Christian beliefs are false, but that the *de jure* question shows that there are good reasons why the question of whether or not the central beliefs of Christianity are true is one that *need not, and indeed ought not, be taken seriously*. Understood in this way, then, the test of a good response to the *de jure* question is that it shows that the *de facto* question ought indeed to be taken seriously.

Nicholas Wolterstorff, as we saw, took the *de jure* question to be one about *entitlement*, that is, the question of whether Christians are entitled to hold their beliefs. In order to assess this challenge, Wolterstorff introduced the following criterion of entitlement by which to test particular beliefs: 'a person S is entitled to his belief that *p* just in case S believes *p*, and there's no doxastic practice D pertaining to *p* such that S ought to have implemented D and S did not, or S ought to have implemented D better than S did' (Wolterstorff, 1995, p. 272). We saw, however, that while by this criterion the Christian believer is entitled to her beliefs, so too is the believer in space aliens (Quinn, 2001), as would the Yorkshire Ripper (Levine, 1998) be entitled to his

beliefs. Plantinga added to the critique of Wolterstorff's proposed solution by pointing out that it is quite conceivable that
an insane person who was nonetheless committed to 'satisfying
his intellectual obligations and carrying out his cognitive duties'
would also be entitled to his beliefs in Wolterstorff's sense, even
though his beliefs were clearly mad (Plantinga, 2000a, pp. 101–
2). In the terms we have been using here, then, it is clear that
showing Christian believers to be Wolterstorff-entitled to their
beliefs is insufficient to the task of undermining the claim that
the truth of Christian belief need not, and indeed ought not, be
taken seriously. If being entitled in Wolterstorff's sense leaves
the Christian on a par with the holder of obviously insane
beliefs, then showing Christian believers to be entitled to their
beliefs does little to endorse the likelihood of the truth of those
beliefs.

William Alston, on the other hand, took the *de jure* question
to be one about *justification*, where justification is understood
in broadly reliabilist terms. Specifically, Alston construed the *de
jure* question in terms of William James' test of justified belief,
in which 'one is justified in engaging in a practice [in this case
the practice of forming beliefs] provided one does not have
sufficient reasons for regarding it as unreliable' (Alston, 1983,
p. 116). Alston's response to the challenge, thus understood,
was based on his concept of 'mystical perception', an awareness
of the presence or activity of God that exists in parallel with
sensory perception. He argued that there exist no good grounds
for considering sensory perception to be reliable that do not
also hold for mystical perception, and that therefore, because
we take it for granted that sensory perception *is* reliable, it must
be accepted that mystical perception, if it exists, is also reliable.
We saw that Alston's theory drew a range of responses, among
the most damaging of which were those that focused on the
centrality of the notion of perception in his model. Most
damaging of all, though, were those challenges, like those based
on the existence of religious pluralism, which questioned just
how far being Alston-justified takes the Christian believer. Here
again we saw that Plantinga was among the critics who, like

Daniels, concluded that 'whether a practice is . . . justified in [Alston's] sense turns out to be of very little interest' (Daniels, 1989, p. 488). As with Wolterstorff's theory, being Alston-justified leaves the Christian believer epistemically indistinguishable from believers in other religions, or from characters such as Plantinga's example of the person who believes in God just to please her friends, or as a result of brainwashing or hypnotism (Plantinga, 2000a, p. 107). Once again, achieving the supposedly desired epistemic state is insufficient to the task of refuting the claim that the truth of Christian belief need not, and indeed ought not, be taken seriously.

The last of the three central proponents of Reformed epistemology we considered was Alvin Plantinga himself. Having rejected, among others, Wolterstorff-entitlement and Alston-justification as being insufficient to the task of responding to the *de jure* challenge, Plantinga proposed instead that the way to meet this challenge is by showing that Christian beliefs, if true, have *warrant* for the believer. In Plantinga's account, as we saw, 'a belief has warrant just if it is produced by cognitive processes or faculties that are functioning properly, in a cognitive environment that is propitious for that exercise of cognitive powers, according to a design plan that is successfully aimed at the production of true belief' (Plantinga, 2000a, p. xi). Answering the question of warrant, Plantinga argued, would address what was left unanswered by the other attempts at responding to the *de jure* question. In other words, for Plantinga the *de jure* question *is* the question of whether Christian beliefs are warranted. His attempt to show that Christian beliefs are warranted (or, more accurately, that it cannot be shown that they are unwarranted without addressing the *de facto* question) was built around his A/C model of belief, which has as its central tenet the idea that, if God exists, there is good reason to think that he has created in us a *sensus divinitatis*, 'a disposition or set of dispositions to form [properly basic] theistic beliefs in various circumstances, in response to the sorts of conditions or stimuli that trigger the working of this sense of divinity' (Plantinga, 2000a, p. 173). Plantinga then extends his A/C model to account for the obvious fact that many people do not believe in God, by adding the consideration that one of the cognitive consequences of original sin is that it results in a malfunctioning *sensus divinitatis*, which in believers is rectified by God primarily through the intervention of the Holy Spirit.

As we saw in Chapters 3 and 4, Plantinga's thesis has stimulated a wide range of critical responses. That is not, of course, unexpected. What is perhaps surprising though, given the nature of Plantinga's critique of Wolterstorff and Alston, is that the most cogent of these responses point to reasons why his extended A/C model, *even if successful*, does not do enough to show that there is good reason for taking the question of the truth of the claims of Christianity seriously. One of those lines of critique is based on the now-familiar point about the existence of religious pluralism, but we saw there are other lines of critique too, such as what I called the ethical objection and the 'further question' objection, that are aimed at establishing this same point. And so it seems that, despite Plantinga's confidence, answering the question of warrant is, on its own, no more a complete response to the *de jure* challenge than answering the questions of entitlement or justification (à la Wolterstorff and Alston) is.

It must be stressed that this is not to say that Plantinga and the others do not provide a partial response to the *de jure* challenge. On the contrary, it seems clear that there are particular versions of the *de jure* question that are (or would be, if they were levelled by anyone) met by the accounts of Christian belief given by Wolterstorff, Alston, and Plantinga. But what cannot be escaped is the fact that if the test of a successful response (and therefore definition) of the *de jure* question is (as Plantinga claims) that it foreclose any question of the validity of Christian belief that is not based on whether Christian belief is *true*, then none of the responses offered by these three thinkers fits the bill. There is more to the *de jure* challenge than Plantinga is willing to concede, and I suggested earlier that we should refer here to the 'expanded' *de jure* objection. Furthermore, what was distinctive about those aspects of the expanded *de jure* question that were unaccounted for by Plantinga's warrant-based response was that they were all primarily about the unbeliever rather than the believer. We saw this, for example in Evan Fales' articulation of what I called the 'further question' challenge to Plantinga's theory: 'Perhaps God has implanted within me a [*sensus divinitatis*] by the light of which I could come to know Him. Perhaps, even, the [Holy Spirit] is at work, labouring to break through that deep, tough encrustation of sin that over-shadows and cripples my cognitive faculties. But how can I know whether this is so?' (Fales, 2003, p. 358) To put this in other terms, while Plantinga's model defends the idea that it is not true of the Christian that she ought not to take seriously the question of the truth of Christian belief, what remains is to show the unbeliever that she too ought to consider the *de facto* question to be a question worth engaging with.

I also suggested, though, that all is not lost for the Reformed epistemologist. I proposed, following an insightful suggestion by C. Stephen Evans, that an expanded account of the pheno-menological aspect of Plantinga's model, the *sensus divinitatis*, could provide a means of 'continuing the conversation' in such a way that it becomes significantly more difficult to maintain that there are no good reasons for taking the question of the truth of Christian belief seriously. While Evans pursued this via a reading of Kierkegaard, I proposed that the moral phenomen-ology of Charles Taylor would provide a valuable resource in this regard.

Taylor's Moral Phenomenology

Charles Taylor's moral phenomenology, as articulated particu-larly though not exclusively in *Sources of the Self*, has been the focus of considerable philosophical attention, and there exist significant disagreements among informed readers of Taylor's work over its interpretation. Nonetheless I have shown that there are good reasons for thinking that Taylor's argument should be read as an argument in favour of Christian theism, one that is directed against the idea that, as Taylor puts it in a recent work, 'conditions have arisen in the modern world in which it is no longer possible, honestly, rationally, without confusions, fudging, or mental reservation, to believe in God. These conditions leave us nothing we can believe in beyond the human – human happiness, potentialities, or heroism' (Taylor, 2003a, p. 52). Read this way, Taylor's argument is very much directed against the *de jure* question, and therefore relevant to the Reformed epistemology project. The argument has as its foundation a transcendental argument, which (as we saw in Chapter 6) offers the potential to offer independent reasons for thinking that Christian beliefs might be the product of a proper functioning *sensus divinitatis*, reasons that are not dependent on the presumption of a functioning *sensus divinitatis* or its precondition, the existence of God.

In order to assess whether Taylor's work does indeed offer some value to the Reformed epistemology project, I articulated the structure of his argument (largely following Melissa Lane in this respect), and then dedicated the bulk of Part 2 to assessing whether the argument withstands the most relevant criticisms levelled against it. The argument, as we saw, consisted of a range of cumulative claims:

(i) we must have a morality (the claim of morality);
(ii) we must have a morality with a certain structure, such that particular values are connected to conceptions of the good, or 'sources' (the claim of structure);
(iii) we must have a morality based on an incomparably higher good (the claim of transcendence); and
(iv) we must understand the structure of our morality and the incomparably higher good on which our morality must be based in the terms of Christian theism (the claim of theism).

In what follows I shall recap on what was achieved in Chapters 6 to 8 regarding these four claims, and thereafter I shall offer an assessment of the overall argument. Finally I turn to the question of what is gained by adding this argument to the Reformed epistemologist's arsenal.

The claim of morality

The claim of morality can be expressed as the claim that human experience has an inescapably moral dimension. This is what grounds Taylor's argument in phenomenology. As Lane put it, this claim 'proceeds by reflecting on our actual moral experience, to find that we always do have moral values. If someone claims to do without morality altogether, the Phenomenologist is consistently able to show up that claim as parasitically reliant on the morality it denies' (Lane, 1992, p. 47). Taylor uses the term 'strong evaluations' to describe these inescapable moral judgements.

Essential to establishing the weight of this claim (itself the essential anchor-point for the remainder of Taylor's theistic argument) is establishing the primacy of phenomenology in ontological explanations of what it is to be human. Indeed, while none of Taylor's critics argue that we are not strong evaluators in Taylor's sense, what is challenged is what weight should be given to this fact. Lane, for one, challenged Taylor's assertion that this seeming inescapability of morality cannot be explained in some reductionist account, as did Gary Gutting in the arguments considered in Chapter 7. We saw, however, that Taylor presented a strong argument in favour of the primacy of phenomenology in questions of morality in his paper 'Ethics and ontology'. He contends that reductive naturalist accounts of morality such as sociobiological accounts that try to reconcile the phenomenology and the ontological account, and projectivist accounts like those put forward by Mackie and Blackburn which try to deny the phenomenology its force, both fail satisfactorily to address the tension between our moral experience and the ontological accounts they propose. Taylor concludes that such accounts cannot provide the best account of our lives (because they do not account for our moral experience), and that therefore they do not undermine the view that phenomenology must take primacy in accounts of this kind.

The claim of structure

Having defended the view that our moral phenomenology should carry significant weight in explanations of what it is to be human, we turned next to face challenges to the claim of structure, that is, the claim that it is an inescapable feature of our moral experience that it take a certain structure, described in Taylor's account as a 'moral framework'.

Once again it was Lane that offered an objection to this aspect of Taylor's argument. Her contention was not that moral frameworks do not exist, but rather that the nature of our experience is insufficient to show that they exist. This, she argued, is because, as Taylor himself points out, 'modern philosophy suffers an "eclipse of our whole awareness of qualitative distinctions", and this prevents us from articulating the sources that are buried within us' (Lane, 1992, p. 50). We saw, however, that Lane's critique was built on a misunderstanding of Taylor's account, in which frameworks remain inescapable even if inarticulately so. Her misreading of the nature of Taylor's historical account compounded the problem, as we saw in Chapter 8. Gary Gutting, on the other hand, expressed himself to be positively disposed towards the notion of moral frameworks. For Gutting, though, these must be understood in terms of ethical naturalism, one that embeds these frameworks within social networks. Gutting's challenge, then, was not to frameworks per se, but to the claim that these frameworks must be understood in transcendent terms. While Taylor's arguments in 'Ethics and ontology' offered significant considerations as to why ethical naturalist accounts like Gutting's face real problems, it was conceded that a sophisticated ethical naturalism like Gutting's could possibly offer an explanation of the moral frameworks of our phenomenology. It became clear, therefore, that discerning between these competing explanations (Taylor's theistic account and Gutting's naturalist account) would of necessity depend on which account seemed to offer the greater explanatory or motivational power. The 'claim of transcendence' became the central focus for this evaluation. Certainly, however, neither Lane nor Gutting's account foreclosed the possibility that moral frameworks function in the way Taylor explains them to (indeed, Gutting co-opts Taylor's account of moral frameworks into his own ethical pragmatism).

The claim of transcendence

The 'claim of transcendence' as we saw, is the claim that we must have a morality based on an incomparably higher good, or, in Taylor's terminology, the claim that 'we cannot make sense of our moral life without something like a hypergood perspective, some notion of a good to which we can grow, and which then makes us see others differently' (Taylor, 1989, p. 71). Not surprisingly it is at this point in the argument that I have been articulating that the resistance begins to stiffen. There are many who feel the same way as Richard Rorty, who challenges this idea and proposes instead that we make sense by 'simply arranging and balancing ordinary goods' (Rorty, 1994, p. 200).

Once again, however, we saw that making a judgement on this issue depends on the motivational power of the account given of the nature of our moral commitments. In Gutting's account the modern awareness of alternative moral perspectives leads people to 'an unwillingness to absolutize moral claims. They say that certain actions are right or wrong, but they seem to find no sense in the idea that morality expresses anything other than the contingent attitudes of their social group. Why should we expect that their descriptions but not those given in traditional terms will turn out to be self-deceptive?' (Gutting, 1999, p. 151). Taylor's account, on the other hand, propounds the view that Christian theism offers 'a fully adequate moral source', while casting doubt on whether the sources of ethical naturalism meet up to this challenge. As he puts it in *Sources*, 'The question is whether, even granted we fully recognize the dignity of disengaged reason, or the good-ness of nature, this is in fact enough to justify the importance we [moderns] put on it, the moral store we set by it, the ideals we erect on it' (Taylor, 1989, p. 317). Which of these accounts is correct? It seems the only way to adjudicate between them is a method Gutting implicitly commends, assessing which account offers the most explanatory power. And so we saw that the claim of transcendence turns out to depend on Taylor's histori-cal account, an account I argued is directed at establishing the claim of theism.

The claim of theism

The previous chapter was dedicated to considering Taylor's historical retrieval. As we have been reminded, the persuasive-ness of the claims of structure and transcendence depend in large part on what Taylor's retrieval can be construed as show-ing. Once again it was Lane who correctly identified Taylor's retrieval as an argument in favour of the claims of transcend-ence and theism, but once again Lane contended that this argu-ment strategy was unsuccessful. We saw that the core of Lane's critique was what she saw as a tension between 'the idea that a source can lose its power for . . . external historical reasons, and the idea that the most adequate source can always be identified by the Best Account' (Lane, 1992, p. 54). Yet again, however, Lane's critique turned out, on investigation, to be based on a misreading of Taylor's argument, primarily a misunderstanding of the role Taylor's historical account plays in *Sources*.

To illustrate the error of Lane's reading, I drew the reader's attention to Stephen Mulhall's insightful reading of the histori-cal part of *Sources of the Self*. Mulhall, we saw, viewed Taylor's history as a case of 'full-blown moral argument' in which the philosophical transitions the history traces are assessed as either epistemic gains or losses. The conclusion of this process, in Mulhall's reading, is to show that only theism provides the resources necessary to account for our moral commitments, and that the transitions away from theism in the history of

Western philosophy, while considered at the time to be epistemic steps forward, have in fact resulted in a loss of understanding of ourselves morally. Mulhall and I are agreed that Taylor's reading is intended as a strong antidote to what he elsewhere calls the 'subtraction story' by which the history of modern secularity is considered to be a process of pure epistemic gain, and where the 'death of God' is the pinnacle accomplishment of those gains. Mulhall concludes that there seems little reason to think that secular moral sources are adequate in accounting for our moral intuitions.

Of course Taylor's account cannot be taken to be the best account unless it is shown to fare well against its best rivals. There exists, to my knowledge, no full-blown naturalist account of the development of the Western self that is consciously intended as a refutation of Taylor's retrieval. Gutting's counter is, therefore, representative of the best available competitor to Taylor's account, which is why the latter part of the previous chapter was dedicated to assessing how well Taylor's account fares in the light of Gutting's response. On completion of that analysis, I concluded that Gutting's arguments do little to undermine Taylor's position.

That said, it must be conceded that, as Pinkard puts it, 'Taylor's theory of the relation of philosophy to history rests on some admittedly controversial claims about what has failed and what has succeeded in that history' (Pinkard, 2004, p. 207). There have been many commentators who have contested various aspects of Taylor's retrieval.[1] And by Taylor's own hermeneutics, no account of this kind can be taken as final, and must always be considered to be open to reinterpretation. What *has* been shown, however, is that Schweiker is not mistaken when he writes that 'Taylor argues, if I understand him rightly, that the endorsement of the worth of existence which grounds the moral life is at least implicitly theological in character'

---

1 See, for example, Wayne Hankey's critique of Taylor's reading of Augustine, 'Between and beyond Augustine and Descartes: more than a source of the self' (Hankey, 2001).

(Schweiker, 1993, p. 627). More importantly, what has been demonstrated is that far more has to be done if it is to be claimed that Taylor's theistic account is untenable, and that it is simply not true that, as Skinner put it, 'anyone who continues to affirm [theism] must be suffering from some serious form of psychological blockage or self-deceit' (Skinner, 1991, p. 148).

What the 'Augmented Model' Achieves

Before addressing just exactly what it is this 'Augmented Model' can be considered to achieve, it is first important to stress what it does not achieve. It is clear that what we do not have here is a proof of the existence of God, nor proof of the truth of the claims of Christianity. Plantinga's model on its own is only intended to show that Christian belief is warranted if true, and while adding Taylor's argument shows that the account given by Christian theism makes good sense, possibly best sense, of our moral phenomenology, this still does not show that God actually exists, that Jesus Christ is the Messiah, that he died and rose again from the dead, and so on.

I don't believe, however, that the above point undermines the effectiveness of the Augmented Model. That it is not a proof of any of the truth claims of Christianity is in fact a point in favour of the Augmented Model. Here we must remind ourselves of just what the Augmented Model is supposed to achieve, that is, what challenge it is supposed to stave off. The expanded *de jure* challenge, we saw, was the claim that the question of whether or not Christianity is true is one that *need not, and indeed ought not, be taken seriously.* Plantinga's extended A/C model of Christian belief shows that it is not true for believers that they ought not to hold Christian beliefs, but we saw that this left a range of questions within the orbit of the *de jure* challenge to the effect that the truth of Christianity is not something that unbelievers ought to take seriously. The reason for adding Taylor's argument, then, is to respond to the latter set of questions. Understood this way, it is clear that the argument need not achieve any high standard of proof. It is sufficient that it show that it is reasonable to believe that Christianity provides a good, possibly the best, account of the nature of our moral phenomenology. If this is conceded then the opponent of Christian theism can no longer honestly claim that she need not consider the question of whether or not Christianity is true.

If I have been successful in my arguments in the second half of this book, then it should be clear that Taylor's argument does, indeed, address the shortcomings faced by Plantinga's model, which we generalized as the problem of answering the question 'Why should the unbeliever take Christian belief seriously enough to consider that the *de facto* question warrants attention, even granting that the Christian believer might well be both justified and warranted in her beliefs?' We have shown that the historical-transcendental argument (as O'Hagan described it) that we have unearthed from within Taylor's work resists the most relevant criticisms that have been levelled against it, and provides a genuine reason to show that the *de facto* question must be taken seriously. That said, it is worth looking back at the specific lines of attack against Plantinga's model that lay behind our generalization, to ensure that those objections are all in fact met by this response.

In Chapter 3 I outlined those objections under four headings: proper basicality, the ethical objection, the 'further question' objection, and the challenge of religious diversity. On analysis, it turned out that the challenges to Plantinga's model on the grounds that it did not show Christian belief to be properly basic turned out to be reasonably easily met, or else they turned out to in fact be objections that fell more properly into the remaining three categories.

The ethical objection was, we saw, difficult to pin down, but it seemed to be primarily aimed at the perceived exclusivism of Christian belief. The basic idea seemed to be that, given the intolerance, hatred and violence that have often been associated with religious exclusivism, beliefs of this kind ought to face greater scrutiny than other kinds of exclusivist beliefs (such as the claims of science). Even if it were necessarily the case that

Christian belief *is* in fact exclusivist – Plantinga and I think it is, but as we shall see Taylor's intuition is that it is not necessarily so – it seems clear that Taylor's argument does enough to overcome honest ethical resistance to taking the question of the truth of Christian belief seriously. For if, as Taylor's argument shows, there is good reason to believe that the Christian account makes best sense of our moral phenomenology, then it seems to me that the ethical imperative must drive the enquirer to an urgent investigation into the question of whether the claims of Christianity are in fact true. For if exclusivist religious beliefs are potentially dangerous and harmful, but cannot be dismissed out of hand as simply irrational, then surely the ethically driven objector must do her best to show those beliefs to be *false*.

The 'further question' objection, while vaguely expressed, turned out to be something like the objection that Stern points out is often directed at broadly reliabilist theories of justification, the objection that 'while certain methods we use might actually *be* truth-conducive (and hence while we might actually *have* justified beliefs), it is not possible for us to *show* or *properly claim* we do, as it is not possible for us to have any non-circular reason for making any such claim, since we must rely on other beliefs of the same sort as grounds for supposing this to be the case . . . [thereby] rendering this legitimating move empty, and leaving us with no reason to take our . . . beliefs to be justified' (Stern, 2000, p. 23). But this is precisely the sort of objection, as Stern also points out, which can be overcome by judicious use of a modest transcendental argument. The purpose of such a transcendental argument is to provide independent reasons for taking some method of belief-formation (in our case, forming Christian beliefs as a result of a properly functioning *sensus divinitatis*) to be reliable. Taylor's argument, while not conclusive, offers sufficient reason to consider the *sensus divinitatis* to be a reliable way of forming true beliefs that it forecloses this particular line of objection. What is left is the *de facto* question, which is precisely what a good answer to the expanded *de jure* question is supposed to achieve.

Conclusion

Finally we must consider the challenge posed by the existence of religious diversity. We need to tread particularly carefully here, given that Plantinga and Taylor differ quite strongly on how they view the relationship of Christianity to other religions. Plantinga, as we have seen, is an unrelenting exclusivist – he believes that Christianity is true, and other religions are not. Taylor, on the other hand, seems to want to affirm a multiplicity of faiths. This is perhaps nowhere clearer than in his discussion of Iris Murdoch's moral philosophy, where he writes of 'that puzzling multiplicity of paths which seems to be a perennial feature of the human condition. Many faiths, not least the one I share in, have spent centuries trying to deny this multiplicity. It is now time to discover, in humility and puzzlement, how we on different paths are also fellow travellers' (Taylor, 1996, p. 19). It is important that we consider just what is implied by this statement. Does Taylor think that all adherents to all faiths are equally correct, and that there are no important differences between them? If that were so, this would obviously be coming very close to conceding the case to those critics of Christian belief who base their objection on the fact of religious diversity. For if all faiths, each of them with their different and conflicting beliefs, are in some sense equally true (I confess that I struggle to see how one could rationally make such a claim), then there is no particular reason for taking seriously the *de facto* question about Christian beliefs.

I think, however, that on reflection it is clear that Taylor is not contending for this levelling view of religion. For to do so would be to fall foul of one of his own principles, albeit one that finds its expression in his political philosophy. Here the principle is similar to, and can be derived from, Taylor's 'starting hypothesis' with respect to the evaluation of cultures other than one's own – 'the presumption of equal worth'. 'As a presumption the claim is that all human cultures that have animated whole societies over some considerable stretch of time have something important to say to all human beings' (Taylor, 1994, p. 66). What this presumption does not amount to, however, is an *a priori* commitment to the value of all cultures. The value of a culture can only be established by investigating it. To value it otherwise would be an insulting form of homogenization, and would amount to an arrogant belief that there is nothing to be learned from that culture. The flip-side of this, however, is that some cultures may fall beyond the pale, and a line will have to be drawn. It seems hard to see why this principle would fall away upon entering into the realm of religion. For again the effect of affirming all faiths equally simply on the basis of principle means that all are in fact rendered equally valueless, and the particular beliefs of each religion, so important to the believers in those religions, are rendered irrelevant. It seems therefore that in the quoted passage Taylor must be expressing something like his 'presumption of equal worth' for different cultures, but that this presumption must then be tested by real engagements in which some (and possibly most) religions will be found wanting. Taylor's generosity to other faiths also, I think, reflects his view that no account is ever complete and closed to reinterpretation.

While my own view is much closer to Plantinga's than to Taylor's on this question, I do not believe that it is necessary for us to choose between them on this in order to make the Augmented Model successful in responding to the challenge posed to Christian belief by the fact of religious diversity. That challenge, we must remember, claims that because Plantinga's model can potentially be co-opted by adherents of many different belief systems (both theistic and non-theistic), the model gives no reason why the truth claims of Christianity in particular ought to be taken seriously. But adding Taylor's argument, which shows that there is good reason to think that Christianity offers a very good account, possibly the best, of the nature of our moral phenomenology, provides exactly the sort of reason needed to show that the objector cannot honestly consider the truth claims of Christianity to be irrelevant, even if it is a form of Christianity that is open (in the Taylorian sense, rather than an *a priori* sense) to what is good in other belief-systems. I personally think there are significant problems with this kind of view, but assuming it can be made to work it would suffice to undermine the *de jure* objection from religious pluralism. And of course Plantinga's more straightforwardly exclusivist view avoids any tension here whatsoever.

It seems, therefore, that appending Taylor's argument to Plantinga's extended A/C model of Christian belief does indeed cover those questions that are part of the expanded *de jure* objection that Plantinga's model on its own does not. But, the question may be asked, does not Taylor's argument suffice on its own? What is gained for Taylor's argument by adding it to Plantinga's model?

The first obvious point is that the Augmented Model offers a more detailed and structured account of the nature of Christian belief. This is important because, while Taylor's argument may show Christian belief to offer a good description of our phenomenology, connecting that phenomenology with the idea of the *sensus divinitatis* makes explicit how such beliefs (if true) have warrant.

In addition, the extended A/C model's developed notion of the noetic effects of sin, and of the necessity of the intervention of the Holy Spirit to rectify the damage so caused, and of the role of Scripture and faith in this process, provide a defensible answer to the question, which must obviously be posed of the Taylorian argument, of why it is so difficult to reach agreement on the best account of human phenomenology. This is not to say that such an answer will be convincing to all, or even most, but rather that it fills a gap in the Taylorian argument in a way that is coherent with the overall argument and which cannot be challenged on the basis of its internal rationality.

In the end, it seems that much of the weight of the Augmented Model is derived from Taylor's important claim that we have 'no good grounds to question the ontology implicit in the terms which allow us our best account of ourselves' (Taylor, 1994, p. 208). While the Augmented Model does not establish conclusively that Christian theism provides such an account, it provides sufficient support for that view to make it impossible to contend that one need not, or even ought not, take the truth claims of Christianity seriously. Its effect, then, is well described by Taylor's words, deployed in a different though related context. The Augmented Model does not 'by itself decide the question whether there is a God or not, whether there is transcendence. But it could open this issue for a more active and fruitful search' (Taylor, 2003a, pp. 66–7).

Bibliography

Abbey, R., 2000, *Charles Taylor*, Teddington: Acumen.

Abbey, R., ed., 2004, *Charles Taylor*, Cambridge: Cambridge University Press.

Adams, R. M., 1994, 'Religious disagreements and doxastic practices', *Philosophy and Phenomenological Research* 54(4), pp. 885–90.

Alston, W., 1971, 'Varieties of privileged access', *American Philosophical Quarterly* 8(3), pp. 223–41.

Alston, W., 1976a, 'Has foundationalism been refuted?', *Philosophical Studies*, 29(5), pp. 287–305.

Alston, W., 1976b, 'Self-warrant: a neglected form of privileged access', *American Philosophical Quarterly* 13(4), pp. 257–72.

Alston, W., 1977, 'Two types of foundationalism', *Journal of Philosophy* 73(7), pp. 165–85.

Alston, W., 1982, 'Religious experience and religious belief', *Noûs* 16, pp. 3–12.

Alston, W., 1983, 'Christian experience and Christian belief', in A. Plantinga and N. Wolterstorff, eds, *Faith and Rationality*, Notre Dame, Ind.: University of Notre Dame Press, pp. 103–34.

Alston, W., 1986a, 'Religious experience as a ground of religious belief', in J. Runzo and C. Ihara, eds, *Religious Experience and Religious Belief*, Lanham, Md.: University Press of America, pp. 31–51.

Alston, W., 1986b, 'Is religious belief rational?', in S. M. Harrison and R. C. Taylor, eds, *The Life of Religion*, Lanham, Md.: University Press of America, pp. 1–15.

Alston, W., 1986c, 'Perceiving God', *Journal of Philosophy* 83, pp. 655–65.

Alston, W., 1988a, 'Religious diversity and perceptual knowledge of God', *Faith and Philosophy* 5, pp. 433–48.

Alston, W., 1988b, 'The perception of God', *Philosophical Topics* 16, pp. 23–52.

Alston, W., 1989, 'Reply to Daniels', *Philosophy and Phenomenological Research* 49(3), pp. 501–6.

Alston, W., 1991, *Perceiving God: the epistemology of religious experience*, Ithaca and London: Cornell University Press.

Alston, W., 1993, 'Epistemic desiderata', *Philosophy and Phenomenological Research* 53(3), pp. 527–51.

Alston, W., 1994a, 'Précis of *Perceiving God*', *Philosophy and Phenomenological Research* 54(4), pp. 863–8.

Alston, W., 1994b, 'Reply to commentators', *Philosophy and Phenomenological Research* 54(4), pp. 891–9.

Alston, W., 1995, 'Epistemic warrant as proper function', *Philosophy and Phenomenological Research* 55(2), pp. 397–408.

Baker, D. P., 1999, 'Taylor and Parfit on personal identity: a response to Lötter', *South African Journal of Philosophy* 18(3), pp. 331–46.

Baker, D. P., 2000, 'Charles Taylor's *Sources of the Self*: a transcendental apologetic?', *International Journal for Philosophy of Religion* 47, pp. 155–74.

Baker, D. P., 2003, 'Morality, structure, transcendence and theism: a response to Melissa Lane's reading of Charles Taylor's *Sources of the Self*', *International Journal for Philosophy of Religion* 54(1), pp. 33–48.

Baker, D. P., 2005, 'Plantinga's Reformed epistemology: what's the question?', *International Journal for Philosophy of Religion* 57, pp. 77–103.

Basinger, D., 2002, *Religious Diversity: A Philosophical Assessment*, Burlington, Vt.: Ashgate.

Beilby, J., ed., 2002, *Naturalism Defeated? Essays on Plantinga's Evolutionary Argument Against Naturalism*, Ithaca and London: Cornell University Press.

Bishop, J., and Aijaz, I., 2004, 'How to answer the *de jure* question about Christian belief', *International Journal for Philosophy of Religion* 56(2–3), pp. 109–29.

Cassam, Q., 1999, 'Self-Directed Transcendental Arguments', in Robert Stern, ed., *Transcendental Arguments: Problems and Prospects*, Oxford: Oxford University Press, pp. 83–110.

Christian, R. A., 1992, 'Plantinga, epistemic permissiveness, and metaphysical pluralism', *Religious Studies* 28, pp. 553–73.

Connolly, W. E., 2004, 'Catholicism and philosophy', in Ruth Abbey, ed., *Charles Taylor*, Cambridge: Cambridge University Press.

Crisp, T. M., 2000, 'Gettier and Plantinga's revised account of warrant', *Analysis* 60(1), pp. 42–50.

Daniels, C., 1989, 'Experiencing God', *Philosophy and Phenomenological Research* 49(3), pp. 487–99.

DeRose, K., 1999, 'Voodoo epistemology', unpublished comments on Alvin Plantinga's *Warranted Christian Belief*; Society of Christian

Bibliography

Philosophers group meeting at the Eastern Division Meetings of the American Philosophical Association, Boston, 29 December 1999, http://pantheon.yale.edu/~kd47/voodoo.htm

Elshtain, J. B., 1999, 'Augustine and diversity', in J. Heft, ed., *A Catholic Modernity? Charles Taylor's Marianist Award Lecture*, Oxford: Oxford University Press, pp. 95–103.

Evans, C. S., 1988, 'Kierkegaard and Plantinga on belief in God: subjectivity as the ground of properly basic religious beliefs', *Faith and Philosophy* 5, pp. 25–39.

Fales, E., 1996a, 'Scientific explanations of mystical experiences, part I: the case of St Teresa', *Religious Studies* 32(2), pp. 143–63.

Fales, E., 1996b, 'Scientific explanations of mystical experiences, part II', *Religious Studies* 32(3), pp. 297–313.

Fales, E., 1996c, *A Defense of the Given*, Lanham, Md.: Rowman & Littlefield.

Fales, E. 2003, Critical notice of *Warranted Christian Belief* by Alvin Plantinga, *Noûs* 37(2), pp. 353–70.

Forrest, P. 2002, Review of *Warranted Christian Belief* by Alvin Plantinga, *Australasian Journal of Philosophy* 80(1), pp. 109–11.

Freud, S., 1961, *Civilization and Its Discontents*, ed. James Strachey, New York: Norton.

Gale, R., 1994a, 'The overall argument of Alston's *Perceiving God*', *Religious Studies* 30, pp. 135–49.

Gale, R., 1994b, 'Why Alston's mystical doxastic practice is subjective', *Philosophy and Phenomenological Research* 54(4), pp. 869–75.

Glover, J., 1999, *Humanity: A Moral History of the Twentieth Century*, London: Jonathan Cape.

Greenway, W., 2000, 'Charles Taylor on affirmation, mutilation and theism: a retrospective reading of *Sources of the Self*', *Journal of Religion* 80, pp. 23–40.

Grigg, R., 1983, 'Theism and proper basicality: a response to Plantinga', *International Journal for Philosophy of Religion* 14, pp. 123–27.

Grigg, R., 1990, 'The crucial disanalogies between properly basic belief and belief in God', *Religious Studies* 26, pp. 389–401.

Gutting, G., 1983, *Religious Belief and Religious Skepticism*, Notre Dame, Ind.: University of Notre Dame Press.

Gutting, G., 1999, *Pragmatic Liberalism and the Critique of Modernity*, Cambridge: Cambridge University Press.

Hankey, W., 2001, 'Between and beyond Augustine and Descartes: more than a source of the self', *Augustinian Studies* 32(1), pp. 65–88.

213

Hart, H., van der Hoven, J., and Wolterstorff, N. eds, 1983, *Rationality in the Calvinian Tradition*, Lanham, Md.: University Press of America.

Hebblethwaite, B., 1994, Review of *Perceiving God: The Epistemology of Religious Experience* by William P. Alston, *Modern Theology* 10(1), pp. 116–19.

Heft, J. L. (ed.), 1999, *A Catholic Modernity? Charles Taylor's Marianist Award Lecture*, Oxford: Oxford University Press.

Helm, P., 2001, Review of *Warranted Christian Belief* by Alvin Plantinga, *Mind* 110(440), pp. 1110–15.

Hester, M., 1990, 'Foundationalism and Peter's confession', *Religious Studies* 26, pp. 403–13.

Hill, D., 2001, 'Warranted Christian belief: a review article', *Themelios* 26(2), pp. 43–50.

Hoitenga, D., 1991, *Faith and Reason From Plato to Plantinga: An Introduction to Reformed Epistemology*, New York: SUNY Press.

Hundert, E. J., 1992, 'Augustine and the sources of the divided self', *Political Theory* 20(1), pp. 86–104.

Jeffreys, D. S., 1997, 'How Reformed is Reformed epistemology? Alvin Plantinga and Calvin's "Sensus Divinitatis"', *Religious Studies* 33, pp. 419–31.

Kerr, F., 2004, 'The self and the good: Taylor's moral ontology', in R. Abbey, ed., *Charles Taylor*, Cambridge: Cambridge University Press, pp. 84–104.

Klaushofer, A., 1999, 'Faith beyond nihilism: the retrieval of theism in Milbank and Taylor', *Heythrop Journal* 40, pp. 135–49.

Koehl, A., 2001, 'Reformed epistemology and diversity', *Faith and Philosophy* 18, pp. 168–91.

Kullman, M., and Taylor, C., 1966, 'The pre-objective world', in M. Natanson, ed., *Essays in Phenomenology*, The Hague: Nijhoff, pp. 116–36.

Laitinen, A., 2000, 'Persoonuus, identiteetti ja etiikka Charles Taylorin, Alasdair MacIntyren ja Paul Ricoeurin filosofiassa', Phil.Lic. thesis, University of Jyväskylä.

Lane, M., 1992, 'God or orienteering? A critical study of Charles Taylor's *Sources of the Self*', *Ratio* 5, pp. 46–56.

LeBlanc, J., 2000, 'Aquinas and Plantinga', http://iago.stfx.ca/people/wsweet/Plantinga-Leblanc.htm

Levine, M., 1997, Review of *Divine Discourse: Philosophical Reflections of the Claim that God Speaks* by Nicholas Wolterstorff, *Mind* 106(422), pp. 359–63.

Levine, M., 1998, 'God Speak', *Religious Studies* 34, pp. 1–16.

Bibliography

MacIntosh, J. J., 2000, 'Locke, Plantinga, and the Aquinas/Calvin Model', http://iago.stfx.ca/people/wsweet/Plantinga-MacIntosh.html

MacIntyre, A., 1981, *After Virtue: A Study of Moral Theory*, London: Duckworth.

MacIntyre, A., 1994, Critical remarks on *The Sources of the Self* by Charles Taylor, *Philosophy and Phenomenological Research* 54, pp. 187–90.

Mackie, J. L., 1977, *Ethics: Inventing Right and Wrong*, London: Penguin.

Marsden, G., 1999, 'Matteo Ricci and the Prodigal Culture', in J. Heft, ed., *A Catholic Modernity? Charles Taylor's Marianist Award Lecture*, Oxford: Oxford University Press, pp. 83–93.

McLeod, M., 1987, 'The analogy argument for the proper basicality of belief in God', *International Journal for Philosophy of Religion* 21, pp. 3–20.

McLeod, M., 1988, 'Can belief in God be confirmed?', *Religious Studies* 24, pp. 311–23.

Mulhall, S., 1996, '*Sources of the Self*'s senses of itself', in D. Z. Phillips, ed., *Can Religion be Explained Away?*, Basingstoke: Macmillan, pp. 131–60.

Nagel, T., 1989, *The View from Nowhere*, Oxford: Oxford University Press.

Nagl, L., ed., 2003, *Religion nach der Religionskritik*, Vienna, Oldenbourg and Berlin: Akademie Verlag.

Odegard, D., 1992, 'Warrant and responsibility', *American Philosophical Quarterly* 29(3), pp. 253–65.

OHagan, T., 1993, 'Charles Taylor's hidden God: Aristotle, Rawls and religion through post-modernist eyes', *Ratio* 6, pp. 74–81.

Pappas, G. S., 1994, 'Perception and mystical experience', *Philosophy and Phenomenological Research* 54(4), pp. 877–83.

Penelhum, T. [date unknown] 'Reflections on Reformed epistemology', http://www.ucalgary.ca/~nurelweb/papers/other/penel.html

Pincoffs, E., 1983, 'Quandary ethics', in S. Hauerwas and A. MacIntyre, eds, *Revisions: Changing Perspectives in Moral Philosophy*, Notre Dame, Ind.: University of Notre Dame Press, pp. 92–112.

Pinkard, T., 2004, 'Taylor, "History," and the history of philosophy', in R. Abbey, ed., *Charles Taylor*, Cambridge: Cambridge University Press, pp. 187–213.

Plantinga, A., 1967, *God and other minds*, Ithaca: Cornell University Press.

Plantinga, A., 1980, 'The Reformed objection to natural theology',

Proceedings of the American Catholic Philosophical Association 54, pp. 49–62.

Plantinga, A., 1981, 'Is belief in God properly basic?', *Noûs* 15, pp. 41–52.

Plantinga, A., 1983a, 'Reason and belief in God', in A. Plantinga and N. Wolterstorff, eds, *Faith and Rationality*, Notre Dame, Ind.: University of Notre Dame Press, pp. 16–93.

Plantinga, A., 1983b, 'The Reformed objection revisited', *Christian Scholars Review* 12, pp. 57–61.

Plantinga, A., 1986a, 'Epistemic justification', *Noûs* 20, pp. 3–18.

Plantinga, A., 1986b, 'Coherentism and the evidentialist objection to theistic belief', in W. Wainwright and R. Audi, eds, *Rationality, Religious Belief, and Moral Commitment*, Ithaca: Cornell University Press, pp. 109–38.

Plantinga, A., 1986c, 'Is theism really a miracle?', *Faith and Philosophy* 3, pp. 109–34.

Plantinga, A., 1986d, 'On taking belief in God as basic', in J. Runzo and C. Ihara, eds, *Religious Experience, Religious Belief*, Lanham, Md.: University Press of America, pp. 1–17.

Plantinga, A., 1986e, 'The foundations of theism: a reply', *Faith and Philosophy* 3, pp. 313–96.

Plantinga, A., 1987, 'Justification and theism', *Faith and Philosophy* 4, pp. 403–26.

Plantinga, A., 1988a, 'Chisholmian internalism', in D. Austin, ed., *Philosophical Analysis: A Defense by Example*, Dordrecht: D. Reidel, pp. 127–51.

Plantinga, A., 1988b, 'Epistemic probability and evil', *Archivo di Filosofia* 56, pp. 557–84.

Plantinga, A., 1988c, 'Positive epistemic status and proper function', in J. Tomberlin, ed., *Philosophical Perspectives*, 2: *Epistemology*, Atascadero: Ridgeview, pp. 1–50.

Plantinga, A., 1990, 'Justification in the twentieth century', *Philosophy and Phenomenological Research* 50 (supplement), pp. 45–71.

Plantinga, A., 1991a, 'The prospects for natural theology', in J. Tomberlin, ed., *Philosophical Perspectives*, 5: *Philosophy of Religion*, Atascadero: Ridgeview, pp. 287–316.

Plantinga, A., 1991b, 'An evolutionary argument against naturalism', *Logos* 12, pp. 27–49.

Plantinga, A., 1991c, 'Warrant and designing agents: a reply to James Taylor', *Philosophical Studies* 64(2), pp. 203–15.

Plantinga, A., 1992, 'Augustinian Christian philosophy', *Monist* 75(3), pp. 291–320.

Plantinga, A., 1993a, *Warrant: The Current Debate*, New York: Oxford University Press.

Bibliography

Plantinga, A., 1993b, *Warrant and Proper Function*, New York: Oxford University Press.

Plantinga, A., 1993c, 'Why we need proper function', *Noûs* 27(1), pp. 66–82.

Plantinga, A., 1995a, 'Pluralism: a defense of religious exclusivism', in T. Senor, ed., *The Rationality of Belief and the Plurality of Faith: Essays in Honor of William P. Alston*, Ithaca: Cornell University Press, pp. 191–215.

Plantinga, A., 1995b, 'Reliabilism, analyses and defeaters', *Philosophy and Phenomenological Research* 55(2), pp. 427–64.

Plantinga, A., 1996, 'Respondeo', in J. Kvanvig, ed., *Warrant in Contemporary Epistemology: Essays in Honor of Plantinga's Theory of Knowledge*, Savage, Md.: Rowman & Littlefield, pp. 307–78.

Plantinga, A., 1997, 'Warrant and accidentally true belief', *Analysis* 57(2), pp. 140–5.

Plantinga, A., 2000a, *Warranted Christian Belief*, New York and Oxford: Oxford University Press.

Plantinga, A. 2000b, 'Pluralism: a defense of religious exclusivism', in P. Quinn and K. Meeker, eds, *The Philosophical Challenge of Religious Diversity*, New York: Oxford University Press, pp. 172–92.

Plantinga, A. 2001a, 'Rationality and public evidence: a reply to Richard Swinburne', *Religious Studies* 37(2), pp. 215–22.

Plantinga, A. 2001b, 'Internalism, externalism, defeaters and arguments for Christian belief', *Philosophia Christi* Series 2, 3(2), pp. 379–400.

Plantinga, A. 2002a, 'Introduction: the evolutionary argument against naturalism: an initial statement of the argument', in J. Beilby, ed., *Naturalism Defeated? Essays on Plantinga's Evolutionary Argument Against Naturalism*, Ithaca and London: Cornell University Press, pp. 1–12.

Plantinga, A. 2002b, 'Reply', *Philosophical Books* 43(2), pp. 124–35.

Plantinga, A. [date unknown] 'Two dozen (or so) theistic arguments', unpublished lecture notes, http://www.homestead.com/philofreligion/files/Theisticarguments.html

Plantinga, A., and Wolterstorff, N., eds, 1983, *Faith and Rationality*, Notre Dame, Ind.: University of Notre Dame Press.

Quinn, P. L., 2001, 'Can God speak? Does God speak?', *Religious Studies* 37, pp. 259–69.

Rorty, R., 1994, 'Taylor on self-celebration and gratitude', *Philosophy and Phenomenological Research* 54(1), pp. 197–201.

Russell, B., 1945, *A History of Western Philosophy*, New York: Touchstone.

Ryan, S., 1996, 'Does warrant entail truth?', *Philosophy and Phenomen-ological Research* 56(1), pp. 183–92.

Schlamm, L., 1993, Review of William Alston, *Perceiving God*, *Religious Studies* 29(4), 560–2.

Schubert, F. D., 1991, 'Is ancestral testimony foundational evidence for God's existence?', *Religious Studies* 27, pp. 499–510.

Schweiker, W., 1993, 'Radical interpretation and moral responsibility: a proposal for theological ethics', *Journal of Religion* 73(4), pp. 613–37.

Sennett, J., 1994, Review of Dewey Hoitenga, *Faith and Reason from Plato to Plantinga: A History of Reformed Epistemology*, *Faith and Philosophy* 11, pp. 342–8.

Silver, D., 2001, 'Religious experience and the facts of religious plural-ism', *International Journal for Philosophy of Religion* 49, pp. 1–17.

Skinner, Q., 1991, 'Who are "we"? Ambiguities of the modern self', *Inquiry* 34, pp. 133–53.

Smith, N. H., 1997, *Strong Hermeneutics: Contingency and Moral Identity*, London and New York: Routledge.

Smith, N. H., 2002, *Charles Taylor: Meaning, Morals and Modernity*, Cambridge: Polity.

Stern, R., ed., 1999, *Transcendental Arguments: Problems and Prospects*, Oxford: Oxford University Press.

Stern, R., 2000, *Transcendental Arguments and Scepticism: Answering the Question of Justification*, Oxford: Oxford University Press.

Steup, M., 1993, 'Proper function and warrant after seven vodka Martinis', *Philosophical Studies* 72, pp. 89–109.

Steup, M., 1995, 'Proper and improper use of cognitive faculties: a counterexample to Plantinga's proper functioning theory', *Philo-sophy and Phenomenological Research* 55(2), pp. 409–19.

Steup, M., 1997, Critical study of William Alston, *Perceiving God*, *Noûs* 31(3), pp. 408–20.

Stroud, B., 1968, 'Transcendental arguments', *Journal of Philosophy* 65, pp. 241–6.

Stroud, B., 1999, 'The goal of transcendental arguments', in R. Stern, ed., *Transcendental Arguments and Scepticism: Answering the Question of Justification*, Oxford: Oxford University Press, pp. 155–72.

Sudduth, M., 2003, 'Reformed epistemology and Christian apologetics', *Religious Studies* 39, pp. 299–321.

Swinburne, R., 2001, 'Plantinga on warrant', *Religious Studies* 37(2), pp. 203–14.

Taylor, C., 1964, *The Explanation of Behaviour*, London: Routledge & Kegan Paul.

Bibliography

Taylor, C., 1978, 'The validity of transcendental arguments in C. Taylor', *Philosophical Arguments*, Cambridge, Mass.: Harvard University Press, pp. 20–33.

Taylor, C., 1989, *Sources of the Self*, Cambridge: Cambridge University Press.

Taylor, C., 1991a, *The Ethics of Authenticity*, Cambridge, Mass.: Harvard University Press.

Taylor, C., 1991b, Comments and replies, *Inquiry* 34, pp. 237–54.

Taylor, C., 1994, *Multiculturalism: Examining the Politics of Recognition*, Princeton, NJ: Princeton University Press.

Taylor, C., 1996, 'Iris Murdoch and moral philosophy', in M. Antonaccio and W. Schwieiker, eds, *Iris Murdoch and the Search for Human Goodness*, Chicago, Ill.: University of Chicago Press, pp. 3–28.

Taylor, C., 1997, 'Leading a life in R. Chang', ed., *Incommensurability, Incomparability, and Practical Reasoning*, Cambridge, Mass.: Harvard University Press, pp. 170–83.

Taylor, C., 1999, 'A Catholic modernity?', in J. Heft, ed., *A Catholic Modernity: Charles Taylor's Marianist Award Lecture*, Oxford: Oxford University Press, pp. 13–37.

Taylor, C., 2000, 'What's wrong with foundationalism?: knowledge, agency and world', in M. Wrathall and J. Malpas, eds, *Heidegger, Coping and Cognitive Science*, Cambridge Mass. and London: MIT Press, pp. 115–34.

Taylor, C., 2001, 'The immanent counter-Enlightenment', in R. Beiner and W. Norman, eds, *Canadian Political Philosophy: Contemporary Reflections*, Oxford: Oxford University Press, pp. 386–400.

Taylor, C., 2003a, 'Closed world structures', in M. Wrathall, ed., *Religion after Metaphysics*, Cambridge: Cambridge University Press, pp. 47–68.

Taylor, C., 2003b, 'Ethics and ontology', *Journal of Philosophy* 100(6), pp. 305–20.

Taylor, C., 2005, 'The immanent counter-Enlightenment: Christianity and morality', *South African Journal of Philosophy* 2005, 24(3), 224–39. (Translation by Ian Jennings of 'Die Immanente Gegenaufklärung: Christentum und Moral', in L. Nagl, ed., *Religion nach der Religionskritik*, Akademie Verlag: Berlin, 2003.)

Taylor, J. E., 1991, 'Plantinga's proper functioning analysis of epistemic warrant', *Philosophical Studies* 64, pp. 185–202.

Taylor, J. E., 1995, 'Plantinga on epistemic warrant', *Philosophy and Phenomenological Research* 55(2), pp. 421–6.

Tien, D. W., 2004, 'Warranted Neo-Confucian belief: religious pluralism and the affections in the epistemologies of Wang Yangming (1472–1529) and Alvin Plantinga', *International Journal for Philosophy of Religion* 55, pp. 31–55.

Tilley, T. W., 1990, 'Reformed epistemology and religious fundamentalism: how basic are our basic beliefs?', *Modern Theology* 6(3),
pp. 237–57.

van Inwagen, P., 1982, 'Abnormal experience and abnormal belief'
(Abstract of Comments), *Noûs* 16, pp. 13–14.
Vogelstein, E., 2004, 'Religious pluralism and justified Christian belief:
a reply to Silver', *International Journal for Philosophy of Religion* 55,
pp. 187–92.

Ward, K., 1994, Review of William Alston, *Perceiving God*, *Philosophy*
69(267), pp. 110–12.
Willard, J., 2003, 'Plantinga's epistemology of religious belief and the
problem of religious diversity', *Heythrop Journal* 44(3), pp. 275–93.
Williams, C., 1994, 'Kierkegaardian suspicion and properly basic
beliefs', *Religious Studies* 30(3), pp. 261–7.
Wolterstorff, N., 1976 (2nd edn 1984), *Reason Within the Bounds of
Religion*, Grand Rapids, Mich.: Eerdmans.
Wolterstorff, N., 1983a, 'Introduction', in A. Plantinga and N.
Wolterstorff, eds, *Faith and Rationality: Reason and Belief in God*,
Notre Dame, Ind.: University of Notre Dame Press, pp. 1–15.
Wolterstorff, N., 1983b, 'Can belief in God be rational if it has no
foundations?', in A. Plantinga and N. Wolterstorff, eds, *Faith and
Rationality: Reason and Belief in God*, Notre Dame, Ind.: University
of Notre Dame Press, pp. 135–86.
Wolterstorff, N., 1986, 'The migration of the theistic arguments: from
natural theology to evidentialist apologetics', in R. Audi and W. J.
Wainwright, eds, *Rationality, Religious Belief and Moral Commit-
ment*, Ithaca: Cornell University Press, pp. 38–81.
Wolterstorff, N., 1989, 'Evidence, entitled belief, and the Gospels', *Faith
and Philosophy* 6, pp. 429–44.
Wolterstorff, N., 1990, 'The assurance of faith', *Faith and Philosophy* 7,
pp. 396–417.
Wolterstorff, N., 1995, *Divine Discourse*, Cambridge: Cambridge
University Press.
Wolterstorff, N., 1996, *John Locke and the Ethics of Belief*, Cambridge:
Cambridge University Press.
Wolterstorff, N., 1998, Reply to Levine, *Religious Studies* 34,
pp. 17–23.
Wolterstorff, N., 2001a, *Thomas Reid and the Story of Epistemology*,
Cambridge: Cambridge University Press.
Wolterstorff, N., 2001b, Response to Helm, Quinn, and Westphal,
Religious Studies 37, pp. 293–306.

Bibliography

Zagzebski, L. (ed.), 1993, *Rational Faith: Catholic Responses to Reformed Epistemology*, Notre Dame, Ind.: University of Notre Dame Press.

Zagzebski, L., 1996, *Virtues of the Mind*, Cambridge: Cambridge University Press.

Zagzebski, L., 2002, 'Plantinga's warranted Christian belief and the Aquinas/Calvin model', *Philosophical Books* 43(2), pp. 117–23.

Index of Names and Subjects